THE
Baseball ◇27 Research
JOURNAL

Editor: Mark Alvarez
Designated Reader: Dick Thompson
Copy Editor: A.D. Suehsdorf

THE BASEBALL RESEARCH JOURNAL (ISSN 0734-6891, ISBN 0-910137-75-7), Number 27. Published by The Society for American Baseball Research, Inc. P.O. Box 93183, Cleveland, OH, 44101. Postage paid at Birmingham, AL. Copyright 1998 by The Society for American Baseball Research, Inc. All rights reserved. Reproduction in whole or in part without written permission is prohibited. Printed by EBSCO Media, Birmingham, AL.

The Society for American Baseball Research

History

The Society for American Baseball Research (SABR) was founded on August 10, 1971, by L. Robert "Bob" Davids and fifteen other baseball researchers at Cooperstown, New York, and now boasts more than 7,100 members worldwide. The Society's objectives are to foster the study of baseball as a significant American institution, to establish an accurate historical account of baseball through the years, to facilitate the dissemination of baseball research information, to stimulate the best interest of baseball as our national pastime, and to cooperate in safeguarding proprietary interests of individual research efforts of members of the Society.

Baseball Research Journal

The Society published its first annual ***Baseball Research Journal*** in January 1972. The present volume is the twenty-seventh. Most of the previous volumes are still available for purchase (see inside back cover). The editorial policy is to publish a cross section of research articles by our members which reflect their interest in history, biography, statistics and other aspects of baseball not previously published.

Interested in Joining the Society?

SABR membership is open to all those interested in baseball research, statistics or history. The 1999 membership dues are $50 US, $60 Canada & Mexico and $65 overseas (US funds only) and are based on the calendar year. Members receive the ***Baseball Research Journal***, ***The National Pastime***, *The SABR Bulletin*, and other special publications. To join SABR, use the form found on the bottom of the publication order form found on the inside back cover. For further information, contact the SABR office at the address or phone below:

SABR
Dept. BRJ
812 Huron Rd E #719
Cleveland, OH 44115
216-575-0500
www.sabr.org
info @ sabr. org

The Best Outfield Ever?

The Phillies of the Gay Nineties

Jerrold Casway

In the history of baseball there have been many great outfield combinations. Any attempt to select the best requires comparative criteria and each outfield has to be evaluated on its offensive play, run production, speed, throwing acuracy, defense, and team value—all taking into account differences in eras, leagues, equipment, and the quality of the playing fields.

The nominees for the unappreciated nineteenth century begin with the 1876-1878 Boston outfield of Jimmy Manning, Jim O'Rourke, and Andy Leonard. They were followed by the Chicago White Stockings outfield of King Kelly and George Gore with Abner Dalrymple or Jimmy Ryan (1880-1881 and 1883-1886). Another great outfield combination was the 1894-1895 Bostons: Hugh Duffy, Tommy McCarthy, and Jimmy Bannon. Some experts might argue that the Baltimore Orioles/Brooklyn Superbas grouping of Willie Keeler and Joe Kelley with Steve Brodie, Jake Stenzel, or Fielder Jones (1894-1898) were tops in the National League. Others would point out the Philadelphia Phillies trio of Billy Hamilton, Ed Delahanty, and Sam Thompson (1891-1895).

In the twentieth century there are plenty of outfield groupings involving great players in varying combinations. There were the Ty Cobb outfields with Sam Crawford and Bobby Veach (1913-1915) and a later one with Harry Heilmann, Veach, and Heinie

Manush (1916-1917, 1921-1922 and 1923-1925). There were also two Babe Ruth trios, the first with Bob Meusel and Earle Combs (1925-1929) and another with Combs and Ben Chapman (1931-1933). Nor can we forget Joe DiMaggio with Charley Keller and George Selkirk (1938-1940) or Keller and Tommy Henrich (1941-1942 and 1946). Following the Yankee tradition, Mickey Mantle played alongside Roger Maris and Hector Lopez, Yogi Berra, or John Blanchard in the early sixties. Across town in the early fifties was Willie Mays, Don Mueller and Monte Irvin. After the Giants relocated to San Francisco the team fielded Mays, Orlando Cepeda with Willie Kirkland and Willie McCovey. For the fans of Boston there was Ted Williams playing alongside Doc Cramer, Joe Vosmik, and Dom DiMaggio in 1939 to 1940 and Williams with Jimmy Piersall and Jackie Jensen in the mid-'50s.

Boston's Tris Speaker, Harry Hooper, and Duffy Lewis played together from 1910 to 1915. The Philadelphia Athletics fielded Al Simmons, Bing Miller, and Mule Haas in 1929 and 1930. The Pittsburgh Pirates had Roberto Clemente, Willie Stargell, and Bill Virdon or Matty Alou from 1965 to 1971 and Dave Parker, Richie Zisk, Willie Stargell, and Al Oliver in the mid-'70s. In the late '30s and early '40s, Ducky Medwick, Terry Moore, Enos Slaughter, and Stan Musial made up great outfields for the St. Louis Cardinals. Fenway Park in the mid-'70s was graced by Dwight Evans, Jim Rice, Fred Lynn, and Carl Yaztrzemski outfields.. Not to be overlooked are the

Jerrold Casway is a professor of history at Howard Community College in Columbia, Maryland, who is completing Ed Delahanty and the Emerald Age of Baseball.

famous Dodger outfield combinations of Duke Snider, Carl Furillo with Gene Hermanski, Andy Pafko, and Jackie Robinson in 1949 to 1953.

Short-term outfield trios worth mentioning were Toronto's George Bell, Jesse Barfield, and Lloyd Moseby (1985-1987); the Pirates 1926 outfield of Paul Waner, Kiki Cuyler, and Max Carey; the 1962 Cincinnati outfield of Wally Post, Vida Pinson, and Frank Robinson; the 1973 Giants assembly of Gary Maddox, Bobby Bonds, and Gary Matthews; the 1973 Red Sox outfield of Reggie Smith, Tony Conigliaro, and Yaztrzemski, or Cleveland's 1995 trio of Albert Belle, Kenny Lofton, and Manny Ramirez. Easily overlooked was the 1901 Phillies outfield of Ed Delahanty, Elmer Flick, and Roy Thomas. Speaking of great outfields on reputation alone, the aging Ty Cobb played alongside the forty-year-old Tris Speaker and young Al Simmons for Connie Mack's 1928 A's.

No debate on the greatest outfield can ignore the players of the Negro Leagues. Ted Knorr, an expert on three generations of ballplayers banned from baseball because of their skin color, reminds us of a number of noteworthy outfield combinations. Among the great African American trios were the Chicago American Giants (1919) consisting of Oscar Charleston, Cristobal Torriente, and Jimmy Lyons; the Pittsburgh Crawfords (1935-1936) of Sam Bankhead, Jimmy Crutchfield, and Cool Papa Bell, and the Harrisburg Giants of 1924-1927, consisting of Charleston, Herbert "Rap" Dixon, and Clarence "Fats" Jenkins. Unfortunately, inadequate record keeping, the lack of fully reported games, and dissimiliar competition make comparisons difficult and inconsistent.

Researcher Knorr tried to remedy this problem by compiling from player interviews and newspaper surveys a ranking of Negro League outfields. Individually, Charleston was seated first, Bell followed in second place, Torriente placed fourth, Dixon and Jenkins were eighth and ninth, Lyons held the tenth position, Bankhead finished eleventh and Crutchfield came in at twenty-fourth. Based on this data, particularly the survey from the Pittsburgh Courier, the Charleston, Torriente, Lyons trio was ranked first and the Bell, Bankhead, Crutchfield group placed second. Ted Knorr goes beyond the Courier and suggests that the Harrisburg Giants outfield deserves consideration on a broader comparative scale. In the chart below, this outfield is compared with some of Knorr's selected great white outfields. His criteria required that the outfield played together for four years and included one Hall of Fame player.

T. Knorr's comparative rankings

Team	Era	Yrs.	HOF	BA	BAn	TPRe	TPRc
Hbg Giants	1924-27	4	1	.353	(.322)	na	na
NY AL	1926-29	5	2	.328	.301	35.5	117.5
Phil. NL	1892-95	5	3	.370	.344	47.2	99.2
Bos. AL	1910-13	6	2	.307	.307	22.8	103.5
Bos. AL	1954-57	5	1	.303	.305	23.7	89.1
Pit. NL	1966-69	5	2	.318	.329	31.9	69
Chi. NL	1928-31	4	2	.333	.304	23.2	44.2
Pit. NL	1959-62	6	1	.285	.289	3.9	30.7
Pit. NL	1929-32	4	1	.327	.299	11.8	25.5
	1976-95	4	1	.261	.261		

Era—Four best consecutive years when the outfield was intact.

Yrs.—Duration the outfield was intact, four year minimum required.

HOF—Number of Hall of Famers, one required.

BA—Composite batting average from Bill James' *Electronic Encyclopedia*.

BAn—Composite batting average normalized, or relative batting average.

TPRe—Total Player Rating from Thorn & Palmer's *Total Baseball* (5th edition).

TPRc—Sum of the accumulated TPR over career of each outfielder.

How authoritative are cross-generational statistics, faded reputations, and the subjective recollections of contemporaries? For whatever it's worth that is the stock-in-trade of comparative baseball researchers.

Undeterred by these pitfalls, I intend to persuade baseball enthusiasts that the best outfield ever assembled belonged to the 1891-1895 Philadelphia Phillies—the trio of Billy Hamilton, Sam Thompson, and Ed Delahanty. They never won a pennant and do not compare with the successes of the great Yankee, Dodger, Boston, or Oriole outfields. Their best finish was third place in 1895, but their all-around play in the field and at the plate makes them the best ever.

The unfortunate thing about this selection is that no one alive ever saw them play and to some unenlightened fans nineteenth-century baseball was something that happened in the dark ages of the national pastime. This Philadelphia outfield also played before mass media attention could fully publicize their skills and performances. All three of them were undemonstrative, and with the possible exception of Delahanty, they never attracted the kind of attention given to King Kelly, Ty Cobb, Babe Ruth, Willie Mays, or Roberto Clemente. But among knowledgeable contemporaries such as Harry Wright, Connie Mack, and John McGraw, this Philadelphia outfield had no peers.

Thompson—In 1887 "Big Sam" Thompson helped the Detroit Wolverines to a pennant and led the league in batting (.372), RBIs (166), slugging (.571), triples (23), and hits (203) in 127 games. He also scored 118 runs and had 29 doubles, 11 dead-ball home runs, and 24 assists from right field. Most of his contemporaries thought Sam's best years were behind him when Detroit sold him and his sore arm to the Phillies in 1888. When this outfield was assembled in 1891, he was already thirty-one.

Hamilton—In 1890, "Sliding Billy" came to Philadelphia from the American Association after Jimmy Fogarty jumped to the Players' League. In Hamilton's rookie N L season, age twenty-four, he batted .325, stole 102 bases and scored 133 runs in 123 games.

Delahanty—If Fogarty had remained with the ball club, Ed Delahanty might not have moved to the outfield. He was purchased by the Phillies in 1888 for $1,800. He was originally a second baseman, but injuries and his move to shortstop in the Players' League retarded his development. "The only Del" was the youngest of the trio. In 1891, at the age of twenty-three, he returned to the Phillies, and by midseason was playing center field regularly. Delahanty was an instant defensive success, and though he hit only .243, his potential as a hitter was widely recognized. In 1892, the last year of the fifty-five foot pitching distance, only six National League batters hit over .300. Three of them were in the new Phillies outfield.

The trio—Sam Thompson played the difficult afternoon-sun right-field position. The Baker Bowl outfield was surrounded by a banked bike track that abutted the short right field Broad Street wall that was topped by a twelve-foot wire-mesh screen. Game descriptions raved about how well Thompson played caroms and managed the grade along the perimeter. By 1892, Thompson's arm was fully recovered, and "Big Sam" threw with a renewed swift accuracy. From 1890 to 1896, Thompson averaged more than 25 assists per season. Few outfielders could match Thompson's normal efficiency. Although nineteenth-century baserunners took more liberties with outfielders, the numbers speak for themselves. Willie Mays never had more than 23 assists in a season, DiMaggio's high was 22, Colavito's best was 16, Clemente's top was 27, and Dwight Evans never had more than 15. At his peak Ty Cobb rivaled Thompson, and only Tris Speaker exceeded them all.

Sam Thompson and his outfield mates also were among the National League's fielding leaders during their tenure together. Their achievements and capabilities have to be weighed against the fact that the Phillies outfielders and their late nineteenth-century peers wore small unpadded gloves that covered only their palms. In 1894, Thompson shattered the top of his pinkie and had to have the tip amputated during the season. He still returned to play in 99 games and hit .404.

Billy Hamilton played center field and for a time moved to left when Delahanty joined the outfield. "Sliding Billy" was among the fleetest players of his era and remains among baseball's greatest base stealers. This speed allowed him to cover the spacious confines of the Broad and Lehigh corner of the ballfield. He was not the fielder Thompson or Delahanty was, but he got to balls that eluded most outfielders. And though his arm did not measure up to those of his outfield mates, from 1890 to 1895 he averaged more than 16 assists a year. His low of eight came in 1893, when he missed the last 49 games of the season and nearly died from typhoid fever.

Although Ed Delahanty broke in as an infielder, his speed, physique, and strong arm were more suited for the outfield. He did not have Hamilton's quickness, but he was considered a fast runner, averaging 31 steals a year during his prime decade. His arm was so strong that runners quickly learned not to take liberties on the basepaths when he had the ball. His assist totals were somewhere between the figures recorded by Thompson and Hamilton. Delahanty's greatest asset was his aggressive outfield play. Newspaper accounts marvelled at how he ran up the terrace into the roped-off crowds of spectators to catch fly balls. He was often compared with Hamilton's predecessor, the flamboyant Jimmy Fogarty, in his ability to chase down hard-hit balls to the deep outfield. Eventually, manager Harry Wright moved Delahanty to left field to offset the problems the lefthanded Billy Hamilton had in getting balls quickly back to the infield.

Offense—The most obvious impact of this great outfield was its offensive production. No outfield in the history of the national pastime has put up better collective numbers. These statistics excluded 1891 when Delahanty was starting to break into the Phillies outfield. The data does take into account the many games missed in 1893 and 1894 due to the illness and injury of Hamilton and Thompson.

The group's overall batting mark for 1892-1895 was .372. They averaged 191 hits, 106 RBIs (Delahanty and Thompson, 126), 133 runs, 32 doubles, 15 triples and nine home runs, and 44 stolen bases per season.

Individually, Hamilton had the highest four-year

average at .376. He was followed by Delahanty at .370, and Thompson at .369. During this span, Delahanty averaged 119 RBIs and Big Sam topped him with 134. Hamilton scored 150 runs a season followed by Delahanty with 130 and Thompson with 120. "King Del" also averaged 38 doubles, 17 triples, and 10 home runs, while Thompson kept pace with 35 doubles, 16 triples and 13 home runs. Hamilton stole an average of 74 bases. Delahanty had 33 and Thompson 24 during their years together. Other marks worthy of recognition were four .400 batting marks, two by Ed Delahanty. In 1895, Sam Thompson knocked in 165 runs. Hamilton scored 192 and 166 runs in consecutive seasons. In their last year together Big Sam hit 27 triples and Hamilton stole 98 bases. In a Dead Ball Era when 20 home runs were akin to 60, "Del" hit 19 in 1893 and Thompson 18 in 1895.

There have beenoutfields that had extraordinary statistics, but nowhere does an outfield trio have such consistently high offensive production and defensive efficiency. Some naysayers would challenge these accomplishments by reminding readers that beginning in 1893 the pitching mound was put back fifteen feet and for a few years hitting boomed. There is no denying these assertions, but these three players vastly exceeded the offensive averages put up by that era's productive hitters. Most remarkably, in 1894 the entire Phillies outfield hit over .400. Even substitute Tuck Turner batted .416 in 80 games.

This outfield should have had at least one more year together, but the Phillies traded the sulking Billy Hamilton to Boston after he hit .389, scored 166 runs and stole 97 bases in 1895. In return they got a much-needed field captain, the veteran third baseman, Billy Nash. In 1896 Hamilton outhit Nash by 120 points. The only consolation was that Nash scouted and signed Napoleon Lajoie to a Phillies contract.

That same year was Sam Thompson's last productive season. He injured his back and played sparingly until he quietly retired during the 1898 season. Ed Delahanty remained with Philadelphia until 1902. Although he was moved to first base in 1900, he returned at midseason the following year to left field after the Phillies signed the sore-armed Hugh Jennings to play first and act as captain. For the rest of the year Delahanty was part of another great outfield with Elmer Flick and Roy Thomas. The following season Ed Delahanty and Flick moved over to the upstart American League. "Del" signed with Washington and Flick played with the Athletics of Philadelphia.

With the exception of the 1926 Pittsburgh outfield of the Waner brothers and Kiki Cuyler; the Cobb, Heilmann, and Manush group of 1923-24, and the Geritol duo of Cobb and Speaker playing with Al Simmons on the 1928 Athletics, no other outfield would put three men in the Hall of Fame. Ed Delahanty was elected in 1945. Billy Hamilton waited until 1961. Sam Thompson, the leading RBI-per-game player in baseball history, was admitted in 1974. In lifetime batting averages the trio historically rank fourth (Delahanty, .346), seventh (Billy Hamilton, .344), and twenty-sixth (Sam Thompson, .331). Other evaluations include Charles Faber's rating system for nineteenth-century ballplayers in his book *Baseball Pioneers*. Offensively, he ranked Sam Thompson as the era's third-best right fielder, behind Willie Keeler and King Kelly. Billy Hamilton, in center field, was ahead of Pete Browning and George Gore. Ed Delahanty topped a list with Jesse Burkett and Hugh Duffy. The two best single-season outfields, according to Faber's measurements, were the 1895 and 1894 Phillies. He also confirmed the dominance of the Philadelphia trio by rating it the best overall career outfield for the nineteenth century. For individual total ranking, using both offensive and defensive factors, Thompson came in second to Keeler in right field, and Hamilton and Delahanty outdistanced their closest rivals.

More contemporary and detailed ratings come from Thorn and Palmer's *Total Baseball* (5th edition) all-time leader career rankings. In eight major offensive categories, the Phillies threesome of Delahanty, Hamilton, and Thompson prevailed over all leading outfield combinations. On the next page are a few revealing comparisons.

If readers put aside their nineteenth century prejudices and the fame of outfields graced by immortal players like Cobb, Ruth, DiMaggio, and Mays, they may appreciate how Delahanty, Hamilton, and Thompson rank as the greatest outfield ever. If any doubt remains there are always the opinions of McGraw, Mack and Harry Wright, who saw plenty of outfield combinations durng their combined eighty years in the game.

Thorn and Palmer's Ratings

	RBI/G	ABW	RBA	AP	OBP	ABR	TA	TPR
Delahanty	10	36	19	24	24	20	14	30
Hamilton	—	58	17	57	4	46	4	114
Thompson	1	87	22	37	—	65	44	98
Musial	75	6	14	12	18	6	15	13
Medwick	30	80	33	89	—	84	—	109
Slaughter/Moore	—	—	—	—	—	—	—	227
Cobb	84	2	1	8	7	4	11	4
Heilmann	19	22	26	30	25	23	27	74
Manush	—	—	81	—	—	—	—	—
Ruth	5	1	27	1	2	1	1	1
Meusel	14	—	—	—	—	—	—	—
Combs	—	—	—	—	49	—	·	331
DiMaggio	4	26	39	17	46	24	16	25
Keller	66	91	—	24	25	93	22	135
Heinrich	—	—	—	—	—	—	75	262
Mays	87	9	77	12	91	9	23	3
Cepeda	77	63	99	89	—	68	—	221
Kirkland	—	—	—	—	—	—	—	—
Speaker	—	10	11	17	8	10	7	6
Hooper	—	—	—	—	—	—	—	—
Lewis	—	—	—	—	—	—	—	—
Clemente	—	51	24	—	—	55	—	35
Stargell	64	24	—	33	—	29	77	73
Virdon/M. Alou	—	—	32	—	—	—	—	—
P. Waner	—	38	34	89	36	38	79	59
Cuyler	—	—	—	—	—	—	67	233
Carey	—	—	—	—	—	—	—	147
Keeler	—	—	13	—	85	96	—	378
Kelley	76	89	98	—	39	78	28	176
Brodie/etc.	—	—	—	—	—	—	—	—
Snider	—	46	—	61	—	48	47	148
Furrilo	—	—	—	—	—	—	—	—
Robinson/Pafko	—	—	54	—	25	—	44	75

RBI/G = RBIs Per Game; ABW = Adjusted Batting Wins; RBA = Relative Batting Average; AP = Adjusted Production; OBP = On-Base Percentage, ABR = Adjusted Batting Runs; TA = Total Average; TPR = Total Player Rating

The Opening Day Woes of the Niekro Brothers

Rough starts

Lyle Spatz

For players and fans alike, Opening Day is perhaps the most delightful day on the baseball calendar. Yet you might have difficulty getting the otherwise highly successful Niekro brothers to agree. For while their 539 major league wins (Phil with 318 and Joe with 221) is the highest aggregate total for pitching brothers, in their thirteen opening-day starts the Niekros combined for a dismal 0-10 record.

Joe started one opener for the Cubs and three for Houston, coming away with three losses and one no-decision. Phil, a Hall-of-Famer, started nine openers: eight for Atlanta and one for the Yankees. He lost seven and had two no-decisions. In fact, Phil's 0-7 mark is the worst opening-day record ever. Only fellow Hall-of-Famer Steve Carlton had more losses, but Carlton at least had three wins to go along with his nine defeats. Two other Hall of Famers, Cy Young and Robin Roberts, matched Phil's seven losses, but each also won five times.

Although Phil is five years older than Joe and reached the major leagues three years earlier, it was the younger brother who made the family's first opening day start. Coming off a 10-7 season as a Cubs rookie in 1967, Joe was named by manager Leo Durocher to pitch the 1968 opener against the Reds at Crosley Field. The game was postponed for two days, first because of rioting in Cincinnati over the assassination of Martin Luther King and then as a sign of respect for his funeral. Niekro began well, allowing only one run through four innings, but after a 43-minute rain delay, the Reds got to him for four runs in the fifth. Cincinnati eventually won, 9-4, behind the pitching of Milt Pappas and George Culver.

Phil's first opening-day start was in 1970 following his first 20-win season (23-13). Atlanta, the defending Western Division champion, was in San Diego to play a Padres team that was beginning just its second season in the National League. Coincidentally, Phil's opponent that evening was righthander Pat Dobson, traded to San Diego from Detroit in exchange for brother Joe. The woeful Padres, losers of 110 games in 1969, would cut their losses to 99 this season, although they would again finish last. They pounded Niekro for five runs and six hits in three innings and defeated the Braves, 8-3. All the Padres' runs off Niekro came in the third. The big blow was a three-run homer by Nate Colbert. Dobson left after eight, and although Ron Herbel entered the game with an 8-2 lead and surrendered a run, he earned a save under the evolving criteria for this new pitching statistic.

Atlanta fell from first place to fifth in 1970, and Niekro slipped from 23-13 to 12-18. His record against the National League champion Reds was 0-3 with a 6.88 ERA, yet he was manager Lum Harris's choice to face the Big Red Machine in the 1971 opener, the first one played at Cincinnati's Riverfront

Lyle Spatz is the chairman of SABR's Baseball Records Committee and the author of New York Yankee Openers (McFarland, 1997). He saw his first opener on April 19, 1949. It was at Ebbets Field, and Joe Hatten and the Dodgers beat Larry Jansen and the Giants, 10-3.

Stadium. Despite a temperature of 46 degrees and a sixteen mile-per-hour wind, a crowd of 51,702 turned out—at the time the largest ever for a baseball game in Cincinnati. The Braves won, 7-4, but the victory went to reliever Cecil Upshaw. This game may have been Niekro's best chance ever to win an opener. His teammates provided him with a 4-0 lead against Gary Nolan in the second

Joe and Phil Niekro knuckle for the camera.

inning, but the Reds rallied to tie it with a run in the fourth and three in the sixth, when Niekro gave up a leadoff single to Tommy Helms, a home run to Tony Perez, and a single to Johnny Bench before giving way to Upshaw. After Bench eventually scored the tying run, Upshaw held the Reds scoreless over the final four innings. Meanwhile the Braves scored a run against Wayne Granger in the seventh and two more against Don Gullett in the eighth.

Niekro pitched the Braves' delayed season-opener in 1972, following the thirteen-day player strike that shut baseball down for the first time ever. Opening-day crowds were generally sparse, with only 16,655 at San Diego Stadium. The Padres, introducing their new brown and yellow uniforms, won their third opener in four years. They broke a 2-2 tie with a four-run sixth inning that finished Niekro and then held on for a 6-5 victory.

After three consecutive years as Atlanta's opening-day pitcher, Phil would start only one more over the next five years, at Houston in 1975. That was Joe's first year with the Astros, but it was Larry Dierker who opposed Phil. The Braves, third in the West in 1974, had compiled a 7-18 record in spring training, the poorest in either league. Playing their first opener since 1953 without Hank Aaron, Atlanta held a 2-0 lead going into the home fifth. This time it was Niekro's defense, more specifically the defense of his battery mate, catcher Vic Correll, that betrayed him. Rob Andrews was on second base with two outs when Correll let a Niekro knuckler get away for a passed ball, as Andrews took third. Cesar Cedeno's squib single scored Andrews, but when Milt May flied out to center fielder Rowland Office, the inning appeared to be over. It wasn't. Plate umpire Doug Harvey ruled that Correll had tipped May's bat and awarded the

hitter first base on the interference. Given new life, the Astros capitalized. Cliff Johnson singled Cedeno home, and Jose Cruz followed with a three-run homer, after which Manager Clyde King replaced Niekro with Roric Harrison. Houston added a final run off Gary Gentry in the seventh and won, 6-2.

The Braves finished last under Dave Bristol in 1976 and 1977, with Niekro leading the league in losses in '77, the first of four consecutive years he would do so. He also led the league in ten other departments in 1977, while becoming, at 38, the second oldest pitcher ever to lead a major league in strikeouts. Early Wynn, of the White Sox, was three months older when he was the American League leader in 1958.

Bobby Cox selected Niekro to face the Dodgers in the 1978 season opener at Fulton County Stadium. His mound opponent was Don Sutton, a pitcher who would retire with similar career statistics and whose name would be often linked with Niekro's. Niekro again had an early lead that he failed to hold. Atlanta led 3-0 on a two-run homer by Dale Murphy and a solo shot by Rowland Office, only to have Davey Lopes tie the game with a three-run blast in the third. The Braves regained the lead on Jerry Royster's home run in the fourth, but Reggie Smith's two-run single in the fifth put the Dodgers ahead to stay. LA got three more in the sixth, and Niekro left without having retired a batter in the inning. The final score was 13-4, and Niekro's opening-day record stood at 0-4.

Phil pitched the best opening game of his career in a night game at Houston in 1979. He went the distance, allowing the Astros just three hits and two runs, both runs coming in the first inning on a single by Enos Cabell. Unfortunately for him, his teammates could score only once against J.R. Richard and Joaquin Andujar, and Niekro came away a 2-1 loser. After the game, Braves' catcher Dale Murphy raved about his battery mate. "If we can get Niekro three runs a game," he said, "he'll win 25 this year." (Niekro didn't win 25, but his 21 wins tied brother Joe for the NL lead, while his 20 losses were the most in either league.) Murphy was back behind the plate after playing most of the previous season at first base. He would be primarily a first baseman this season, too, before switching permanently to the outfield in 1980.

If 1979 was Niekro's best opening-day performance, 1980 may have been his worst. He allowed six runs (only four were earned) in two innings of work as the Braves fell at Cincinnati, 9-0. Frank Pastore, substituting for Tom Seaver, who had the flu, pitched a three-hitter and sent Atlanta to its ninth consecutive opening-day defeat. George Foster was the Reds' big gun, reaching Niekro for a two-run double in the first and a two-run homer in the second.

Phil now had made seven opening-day starts for Atlanta and lost six of them with one no-decision. He didn't make another one until 1983 when Manager Joe Torre of the defending NL West champions selected him to open against the Reds at Riverfront Stadium. The game had a familiar pattern. The Braves got Niekro an early lead, which he failed to hold, which in turn led to an Atlanta loss. This time they jumped ahead, 3-0, against Mario Soto, but by the time Niekro departed after seven, the score was tied at 4-4. Steve Bedrosian gave up a run in the eighth, and the Reds, coming off their first last-place finish since 1937, held on to win. Tom Hume relieved Soto in the ninth and set the Braves down in order to earn the save. Niekro had allowed just four hits but two of them were home runs, a two-run shot by Ron Oester and a solo blast by Gary Redus.

Things got even worse for the Niekros the next day. Joe, starting for the Astros at home against the Dodgers, gave up four runs in the first inning and a total of six (five earned) in three innings. Los Angeles crushed Houston, 16-7, the most runs the Dodgers had ever scored in a game against the Astros. Amazingly, thanks to a five-run Houston third that tied the score at 6-6 when he departed, Niekro escaped without the loss. LA scored six runs against loser Frank LaCorte in the sixth and then added four more off Frank DePino and Julio Solano.

The Astros had wanted to start Nolan Ryan in this game to give him a chance to break the major league strikeout record at home. But when Ryan was stricken with a case of prostatitis a few days before the opener, manager Bob Lillis turned to Niekro. Dodger manager Tommy Lasorda started Fernando Valenzuela, but Fernando had no more success than Niekro, lasting only 2-2/3 innings.

Things had been much different when these two met on Opening Day 1981 at Dodger Stadium. Joe, 20-12 in 1980, had concluded the regular season with a 7-1 victory in the playoff game that gave Bill Virdon's Astros their first Western Division title.

Valenzuela, on the other hand, was a twenty-year-old (so he claimed) rookie substituting for Jerry Reuss, who was out with a pulled calf muscle. Making his first major league start, Fernando blanked Houston, 2-0, on five hits, launching the "Fernandomania" that culminated in his becoming the first pitcher to win Rookie of the Year honors and the Cy Young Award in the same season. Joe allowed eight hits and both runs and took his second opening-day defeat.

His third would come in 1984 against Montreal in the Astrodome, the Expos' first win against Niekro in five years. He and Montreal's Charlie Lea were tied at 1-1 after seven, but the visitors scored three in the eighth against Niekro and reliever Bill Dawley on their way to a 4-2 victory. Although Joe would pitch four more seasons, this would be his final opening-day start. The following season, 1985, Phil would have his final try at winning a season-opener.

He was beginning his second year with the Yankees when Manager Yogi Berra chose him to replace the injured Ron Guidry in the opener at Fenway Park. Having celebrated his forty-sixth birthday two days earlier, Niekro became the second-oldest major league pitcher ever to start an opener. Only Jack Quinn of the 1931 Dodgers was older. His opponent was Dennis "Oil Can" Boyd, a twenty-four-year-old who had been only four years old when Niekro reached the majors back in 1964. Niekro had won 284 games in his twenty-one major league seasons, but with today's 9-2 loss to the Red Sox he suffered his 239th defeat and seventh on Opening Day. Staked to a 2-0 lead, he was unable to control his knuckler, walking five men including two with the bases loaded. He also allowed home runs to Tony Armas and Dwight Evans and left after four innings trailing, 5-2.

Obviously, the Niekros's opening-day totals compare poorly to those of other pitching brothers. For instance, the Perrys, who rank second on the list of most wins by brothers with 529, compiled a solid 7-4 mark in season openers: Gaylord won four and lost three, while Jim won three and lost only one. The Coveleskis and the Forsches are two other pairs of brothers who each contributed at least one opening-day win. Stan and Harry Coveleski combined for five wins (against four defeats), with Stan winning four of them, and Bob and Ken Forsch teamed up to win three openers while losing five.

So while the Niekros can look back on very successful major league careers, you can excuse them if they have less than fond memories of Opening Day.

The "Should-Have-Hit 500" Club

Don't count on anything in baseball

Charles Blahous

More exclusive than 3,000 hits and a surer guarantee of Hall of Fame induction than 300 wins, 500 home runs may define the most prestigious statistical club in baseball. Only fifteen players in baseball history have hit the mark, and none was denied entrance to the Hall of Fame.

The era in which we live presents the most impressive list of aspirants to this distinction in more than a generation. The recent seasons of Barry Bonds, Mark McGwire, and Ken Griffey, Jr. make them overwhelming favorites to reach the target. Plausible candidates are Albert Belle, Juan Gonzalez, Frank Thomas, Sammy Sosa, and Jose Canseco. Not since the mid-1960s—the era of Aaron, Mays, Robinson, Killebrew, Jackson, Mantle, McCovey, Banks, and Mathews—have so many men who seem likely to hit 500 homers played simultaneously .

Still, as long as the current crop of players has yet to reach the magic 500 total, there is a chance that misfortune will befall some of them—an injury, a sudden loss of productivity, or some other unforeseen event. And baseball history contains several reminders that there never was a player who was fully guaranteed to make it.

This article will make use of a Bill James formula known as the Favorite Toy. This statistical tool estimates the chances that a player will reach a career milestone, based on his performance to date.

Essentially, the way the Favorite Toy works is this:

A player is assigned a number of "remaining seasons" equal to 0.6 times the number of years until the player turns forty. An additional adjustment is that any player still playing regularly is considered to have at least 1.5 seasons remaining.

The factor of 0.6 is a statistical averaging of various possible outcomes. It factors in the projected erosion of the player's skills, as well as the chance that he may suffer a critical injury, in order to estimate the extent of his decline as he ages. Thus, for every year that a player continues to chug along at a steady pace of performance as he approaches the age of forty, his lifetime projections will improve.

The player's established performance level is then computed by taking three times the production in his most recent year, adding two times his production in the previous year, plus the production in the year before that, with the entire sum divided by six. This yields an established level of performance that weights the current year most heavily, but corrects to a degree for the event that the current year may represent a fluctuation from his standard level of ability.

A player's projected remaining home runs are estimated as his number of remaining years times this established performance level. This is then divided by the number of home runs needed to reach 500 to produce a quotient, from which 0.50 is subtracted to yield the percentage likelihood of reaching the target. Additional corrections to the formula are also made in the case of a projection that approaches 100 percent probability of success. Although this figure is not

Charles Blahous is policy director for U.S. Senator Judd Gregg.

a reliable projection of a player's future performance, it does yield a reasonable estimate of his eventual career total, to the extent that such a guess can plausibly be made on the basis of his totals to date.

The Favorite Toy can survey the past as well as the future. You can use it to identify the players who at one time had the greatest chances of reaching 500 home runs. The top ten such players who failed to reach the target, ranked by their onetime degree of certainty of getting there, are presented in the table at the bottom of the next page. I call this collection of frustrated expectations the "Should-Have-Hit 500" Club.

There is a different story behind each of these names, but they share one thing in common. Fans would have been fully justified in regarding each of these players as likely candidates to hit 500 homers. Their fates are warnings to such players as Barry Bonds and Ken Griffey Jr.— and their fans— that nothing is sure in baseball.

Clearly, this formula does not aim to identify the Tony Conigliaros and Bob Horners, who had brief impressive starts but left their potential largely unrealized. Here instead are players who succeeded for long enough to establish a credible challenge to 500, before failing for a variety of reasons. We will begin with the fainter hopes, and progress to those who had the best chances of all.

At the end of the 1979 season, Pirates captain Willie Stargell celebrated his MVP contribution to a World Series victory. He had a career total of 461 home runs, and had played mostly as a regular in 1979 (424 at-bats). His home-run production was still

Hank Greenberg

adequate—32 dingers in 1979, 28 the previous year. The system figures that he had a good season and a half left in him, enough to give him a 55.8 percent chance of reaching 500. Instead, Stargell gracefully accepted a reserve role the following season, bypassing all chances to pursue 500 by either moving to the AL as a DH, or exploiting his popularity and his relationship with manager Chuck Tanner to hold an enduring starting job in Pittsburgh. He may be the one player on this list who lost his chance more due to his unselfish personality than to an unforeseen difficulty.

Orlando Cepeda finished the 1963 season, age twenty-five, with an impressive career total of 191 home runs. At the same age, Hank Aaron had 179. Cepeda already had one home run crown under his belt (46 homers at the tender age of twenty-three), and showed no sign of slowing down. The formula projected his chances of reaching 500 to be 55.8 percent, based on his established level of 36.3 per year, and a long stretch of time to hit the final 309 homers he needed.

Cepeda was one of several players on the list whose impressive projections resulted from salubrious years for hitters that were followed by years in which pitchers reasserted themselves. But it was knee injuries specifically that accelerated Cepeda's decline, and aside from his MVP season in 1967, he never again approached his earlier levels of performance. He finished with 379 home runs.

Jim Rice's career total of 382 home runs was compiled in a career similar to Cepeda's. Rice bolted out of the starting gate, helping to lead the Red Sox to the

World Series in his first full season, and winning back-to-back home run titles in 1977 and 1978, swatting 46 dingers in the latter year. It was when he added another 39 home runs in 1979 that his chances to hit 500 burned brightest—55.9 percent. He had 172 homers at the age of twenty-six and was dominating AL power production. But his decline began almost immediately and was practically irreversible, save for a 39-homer season in 1983. When he left baseball after 1989, a career of seemingly assured greatness had been reduced to one unlikely to receive Hall of Fame recognition.

Hank Greenberg was one of the mightiest hitters in an era of mighty hitters. He posed the last challenge of significance to Babe Ruth's single-season home run record (58 in 1938). before Maris. From 1937 to 1940 alone he smashed 172 home runs, giving him a career total of 247 at the age of twenty-nine. With his efficient home run pace, he was an outstanding candidate to hit 500, with a 57.4 percent chance as measured by the Favorite Toy.

But Greenberg lost out to World War II. He was the first of many superstars to serve in the military during the war, and he may have been the one whose career totals were most affected as a result. Though in his first full season back (1946), he hit 44 home runs, his career ended shortly thereafter with a total of 331.

Dale Murphy's chances of hitting 500 never looked so good after 1987, an outstanding year for power hitters. He hit 44 that season, giving him 310 homers at the age of thirty-one. With only 190 to go, and a pace of better than 37 per year, the system gave him a 57.5 percent chance to make it. But Murphy slipped to a .224 average the following season and never regained his stroke. After bouncing to the Phillies and Rockies, Murphy departed from baseball with 398 home runs and his once seemingly certain Hall of Fame selection in doubt.

Few players fit the stereotype of the bulky, rapidly-deteriorating slugger better than Rocky Colavito. After 1962, he seemed well on his way to 500 homers and the Hall of Fame. Rocky then had 246 home runs, and had hit more than 35 in each of the previous five years (including 40 or more three times). His chances went south with a subpar 22-homer year in 1963. He was, like Cepeda, blocked from full recovery by an emerging era of dominant pitching. He would have a few more strong seasons, but lasted only a short while in part-time roles with the White Sox, Dodgers, and Yankees, before leaving baseball for good at the age of thirty-five with 374 home runs.

It may come as a surprise that Roger Maris's chances of hitting 500 were once considered quite good by the Favorite Toy. After his record-breaking 61-home-run season at the age of twenty-six, Maris could boast an impressive pace and plenty of time in which to accrue homers. His chances peaked at 63.4 percent. The system cannot know, however, that 1961 was an especially unrepresentative year, the most extreme one-year dilution of pitching talent to date, producing several other monster hitting years in addition to Maris's. Even considering some expected

The "Should Have Hit 500" Club

	Player	Year	Age	HRs	Projected	%	Total
1.	Lou Gehrig	1938	35	493	598	99.4	493
2.	Ralph Kiner	1951	28	257	586	85.0	369
3.	Duke Snider	1957	30	316	564	84.8	407
4.	Roger Maris	1961	26	158	546	63.4	275
5.	Rocky Colavito	1962	28	246	529	61.5	374
6.	Dale Murphy	1987	31	310	514	57.5	398
7.	Hank Greenberg	1940	29	247	519	57.4	331
8.	Jim Rice	1979	26	172	519	55.9	382
9.	Orlando Cepeda	1963	25	191	518	55.8	379
10.	Willie Stargell	1979	39	461	502	55.8	475

decline, however, his subsequent development can only be viewed as unrealized potential, and he departed baseball with fewer home runs—275—than anyone else on this list.

The hitters who can truly be said to have been overwhelmingly likely to hit 500 home runs, yet failed to do so, number only three. These sluggers weren't simply good candidates. They seemed like safe bets.

One of these was Duke Snider. Snider was thirty at the end of the 1957 season, the Dodgers' last year in Ebbets Field, with 316 home runs. It was his fifth consecutive season of 40 or more. Bill James notes that during the four years that Snider, Mays, and Mantle were patrolling center field in New York, it was Snider who led them in home runs and RBI. Hitting at his projected pace, he would need fewer than five seasons to reach 500. His chances were estimated to be 84.8 percent.

But decline for Snider was swift and sudden. His home run production dropped to 15 in 1958, the first year that the Dodgers played in Los Angeles. He began to have back trouble, and never fully adjusted to the move away from Ebbets. After 1959, he was no longer a true regular, and was reduced to part-time stints with the Mets and Giants before leaving baseball for good with 407 homers.

Surer still, however, seemed the chances of Ralph Kiner, the only player ever to lead the league in home runs in each of his first seven years. Ralph Kiner's career was not quite like any other in baseball history. After his 1951 season, his career total stood at 257 home runs and his age at twenty-eight. By leading the league again in 1952, his chances of reaching 500 actually went down. His peak chances of reaching 500 compute to 85.0 percent, and is not higher only because a player is not permitted under the formula to have a better than 97 percent chance of reaching a goal for every year of production needed to achieve it.

Kiner hardly became an unproductive player overnight. After his league-leading 37 homers in 1952, he

Ralph Kiner

was traded to the Cubs in midseason in 1953, hitting 35 homers for the year. But his power declined further in 1954 and 1955, and a back sprain forced his retirement after the 1955 season. He was only thirty-two when he faced his last major league pitch. He had 369 home runs. Even with his power decline he still had reasonable, though not probable, chances of hitting 500 right up to the time of his retirement. Though eventually elected to the Hall of Fame in 1975, his sudden decline has blurred the memory of the devastating hitter he once was.

In a class by himself is Lou Gehrig. He was right on the doorstep of 500 when he was struck down by his fatal illness. Gehrig had 493 homers at the age of thirty-five, and projected to hit a full 105 more, putting him on the verge of 600. Five hundred seemed a virtual certainty, a 99.4 percent chance by the formula. But he would never hit another. Gehrig's sudden tragedy, occurring as it did in the midst of rare productivity, permitted his greatness to be perceived despite his sudden disappearance from the game, and he was elected almost immediately to the Hall of Fame. As he would die not long after his retirement from baseball, his failure to hit 500 home runs was seldom thought of, being among the least of the tragedies to befall him.

The players in the "Should-Have-Hit 500" Club stand in mute testimony to the twists of fate in baseball, of which fans of Bonds, McGwire, Griffey, Belle, Gonzalez, and Thomas should be fully aware. There is poignancy in the careers of players whose futures at one time seemed to burn so bright, but who fell short of the heights expected of them. But all disappointments are relative. Each of these players had a great career. The least successful among them broke Babe Ruth's single-season home run record, and the greatest, his career stopped by tragedy, still proclaimed himself "the luckiest man on the face of the earth."

The 400 Home Run Club

A different perspective

Ron Kaplan

There are twenty-five batters in major league history who have hit 400 or more home runs. More elite are the fifteen in the "500 Club." But as great as these players are, they didn't do it by themselves. Someone had to throw the ball.

Only eight pitchers in major league annals can claim that they were among the select few to have given up more than 400 home runs. The saying goes that a pitcher has to be pretty good to lose a large number of games on a yearly basis. The same can be said for these home run hurlers. In fact, six of the eight are members of the Hall of Fame.

The only pitcher to have allowed more than 500 home runs is Robin Roberts, the reverse Babe Ruth. Roberts led the National League in homers allowed from 1954 through 1957, yet still managed to post 286 victories to go along with 2,357 strikeouts. He was elected to the Hall of Fame in 1976.

Ferguson Jenkins, who won 20 or more for the Cubs for six consecutive seasons (elected in 1991), follows Roberts with 484 taters tossed. He also rang up 3,192 strikeouts to put him in ninth place on that all-time list.

Following close behind Jenkins is Phil Niekro (elected 1997), who fluttered his knuckleballs for the Braves, Yankees, Indians, and Blue Jays. Over twenty-four big league seasons, he collected 318 wins (fourteenth place all time), 3,342 strikeouts (eighth),

pitched over 5,400 innings (fourth)—and yielded 482 homers. He and brother Joe, who also had a long if not as distinguished career, combined for 758 homers, beating out Gaylord (who just missed the magic number with 399) and Jim (308) Perry's combined 707 for most generous siblings.

Don Sutton (elected 1998) allowed 472 souvenirs to go along with his 324 victories (tied for twelfth place), while on the mound for the Dodgers, Astros, Brewers, Athletics, and Angels. His 3,574 strikeouts places him fourth in that department.

Frank Tanana, who combined with Nolan Ryan to make perhaps the most dynamic strikeout tandem in major league history, is fifth on the "long gone" list with 448 homers. Tanana pitched for the Angels, Red Sox, Rangers, Tigers, Mets, and Yankees, in his twenty-one seasons. With a record of 240-236, it's unlikely that he will join his old teammate in Cooperstown. (By comparison, Nolan allowed "only" 321 home runs over his illustrious career.)

Warren Spahn (elected in his first year of eligibility in 1973), who holds the record for most 20-win seasons (thirteen) and the all-time victory record for lefthanders (363), also allowed 434 batters to circle the bases. And he didn't even hit his stride until 1956 when, at age 35, he rang up six straight seasons of twenty-plus wins. As further proof of his stout constitution, Spahn led the league in complete games between ages 36-41.

Bert Blyleven, the perennially altruistic hurler, comes next with 430. He holds the single-season

Ron Kaplan has written about baseball for such publications as The Elysian Fields Quarterly, Nine, BookPage, *and* The Mystery Review.

record with fifty homers allowed in 1986. In twenty-one seasons, the product of Zeist, Holland, won 287 and lost 250.

Steve Carlton (elected 1994 in his first year on the ballot), the enigmatic lefty of Phillies and Cardinals fame, rounds out the select group with 414. In 1972, Carlton was the unanimous winner of the Cy Young Award (his first of four) on the basis of 27 wins, 310 strikeouts, and an ERA of 1.97 for a last-place Phillies club. He gave up a mere seventeen homers that season. In 1969 against the New York Mets, Carlton set the National League mark with 19 strikeouts in a game, but he nevertheless lost the contest, 4-3, on pair of two-run homers.

As of this writing only two active pitchers have given up more than 300. It is unlikely that either Dennis Martinez (364) or Dennis Eckersly (336) will be around long enough the crack the barrier.

The members of the 400 club were no slouches at the plate either. Spahn took his revenge on fellow hurlers with thirty-five homers, second only to Wes Ferrell's thirty-eight. Jenkins and Carlton each popped thirteen round trippers, and Niekro cranked out seven. Tanana and Blyleven can be forgiven, since they spent most of their careers in the American League. Only Sutton, a long-time NL-er, failed to hit even one.

Looking strictly at the cold, hard numbers and the unlikelihood that today's pitchers will enjoy such lengthy careers, you have to consider that while the number of batters in the 500 Club will increase, membership in the pitchers' "400" is most likely closed.

300 Home Run Pitchers

Gaylord Perry	399
Jim Kaat	395
Jack Morris	389
Charlie Hough	383
Tom Seaver	380
Catfish Hunter	374
Jim Bunning	372
*Dennis Martinez	364
Mickey Lolich	347
Luis Tiant	346
Early Wynn	338
*Dennis Eckersley	336
Doyle Alexander	324
Nolan Ryan	321
Juan Marichal	320
Pedro Ramos	315
Jim Perry	308
Jim Palmer	303
Murry Dickson	302
Tommy John	302
* Active	

59 in '21

What if the Babe had had one more game?

Jim Rygelski

After Cardinals slugger Mark McGwire hit his 57th homer in the second-to-last game of 1997, a St. Louis television station showed a list of the best single-season totals. It ranked McGwire's 57 as fifth-best behind Roger Maris's 61 in 1961, Babe Ruth's 60 in 1927, and the 58 of both Hank Greenberg (1938) and Jimmie Foxx (1932). Absent from that home run list was Ruth's 1921 total of 59.

Ruth's 1921 season was probably his best overall, but since he hit *only* 59 homers, the accomplishments of his second season in Yankee pinstripes are largely overlooked in favor of the famous 1927.

In 1921, Ruth's 59 homers (and career best 171 RBI and 177 runs scored, made possible by a .378 batting average, 44 doubles, 16 triples, and 144 walks) helped the Yankees win their first pennant and proved to any skeptics that his 54 homers the years before weren't a fluke. That year also marked the third straight in which Ruth set the single-season home run record (including his 29 with the Red Sox in 1919).

But one other significant though rarely discussed fact emerged from Ruth's 1921: The Babe became—and remains—the only person to bid for the single-season homer record (those who have hit 56 or more) whose team didn't play a full schedule. A rainout never made up held the Yankees to 153 games.

"Iffy" history can be a dangerous thing if it gets out of hand (or so I remind my fellow Cardinals fans

Jim Rygelski is an editor for a chain of weekly newspapers in St. Louis, Missouri.

when they put too much weight on umpire Don Denkinger's infamous call in the 6th game of the 1985 World Series). Yet it's interesting to speculate on what might have happened if that rained-out September 4 game had been made up.

The washout—The 1921 Yankees were involved in an exciting pennant race as they began their last scheduled game against the Senators in Washington on September 4. Ruth entered with 50 home runs, four behind his own record from the year before, which he would top eleven days later. He singled with two out in the first off southpaw Tom Zachary, the same hurler he would hit his 60th homer off in 1927. The Babe, who stole a career high 17 bases that year, was thrown out trying to swipe second. After the Senators went out in their half of the first, rain washed out the contest. Newspapers speculated that the game would be replayed, but it never was. The Yankees finished 4-1/2 games up on Cleveland, and there was no point to replaying the Nats.

A wire-service story in newspapers of October 3 quoted the Babe as saying he was disappointed he hadn't reached the 60-homer mark he'd set for himself. "We'll go gunning for that 60 mark next season," he said. He didn't lament the fact that the Yankees had played one fewer game than scheduled because of the rainout.

To demonstrate what Ruth might have lost with that rainout consider that the first week of September was one of his more productive stretches in 1921,

The Babe hammers one in '21.

was tied for fifth of all those—including Senators—who ever played there.

The Babe's pace—Home run "averages" (usually stated as a home run for every so many times at bat) are deceiving since most sluggers hit theirs in clusters. Ruth in 1921 was no different. Yet his 1921 home-run-hitting pace was probably the most consistent of any of the single-season challengers.

Ruth's 1921 pace also was vastly different from his 1927 assault on the record, in which he had to hit a major league record 17 in the final month to reach 60. In 1921, Ruth hit 10 or more home runs in each of five months, May through September; in 1927 he did so in only two. And in 1921 he hit home runs in 54 of his team's games, a mark that only Maris has tied.

Ruth's 1927 home run pace was never ahead of his pace of 1921. Going into the 154th game of 1927 he was tied with his 1921 output. (Ruth hit his final home run of 1927 in the Yankees' 154th contest, which was the second-last played that year because of a tie earlier in the campaign. The batting records from the tie counted, but Ruth didn't hit a homer in it.)

If the Yankees had replayed the 1921 game and Ruth had hit one out, the best he would have done was tie the mark in 1927. If he'd hit two, he'd still share the record. Which Ruthian "pace" would the media have chosen for his pursuers?

In 1961 much was made of the fact that when Maris hit his 40th home run in this team's 95th game, he was 25 games ahead of Ruth's 1927 pace. But Maris's 1961 cadence was behind Ruth's 1921 pace at most points, and Maris's 40th would have put him only four games ahead of Ruth—his largest lead. By the time Maris hit his 41st he was five behind the Babe of 1921. Until he began a 15-homer-in-22-game surge that allowed him to pass both Ruth and Maris, McGwire in 1998 was one HR (47) behind Ruth in 1921 (48) after 123 games.

And had the Babe hit three, or four in that 1921 game that could have been replayed? Ah, the what-ifs. But let's remember that great season of 1921, when Babe Ruth hit more homers in a season one game short than anybody but he and Roger Maris had ever managed in a season of any length up to 1998.

following his longest homerless drought (nine games) of the season. He hit home runs on September 2 and 3 (both against the Senators in New York), and went on to club them on September 5 in Boston; September 7 against the Red Sox in New York, and on September 8 and 9 against the A's in Phliadelphia.

Ruth in Griffith Stadium—Maybe it wouldn't have mattered if the rainout had been made up. Ruth hit only three homers in Washington's Griffith Stadium that year, tied for his lowest road total that season, and had hit none there after May. While it was only 320 feet down the right field line, the ballpark's thirty-foot wall did provide a challenge.

But Ruth could hit them out of Griffith. His 34 career homers there is tops for any visiting player, according to the SABR publication *Home Runs in the Old Ballparks* (1995), edited by David Vincent. And, according to those same figures, Ruth's career total

The Over-50 Club

Ev Parker

The annual meeting started
In that place where old sluggers go.
Hank Greenberg read the roll-call,
And he read it very slow.

For Hank had looked around the room,
And he knew a timeless truth,
No Over-50 Club could meet,
Without a Babe named Ruth.

"Where the hell is he this year?"
Hack Wilson and Double X moaned.
"Do we really need these meetings?"
Mickey and Roger groaned.

But a whiff of pure Havana,
Preceded The Babe's arrival,
A smile behind a long cigar,
The Game owed him survival.

Smiling The Babe bade the meeting start,
A report by Johnny Mize,
The state of baseball in '98,
Everyone showed surprise.

The Big Cat said, "No beanballs,
Much less brushbacks at the knuckles,
And umps won't call a strike
If the ball's above their buckles."

"The apple," John said, "travels
Like a golf ball off a tee,
Homers hit off the wrong foot,
It's really sad to see."

Then bedlam reigned—"No dusters?"
"No high strikes if you please?"
"Pitchers must hit the sweet spot,
The belt down to the knees?"

Hank Greenberg merely shook his head,
Double X about to swoon.
Each man in that place where old sluggers go,
Knew they'd been born too soon.

Then up piped the Old Bambino
With a Ruthian retort,
"Some kid will hit a hundred soon,
And find he's a homer short."

For **Ev Parker**, SABR proved there is life after N.Y.P.D. "Much thanks to
Bill Deane, Norman Macht, Larry Ritter, and Lyle Spatz, who encouraged me
to express my love for the game the best way I know how—through poetry."

Only the Best

The Sporting News All-Stars 1925-1960

Eric Marshall White

The period 1925 to 1960 was a "golden era" for baseball. It spanned the glory days of Ruth and Gehrig and the emergence of Mays and Aaron. During this period, *The Sporting News* (TSN) was considered the "Bible of Baseball." Under publisher J. G. Taylor Spink, it featured baseball subjects on its front page every week of the year and became the game's most popular and respected publication. TSN was a great innovator in sports journalism. Realizing early on that special recognition of the game's brightest stars sparked fan interest and led to greater readership and sales, TSN selected league MVPs from 1929 to 1945, a Major League Player of the Year beginning in 1936, a Rookie of the Year beginning in 1946, and a Player and Pitcher of the Year for each league beginning in 1948. With the exception of the league MVP awards, each of these honors was an important innovation and a major step in the formation of the annual honors familiar to today's fans.

TSN's most eagerly awaited off-season feature, however, was the announcement of its Major League All-Star Team, introduced in 1925. For thirty-six years, TSN ran a national poll of experienced baseball writers to nominate the game's eight best position players and its two or three top pitchers. Unlike its contemporary MVP award, which was sometimes voted on by as few as eight writers, or the slightly later All Star Game rosters, which involved open fan balloting, these honors were decided by hundreds of

Eric Marshall White, Ph.D., is curator of rare books at Bridwell Library, Southern Methodist University, in Dallas.

highly qualified voters. (The 1950 *Sporting News Baseball Guide* mentions that 346 writers participated in the 1949 voting.) Members of TSN's postseason all-star team could not qualify on the basis of a hot first half or their established popularity with fans. They had to perform spectacularly over a whole season. And there was only one spot per position for the combined leagues. Being the best shortstop in your league often wasn't good enough.

One measure of the importance and prestige that were attached to these honors is the fact that four Hall of Fame plaques (Musial's, Medwick's, Cuyler's, and Ruffing's) mention how many times the player made the team. In the last thirty years, however, fan and media interest in TSN's all-star teams has dropped off dramatically. The reason, I believe, is twofold. First, TSN is no longer fandom's number one source for baseball information. Second, in 1961 the roster was expanded to create a squad for each league. The teams now include designated hitters and relief pitchers.

Despite this dilution of quality and prestige, we can look to TSN's Major League All-Star Teams of 1925 to 1960 as a uniform standard of excellence at each position, and we can review who was considered the best of the best. Equally important, we can look more closely at some of the more controversial choices to better understand those qualities (besides raw statistics) that made these stars shine brightest in the eyes of the voters. Here, ladies and gentlemen, are the original TSN Major League All-Stars:

1925
1B	Bottomley
2B	Hornsby
SS	Wright
3B	Traynor
OF	Cuyler
OF	Carey
OF	Goslin
C	Cochrane
P	Johnson
	Rommel
	Vance

1926
1B	Burns
2B	Hornsby
SS	Sewell
3B	Traynor
OF	Goslin
OF	Mostil
OF	Ruth
C	O'Farrell
P	Pennock
	Uhle
	Alexander

1927
1B	Gehrig
2B	Hornsby
SS	Jackson
3B	Traynor
OF	Ruth
OF	Simmons
OF	P. Waner
C	Hartnett
P	Root
	Lyons

1928
1B	Gehrig
2B	Hornsby
SS	Jackson
3B	Lindstrom
OF	Ruth
OF	Manush
OF	P. Waner
C	Cochrane
P	Grove
	Hoyt

1929
1B	Foxx
2B	Hornsby
SS	Jackson
3B	Traynor
OF	Simmons†
OF	Wilson
OF	Ruth
C	Cochrane
P	Grove
	Grimes

1930
1B	Terry†
2B	Frisch
SS	Cronin†
3B	Lindstrom
OF	Simmons
OF	Wilson
OF	Ruth
C	Cochrane
P	Grove
	Ferrell

1931
1B	Gehrig†
2B	Frisch
SS	Cronin
3B	Traynor
OF	Simmons
OF	Averill
OF	Ruth
C	Cochrane
P	Grove
	Earnshaw

1932
1B	Foxx†
2B	Lazzeri
SS	Cronin
3B	Traynor
OF	O'Doul
OF	Averill
OF	Klein†
C	Dickey
P	Grove
	Warneke

1933
1B	Foxx†
2B	Gehringer
SS	Cronin
3B	Traynor
OF	Simmons
OF	Berger
OF	Klein
C	Dickey
P	Crowder
	Hubbell†

1934
1B	Gehrig†
2B	Gehringer
SS	Cronin
3B	Higgins
OF	Simmons
OF	Averill
OF	Ott
C	Cochrane
P	Gomez
	Rowe
	Dean†

1935
1B	Greenberg†
2B	Gehringer
SS	Vaughan†
3B	Martin
OF	Medwick
OF	Cramer
OF	Ott
C	Cochrane
P	Hubbell
	Dean

1936
1B	Gehrig†
2B	Gehringer
SS	Appling
3B	Higgins
OF	Medwick
OF	Averill
OF	Ott
C	Dickey
P	Hubbell†*
	Dean

1937
1B	Gehrig
2B	Gehringer†
SS	Bartell
3B	Rolfe
OF	Medwick†
OF	J. DiMaggio
OF	P. Waner
C	Hartnett
P	Hubbell
	Ruffing

1938
1B	Foxx†
2B	Gehringer
SS	Cronin
3B	Rolfe
OF	Medwick
OF	J. DiMaggio
OF	Ott
C	Dickey
P	Ruffing
	Gomez
	Vander Meer*

1939
1B	Foxx
2B	Gordon
SS	Cronin
3B	Rolfe
OF	Medwick
OF	J. DiMaggio†*
OF	Williams
C	Dickey
P	Ruffing
	Feller
	Walters†

1940
1B	McCormick†
2B	Gordon
SS	Appling
3B	Hack
OF	Greenberg†
OF	J. DiMaggio
OF	Williams
C	Danning
P	Feller*
	Walters
	Derringer

1941
1B	Camilli†
2B	Gordon
SS	Travis
3B	Hack
OF	Williams*
OF	J. DiMaggio†
OF	Reiser
C	Dickey
P	Feller
	Wyatt
	T. Lee

1942
1B	Mize
2B	Gordon†
SS	Pesky
3B	Hack
OF	Williams*
OF	J. DiMaggio
OF	Slaughter
C	Owen
P	M. Cooper†
	Bonham
	Hughson

1943
1B	York
2B	Herman
SS	Appling
3B	B. Johnson
OF	Wakefield
OF	Musial†
OF	Nicholson
C	W. Cooper
P	Chandler†*
	M. Cooper
	Sewell

1944
1B	Sanders
2B	Doerr†
SS	Marion†*
3B	Elliott
OF	Musial
OF	Wakefield
OF	F. Walker
C	W. Cooper
P	Newhouser
	M. Cooper
	Trout

1945
1B	Cavarretta
2B	Stirnweiss
SS	Marion
3B	Kurowski
OF	Holmes†
OF	Pafko
OF	Rosen
C	Richards
P	Newhouser*
	Ferriss
	Borowy

1946
1B	Musial*
2B	Doerr
SS	Pesky
3B	Kell
OF	Williams
OF	D. DiMaggio
OF	Slaughter
C	A. Robinson
P	Newhouser
	Feller
	Ferriss

1947
1B	Mize
2B	Gordon
SS	Boudreau
3B	Kell
OF	Williams*
OF	J. DiMaggio
OF	Kiner
C	W. Cooper
P	Blackwell
	Feller
	Branca

1948
1B	Mize
2B	Gordon
SS	Boudreau+*
3B	Elliott
OF	Williams
OF	J. DiMaggio
OF	Musial+
C	Tebbetts
P	Sain+
	Lemon+
	Brecheen

1949
1B	Henrich
2B	J. Robinson
SS	Rizzuto
3B	Kell
OF	Williams+*
OF	Musial
OF	Kiner
C	Campanella
P	Parnell
	Kinder+
	Page

1950
1B	Dropo
2B	J. Robinson
SS	Rizzuto+*
3B	Kell
OF	Musial
OF	Kiner+
OF	Doby
C	Berra
P	Raschi
	Lemon+
	Konstanty+

1951
1B	Fain+
2B	J. Robinson
SS	Rizzuto
3B	Kell
OF	Musial+*
OF	Williams
OF	Kiner
C	Campanella
P	Maglie
	Roe+
	Reynolds

1952
1B	Fain
2B	J. Robinson
SS	Rizzuto
3B	Kell
OF	Musial
OF	Sauer+
OF	Mantle
C	Berra
P	Roberts+*
	Shantz+
	Reynolds

1953
1B	Vernon
2B	Schoendienst
SS	Reese
3B	Rosen+*
OF	Musial
OF	Snider
OF	Furillo
C	Campanella+
P	Roberts
	Spahn+
	Porterfield+

1954
1B	Kluszewski
2B	Avila+
SS	Dark
3B	Rosen
OF	Mays+*
OF	Musial
OF	Snider
C	Berra
P	Lemon+
	Antonelli+
	Roberts

1955
1B	Kluszewski
2B	Fox
SS	Banks
3B	Mathews
OF	Snider+*
OF	Williams
OF	Kaline+
C	Campanella
P	Roberts+
	Newcombe
	Ford+

1956
1B	Kluszewski
2B	Fox
SS	Kuenn
3B	K. Boyer
OF	Mantle+*
OF	Aaron+
OF	Williams
C	Berra
P	Newcombe+
	Ford
	Pierce+

1957
1B	Musial+
2B	Schoendienst
SS	McDougald
3B	Mathews
OF	Mantle
OF	Williams+*
OF	Mays
C	Berra
P	Spahn+
	Pierce+
	Bunning

1958
1B	Musial
2B	Fox
SS	Banks+
3B	Thomas
OF	Williams
OF	Mays
OF	Aaron
C	Crandall
P	Turley+*
	Spahn+
	Friend

1959
1B	Cepeda
2B	Fox+
SS	Banks+
3B	Mathews
OF	Minoso
OF	Mays
OF	Aaron
C	Lollar
P	Wynn+*
	Jones+
	Antonelli

1960
1B	Skowron
2B	Mazeroski*
SS	Banks
3B	Mathews
OF	Minoso
OF	Mays
OF	Maris+
C	Crandall
P	Law+
	Spahn
	Broglio

† = League TSN Most Valuable Player Award (awarded until 1945)
* = TSN Major League Player of the Year Award (awarded from 1936)
+ = League's TSN Player/Pitcher of the Year Award (awarded from 1948)

Nearly all the great names are here, plus a few you may not recognize. For me, the most obscure was that "Mostil" on the 1926 team. Johnny "Bananas" Mostil, I have since learned, was a gazelle in center for the White Sox, a .301 career hitter who could steal forty bases, lead the league in walks, and score 135 runs. Mostil's tragic slide into obscurity began during spring training at Shreveport in 1927, when he inexplicably attempted suicide with a razor, barely surviving his many wounds. One story had it that he couldn't live with the pain of chronic neuritis. Others rumored that he had been caught fooling around with a teammate's wife and feared exposure and deadly retribution. A mystery man, indeed.

The thirty-six all-star teams yielded 386 spots, of which 253 (nearly two-thirds) were taken by today's Hall-of-Famers—including the entire 1928 and 1929 teams! On average, the typical Hall of Famer was elected to TSN's all-star team three times—a useful piece of trivia. There were very few one-year wonders here. The other 133 spots were taken most often by players who had distinguished careers, but who do not quite fit the definition of an immortal.

First Base		Second Base		Shortstop		Third Base		Outfield						Catcher	
Gehrig	6	Gehringer	6	Cronin	7	Traynor	7	Williams	13	Medwick	5	Snider	3	Cochrane	7
Foxx	5	Gordon	6	Banks	4	Kell	6	Musial	9	Averill	4	P. Waner	3	Dickey	6
Kluszewski	3	Hornsby	5	Rizzuto	4	Mathews	4	DiMaggio	8	Kiner	4			Berra	5
Mize	3	Fox	4	Appling	3	Hack	3	Ruth	6	Ott	4			Campanella	4
Musial	3	J. Robinson	4	Jackson	3	Rolfe	3	Simmons	6	Aaron	3			W. Cooper	3
								Mays	5	Mantle	3				

Pitcher (RH)		Pitcher (LH)	
Feller	5	Grove	5
Roberts	4	Hubbell	4
M. Cooper	3	Spahn	4
Dean	3	Newhouser	3
Lemon	3		
Ruffing	3		

italics = Not a member of the Hall of Fame.

First base—Lou Gehrig and Jimmy Foxx dominated the voting at first base. Although Gehrig is rightly considered the greatest of all time at his position, people forget that Foxx was right with him in just about everything he did—everything but The Streak. The surprise here is Ted Kluszewski, who will probably never reach Cooperstown. Missing from the list is Hank Greenberg, who was just plain unlucky. Besides losing four years to World War II, he faced insurmountable competition at his position in five of his best seasons.

Second base—Despite the fact that Rogers Hornsby would have been the obvious choice at second base for several years before 1925, the leaders here were Charlie Gehringer, who was the very image of perfection and consistency on both offense and defense, and Joe Gordon. An acrobatic wizard around the keystone, "Flash" Gordon used his glove and powerful bat to help the Yankees and Indians to six pennants. The MVP of 1942, he was named to TSN's all-star team six times, by far the highest total of any player *not* in the Hall of Fame. His six wins equals the combined peacetime honors of Frankie Frisch, Tony Lazzeri, Billy Herman, Bobby Doerr, Red Schoendienst, and Bucky Harris. (If I had to draw a single conclusion from the TSN polls, it would be that you shouldn't have Doerr in Cooperstown without Gordon.) Jackie Robinson's four-fold distinction is amazing, given that he was a regular at second base for only five seasons.

Shortstop—Among shortstops, Joe Cronin's seven all-star team appearances justify the conclusion that he was the greatest player at his position between Honus Wagner and Cal Ripken. Ernie Banks started fast with four selections by 1960. Confounding the critics of his weaker bat, Phil Rizzuto tallied four berths, hard evidence that he was rated higher than PeeWee Reese at the time. Winning the World Series every year does wonders for your reputation.

Third base—The top performance by a third-sacker belongs to Pie Traynor, who used to be rated the best of all time. Although that lofty title is now generally bestowed upon Mike Schmidt, there is no denying that Traynor impressed his contemporaries. Despite a relative lack of competition after the peak years of Red Rolfe and Stan Hack, George Kell's strong showing amply supports his Cooperstown enshrinement. Surprisingly, Eddie Mathews produced "only" four all-

1953, '54, '56, and '58, Mathews was nudged out each year by other members of baseball's first generation of hard-hitting third basemen.

Outfield—*The Sporting News* selected three outfielders to its all-star teams, regardless of whether they played right, center, or left. The first outfielder to dominate the competition was none other than Babe Ruth, who was selected six times in the final decade of his career. Al Simmons was clearly the other illustrious outfielder of the period, followed by Ducky Medwick. The next generation produced the most prolific of all TSN all-stars: the outfield of Ted Williams, Joe DiMaggio, and Stan Musial. Despite a combined nine-plus seasons lost to military service, this trio occupied thirty positions in the all-star outfields. Joltin' Joe was TSN's top vote-getter from 1937 through 1941, and twice he was named by every writer in the national poll. Teddy Ballgame, despite his conflicts with the press, was elected to the team a record thirteen times. Stan the Man was nearly as impressive, considering the additional honors he received at first base.

Among the great young outfielders who starred in the '50s, three went on to win additional honors in the two-team formula after 1960. Mickey Mantle made the team in his sophomore year and in his first two MVP seasons, and he rated three more berths in the '60s. Willie Mays was the most decorated of all recent stars, taking the laurel five times through 1960 and six times in the next decade. That edged out the strong showing of Hank Aaron, who was an all-star three times in the '50s and six more times thereafter—and that's not counting his overlooked MVP season in 1957!

Catcher—Two pairs of catchers dominated the 1925-1960 era. First it was Mickey Cochrane and Bill Dickey, then came Yogi Berra and Roy Campanella. Only one other Hall-of-Fame catcher, Gabby Hartnett, ever made the team! Even he was able to interrupt the Cochrane-Dickey show only two times, ten years apart. Later, it was either Berra or Campanella, and even then, there wasn't enough room for the two of them: Campy's success meant that Yogi was left off the team in two of his MVP years. Now that's what I call a great head-to-head rivalry! In the hiatus between these historic duels, the best performance was that of Walker Cooper, a rock of Gibralter with timely power.

Pitcher—The strongest performances among pitchers begin with that of Lefty Grove, whose unmatched run of five consecutive selections goes a long way toward justifying the claim that he was the greatest pitcher in modern baseball. During his streak, Grove compiled an incredible 128-33 record with four ERA titles. The next year he put up a 24-8 mark and was left off the team! Next came Bob Feller, who, despite his military service, was an all-star in five seasons and the AL Pitcher of the Year in a sixth. Carl Hubbell, Robin Roberts, and Warren Spahn were impressive with four selections each, and Spahnie went on to make the NL team at the age of forty in 1961. Joining these Hall of Famers with three all-star berths was Walker Cooper's brother, Mort.

Beyond the numbers—Clearly, a dream team of the most prolific TSN all-stars of 1925 to 1960 would be a threat to win 150 games in any fantasy league. On the other side of the coin, several Hall-of-Famers never made the team despite playing a healthy decade in the relevant period. While this may raise the question of how a player can be considered an immortal now if he was never considered a true star when he played, what intrigues me most about TSN's voting is its potential as a measure of just how contemporary experts went about rating players. That is, as an answer to the question, "By what criteria were they judged?"

The voting for TSN's All-Stars provides an invaluable historical record of how experienced baseball writers rated the men who played in front of them. As Bill James noted in *Whatever Happened to the Hall of Fame?*, "If a player's defensive skills or clutch performance or leadership qualities were outstanding enough to cause him to rate higher than his statistics show, this voting should reflect that." What is surprising, however, is the degree to which the voting directly contradicted the raw statistical "evidence." For instance, consider the hitting statistics posted by the catchers listed below (admittedly, triple-crown stats are not the best way to rate catchers, but it's something to go on, and we all know how much these numbers weigh in today's MVP award debates):

Year	Catcher	HR	RBI	BA
1925	Hartnett	24	67	.289
	Cochrane	6	55	.331
1926	Hargrave	6	62	.353
	O'Farrell	7	68	.293
1927	Cochrane	12	80	.338
	Hartnett	10	80	.294
1928	Hartnett	14	57	.302
	Cochrane	10	57	.293
1930	Hartnett	37	122	.339

	Cochrane	10	85	.357
1932	Cochrane	23	112	.293
	Dickey	15	84	.310
1934	Hartnett	22	90	.299
	Dickey	12	72	.322
	Cochrane	2	76	.320
1935	Hartnett	13	91	.344
	Dickey	14	81	.279
	Cochrane	5	47	.319
1937	Dickey	29	133	.332
	Hartnett	12	82	.354
1938	York	33	127	.298
	Lombardi	19	95	.342
	Dickey	27	115	.313
1940	Lombardi	14	74	.319
	Danning	13	91	.300
1942	W. Cooper	7	65	.281
	Dickey	2	37	.295
	Owen	0	44	.259
1945	Lombardi	19	70	.307
	Richards	3	32	.256

Based on these numbers, most of today's fans would take the guy listed first in each year. Amazingly, however, in all of these seasons, the player with the superior numbers was beaten out for TSN's All-Star honors by the *bottom* man in each group. Now, I do not believe for a moment that this means that the voters were blind to offensive statistics. But I do believe that they were able to see a lot on the field of play that we can't see in the hindsight of numbers. Although it is possible that the writers in those days generally gave too much credit for "intangibles," at least here we can surmise who was getting credit for them and who was not. Then again, those tangible offensive events did not simply accumulate in a vacuum. Sometimes they helped the team win, sometimes they went to waste. The writers saw it all first hand, so it should be no surprise that the All Star nearly always played on the team that finished higher in the standings. For what it is worth, in Cochrane's seven all-star seasons, he led the contending catchers in team standings seven times (one tie), including five pennants. In contrast, the traditional defensive stats don't reveal much here, certainly not as much as team standings. Although defense clearly won the day for O'Farrell (1926) and Owen (1942), Cochrane was the all-star several times despite having also-ran defensive stats. This fact tends to reinforce the notion that he was (and was seen as) a peerless leader with clutch ability, speed afoot, tactical savvy, and competitive fire, who did whatever it took to win ballgames. These intagibles were his hallmark, and they won him the BBWAA MVP award in 1934 over Gehrig's triple crown.

Clearly, we are dealing with an authoritative source of information here. Even without television, scribes of that period actually saw more of Cochrane and

Hartnett than today's media people see of Rodriguez and Piazza. With only eight teams in the league, a writer covering the Red Sox could watch an opposing team twenty-two times during the season, and he might catch some NL action whenever the Braves were in town. This extensive pressbox observation, not highlight films, computerized statistical updates, or endorsement hype, was the foundation of the voter's opinion. You have to respect that.

Snubs and logjams—Although TSN's voters could see beyond the numbers, there are still some cases in which it appears that justice was not served. By this I do not mean to rehash the many great performances that went unrewarded, such as Harry Heilmann's stratospheric batting marks in 1925 and 1927. Rather, I'm thinking of those instances in which the voting contradicted the results of other award polls. Ten times, an MVP selected by the Baseball Writers Association of America or its predecessors was surpassed in TSN's all-star poll by another player at the same position. Ironically, in three seasons TSN could not find room on the team for its own award winner because of insurmountable competition from the other league. All of these "snubs" were the unavoidable result of a difference of opinion in the face of very stiff competition.

Year	Player	Other honors
1925	Roger Peckinpaugh	American League Award
1928	Jim Bottomley	National League Award
1931	Chuck Klein	TSN's NL MVP
1935	Gabby Hartnett	BBWAA's NL MVP
1938	Ernie Lombardi	BBWAA's MVP, TSN's NL Player of the Year
1947	Bob Elliott	BBWAA's NL MVP
1949	Howie Pollet	TSN's NL Pitcher of the Year
1951	Yogi Berra	BBWAA's AL MVP
1955	Yogi Berra	BBWAA's AL MVP
1957	Henry Aaron	BBWAA's NL MVP
1960	Chuck Estrada	TSN's AL Pitcher of the Year

However, another species of controversy, known as "inherent contradiction," arose throughout the history of the voting. The following players were honored by TSN as their league's outstanding player, yet their presumably rightful place on the all-star team was given to a usurper from the same circuit.

Year	Player	Other honors	Usurper
1937	Johnny Allen	TSN's Major League Player of Year	Hubbell, Ruffing
1944	Eddie Mayo	TSN's AL Player of the Year	Stirnweiss
1949	Enos Slaughter	TSN's NL Player of the Year	Musial, Kiner
1951	Bob Feller	TSN's AL Pitcher of the Year	Reynolds
1952	Luke Easter	TSN's AL Player of the Year	Williams
1958	Jackie Jensen	BBWAA's MVP, TSN's AL Player of the Year	Williams
1960	Dick Groat	BBWAA's MVP, TSN's NL Player of the Year	Banks

This kind of contradiction raises the question, "If Johnny Allen was the best pitcher in the world in 1937, how could Hubbell and Ruffing supercede him as the All Stars?" The most likely answer resides in the fact that the all-star team resulted from a broad-based poll and the other award was probably a decision made by TSN's editorial board. The ultimate contradiction came in 1960, when TSN and the BBWAA chose Dick Groat as the best player in the NL, but they put a different guy in the same league on the all-star team. The Major League Player of the Year (but apparently not the top player in the NL) was Groat's teammate, World Series hero Bill Mazeroski. You figure it out.

With all these contradictions in mind, I remain inclined to trust TSN's polls, and to conclude that in nearly every case, their voters knew what they were doing, regardless of the MVP awards and the like. Two of the rare exceptions come from the early history of the voting, when it seems that a uniform definition of what constituted an "All Star" had not been adopted yet. This would explain the suspiciously sentimental choices of aging Walter Johnson over Stan Coveleski in 1925, and of World Series hero Grover Alexander over several better-qualified hurlers the next year. Nevertheless, the only instance in the history of TSN's Major League All-Star Team in which I suspect a blatant goof, or at least a convenient fudging of facts, was in the strange case of the 1938 team. This roster, which failed to extend invitations to an MVP catcher, a first baseman with 58 homers, and two hurlers who led their leagues in both ERA and winning percentage, also featured a highly controversial selection at third base and an inexplicable pick in the outfield. At first glance, the root of the problem appears to have been at third base, where Red Rolfe got the nod despite Harland Clift's immensely superior numbers. The thing is, TSN selected Mel Ott for the outfield even though he played 113 games at third base. Perhaps the unspoken consensus was that although Ott was too potent at the plate to leave off the club, he was too green at third to merit all-star status. Granted, Ott was the NL's outstanding hitter in 1938, but how could he have been considered one of the top three outfielders in the game if he played less than a quarter of the season there? The real loser was not Clift, but someone who could have been the third legitimate outfielder. Nominees anyone?

Well, there you have it—thirty-six years of performance ratings at every position endorsed by a large community of baseball experts, with an extremely high level of credibility throughout. I hope you've found it all as provocative and revealing as I have. Regardless of who did and didn't make the rosters, and regardless of who is or is not yet elected to the Hall of Fame, we can still enjoy looking over the old TSN Major League All-Star rosters, embark on a nostalgic trip back to the diamonds of summers long ago, and remember (even if only vicariously) the great players in their finest seasons.

Bibliography:

The Sporting News - Centennial Issue (April 1, 1986).

The Sporting News, Daguerreotypes, 8th ed. (St. Louis, 1990).

Bill James, Whatever Happened to the Hall of Fame? (New York, 1994).

J. G. Taylor Spink, The Sporting News Dope Book 1962 (St. Louis, 1962).

J. G. Taylor Spink, The Sporting News Baseball Guide 1950 (St. Louis, 1962).

Bill James, The Bill James Historical Baseball Abstract, revised ed. (New York, 1988).

AL Pitching vs. Roger Maris in 1961

In 1961, when Roger Maris set the single-season's home run record that was just broken this past summer, forty-eight different pitchers were co-responsible. Thirty-seven were nicked only once. Nine were roughed up twice. Jim Perry of the Indians and Pete Burnside of the Senators were taken deep three times. The most notable pitching victim on Roger's hit list was fading future Hall of Famer Early Wynn. Several other quality pitchers tossed him gopher balls: Camilo Pasqual, Mudcat Grant, Billy Pierce, Milt Pappas, Juan Pizzaro, and Bill Monbouquette among them.

Against expansion clubs, Roger hit thirteen blasts. He had nine against the new Senators, but only four against the Angels. He whacked out thirteen against the White Sox, by far his favorite victims. He hit eight against both Detroit and Cleveland. Boston allowed seven. Kansas City surrendered five. Minnesota pitching gave up only four, and the Orioles held him to a stingy three.

The pitchers stung twice were Pedro Ramos, Gary Bell, Gene Conley, Frank Lary, Pierce, Cal McLish, Monbouquette, Eli Grba, and Ray Herbert.

—Jim Amato

Give the Ump His Due

OLLIE ANDERSON
WESTERN LEAGUE UMPIRE
OFFICIATED IN 4544 GAMES
WITHOUT MISSING AN ASSIGNMENT
This will be his 28th season

Submitted by **Fr. Gerry Beirne**, *from one of several scrapbooks from the 1920s, '30s, and '40s he has come into possession of. This clipping is from 1931.*

Major League Career Hitting Records

A chronological view

Tom Ruane

Record books tend to have a poor sense of history. Once a mark has been broken, no matter how long it sat atop the heap, it is discarded and replaced by the new standard. There is no mention in *The Sporting News Complete Baseball Record Book*, for example, of the fact that Roger Connor held the record for career home runs from 1895 to 1921. Or that Cap Anson was the lifetime leader in hits from 1880 to 1923.[1] If records are made to be broken, the lifetime hitting marks of the nineteenth century were certainly put to their correct use.[2] Of all the major hitting records in place at the turn of the century, only one would survive to the Depression and that would fall in 1933, the year Babe Ruth finally eclipsed Anson's RBI total.

As a result, none of the record-breaking accomplishments of the game's early stars is included in the current record books. This article will attempt to remedy this by providing a chronology of the record holders in each hitting category.[3] Whenever a record is broken, there is a line in the chart identifying the year, total, and the player. If a player simply extended his own record for several years, only the first and last years are included and the elision is indicated by a "…" after the first year. For example, the lines:

1885	1064	Jim O'Rourke
1886	1182	Cap Anson…
1897	2523	Cap Anson

from the Games Played chart means that O'Rourke took over the career lead in games in 1885, had his record topped by Anson the following year, who kept extending his own mark every year until 1897. With averages, a lower number sometimes succeeds a higher number when the player holding the record retains it although his personal record declines. This shows up first in the On-Base Percentage chart, first with John McGraw, then with Ruth and Ted Williams.

The charts:

Games Played

Year	Total	Player(s)
1871	33	Dave Eggler, Bob Ferguson, John Hatfield, Dickey Pearce, and Joe Start
1872	89	Dave Eggler and John Hatfield
1873	142	Dave Eggler
1874	210	Harry Schafer and Al Spalding
1875	286	Andy Leonard
1876	350	Andy Leonard and Al Spalding
1877	410	Al Spalding
1878	468	Andy Leonard
1879	539	Tom York
1880	597	Joe Start
1881	677	Tom York
1882	758	Joe Start and Tom York
1883	858	Tom York
1884	952	Jim O'Rourke
1885	1,064	Jim O'Rourke
1886	1,182	Cap Anson…
1897	2,523	Cap Anson

Tom Ruane lives in Poughkeepsie, New York.

Year	Total	Player(s)
1915	2,595	Honus Wagner...
1917	2,792	Honus Wagner
1926	2,806	Ty Cobb...
1928	3,035	Ty Cobb
1974	3,076	Hank Aaron...
1976	3,298	Hank Aaron
1983	3,308	Carl Yastrzemski
1984	3,371	Pete Rose...
1986	3,562	Pete Rose

At-Bats

Year	Total	Player(s)
1871	168	John Hatfield
1872	455	John Hatfield
1873	710	John Hatfield, Al Spalding
1874	1,069	Al Spalding
1875	1,427	Andy Leonard
1876	1,730	Andy Leonard
1877	2,004	George Wright...
1879	2,659	George Wright
1880	2,789	Joe Start...
1883	3,863	Joe Start
1884	4,254	Jim O'Rourke...
1886	5,171	Jim O'Rourke
1887	5,600	Cap Anson...
1897	10,274	Cap Anson
1917	10,430	Honus Wagner
1926	10,591	Ty Cobb...
1928	11,434	Ty Cobb
1974	11,628	Hank Aaron...
1976	12,364	Hank Aaron
1982	12,544	Pete Rose...
1986	14,053	Pete Rose

Runs Scored

Year	Total	Player(s)
1871	66	Ross Barnes...
1877	600	Ross Barnes
1879	655	Ross Barnes
1881	697	Ross Barnes
1882	732	Jim O'Rourke...
1893	1,731	Jim O'Rourke
1894	1,770	Cap Anson...
1897	1,996	Cap Anson
1925	2,040	Ty Cobb...
1928	2,246	Ty Cobb

Hits

Year	Total	Player(s)
1871	66	Cal McVey
1872	160	Ross Barnes...

Year	Total	Player(s)
1877	691	Ross Barnes
1878	761	Cal McVey
1879	866	Cal McVey
1880	897	Cap Anson...
1897	3,415	Cap Anson
1917	3,415	Cap Anson, Honus Wagner[4]
1923	3,453	Ty Cobb...
1928	4,189	Ty Cobb
1985	4,204	Pete Rose
1986	4,256	Pete Rose

Doubles

Year	Total	Player(s)
1871	11	Cap Anson
1872	38	Ross Barnes...
1877	122	Ross Barnes
1879	135	Cal McVey
1880	140	Jim O'Rourke
1881	161	Jim O'Rourke
1882	188	Cap Anson...
1897	582	Cap Anson
1913	605	Nap Lajoie...
1916	657	Nap Lajoie
1925	675	Tris Speaker...
1928	792	Tris Speaker

Triples

Year	Total	Player(s)
1871	10	John Bass
1872	11	Ross Barnes, George Hall, Lip Pike, Tom York
1873	21	Ross Barnes
1874	32	George Wright
1875	39	George Wright
1876	48	George Hall
1877	56	George Hall
1879	60	Tom York...
1884	86	Tom York
1885	95	Jim O'Rourke...
1887	114	Jim O'Rourke
1888	125	Roger Connor...
1897	233	Roger Connor
1905	237	Jake Beckley
1906	243	Jake Beckley
1913	251	Sam Crawford...
1916	309	Sam Crawford

Home Runs

Year	Total	Player(s)
1871	4	Levi Meyerle, Lip Pike, Fred Treacey

Year	Total	Player(s)
1872	10	Lip Pike...
1877	20	Lip Pike
1880	23	Charley Jones
1882	24	Jim O'Rourke
1883	33	Charley Jones
1884	40	Charley Jones
1885	50	Harry Stovey
1886	57	Harry Stovey
1887	65	Dan Brouthers
1888	74	Dan Brouthers
1889	89	Harry Stovey...
1893	122	Harry Stovey
1895	126	Roger Connor...
1897	138	Roger Connor
1921	162	Babe Ruth...
1935	714	Babe Ruth
1974	733	Hank Aaron...
1976	755	Hank Aaron

Runs Batted In[5]

Year	Total	Player(s)
1871	44	Rynie Wolters
1872	99	Lip Pike...
1874	200	Lip Pike
1875	275	Cal McVey...
1879	447	Cal McVey
1881	518	Cap Anson...
1897	2,076	Cap Anson
1933	2,128	Babe Ruth...
1935	2,213	Babe Ruth
1975	2,262	Hank Aaron
1976	2,297	Hank Aaron

Walks

Year	Total	Player(s)
1871	18	Ed Pinkham
1872	31	Denny Mack
1873	46	Denny Mack
1874	48	Ross Barnes...
1877	82	Ross Barnes
1879	98	Ross Barnes
1880	102	Jim O'Rourke...
1882	142	Jim O'Rourke
1883	157	Jim O'Rourke, Tom York
1884	192	Jim O'Rourke
1885	241	George Gore...
1887	385	George Gore
1888	447	Ned Williamson
1889	499	George Gore...
1891	650	George Gore
1892	724	Roger Connor...

Year	Total	Player(s)
1897	1,002	Roger Connor
1899	1,016	Billy Hamilton...
1901	1,187	Billy Hamilton
1923	1,199	Eddie Collins...
1929	1,499	Eddie Collins
1930	1,561	Babe Ruth...
1935	,2056	Babe Ruth

Strikeouts[6]

Year	Total	Player(s)
1871	7	Ralph Ham, Denny Mack, Lip Pike
1872	16	Denny Mack
1873	25	Denny Mack
1876	30	Denny Mack
1877	55	Lew Brown...
1879	120	Lew Brown
1880	127	Will White
1881	183	Pud Galvin...
1885	418	Pud Galvin
1886	478	John Morrill...
1890	656	John Morrill
1895	659	Tom Brown
1896	708	Tom Brown
1926	743	Babe Ruth...
1935	1,330	Babe Ruth
1964	1,348	Mickey Mantle...
1968	1,710	Mickey Mantle
1978	1,746	Willie Stargell...
1981	1,912	Willie Stargell
1982	1,966	Reggie Jackson...
1987	2,597	Reggie Jackson

Stolen Bases[7]

Year	Total	Player(s)
1871	20	Mike McGeary
1886	68	Harry Stovey
1887	189	Arlie Latham...
1896	738	Arlie Latham
1897	787	Billy Hamilton
1898	58	Ed Delahanty[8]
1899	116	John McGraw...
1901	169	John McGraw
1902	202	Sam Mertes...
1904	294	Sam Mertes
1905	349	Honus Wagner...
1916	698	Honus Wagner
1917	703	Ty Cobb, Honus Wagner
1918	737	Ty Cobb...
1928	891	Ty Cobb
1977	900	Lou Brock...
1979	938	Lou Brock
1991	994	Rickey Henderson...
1996	1,186	Rickey Henderson

Caught Stealing[9]

Year	Total	Player(s)
1912	34	Ty Cobb
1913	63	Clyde Milan...
1916	124	Clyde Milan
1920	136	Clyde Milan
1921	141	Clyde Milan
1922	151	Ty Cobb...
1928	212	Ty Cobb[10]
1974	231	Lou Brock...
1979	307	Lou Brock

Sacrifice Hits[11]

Year	Total	Player(s)
1894	26	Patsy Donovan
1895	46	Hughie Jennings...
1897	74	Hughie Jennings
1898	89	Dummy Hoy
1899	111	Bones Ely...
1901	134	Bones Ely
1902	154	Willie Keeler...
1910	366	Willie Keeler
1921	377	Eddie Collins...
1927	511	Eddie Collins

Sacrifice Flies[12]

Year	Total	Player(s)
1954	19	Gil Hodges...
1957	37	Gil Hodges
1958	43	Frank Thomas...
1960	50	Frank Thomas
1961	54	Minnie Minoso, Frank Thomas
1962	60	Frank Thomas
1963	62	Hank Aaron, Ernie Banks, Frank Thomas
1964	68	Ernie Banks
1965	75	Ernie Banks
1966	80	Hank Aaron, Ernie Banks
1967	86	Hank Aaron...
1976	121	Hank Aaron
1993	123	Robin Yount
1996	125	Eddie Murray

Intentional Walks[13]

Year	Total	Player(s)

Year	Total	Player(s)
1955	25	Ted Kluszewski
1956	47	Ted Kluszewski
1957	61	Ted Williams
1958	79	Stan Musial...
1960	97	Stan Musial
1961	116	Ernie Banks...
1967	183	Ernie Banks
1968	200	Hank Aaron...
1976	293	Hank Aaron

Hit By Pitches[14]

Year	Total	Player(s)
1884	15	Ed Swartwood
1885	27	Bill Gleason
1886	34	Bill Gleason
1887	43	Fred Mann
1888	65	Curt Welch...
1892	171	Curt Welch
1893	180	Tommy Tucker...
1899	272	Tommy Tucker
1901	275	Hughie Jennings...
1903	287	Hughie Jennings

Grounded into Double Plays[15]

Year	Total	Player(s)
1933	26	Ernie Lombardi...
1947	261	Ernie Lombardi
1970	266	Hank Aaron...
1976	328	Hank Aaron

Game Winning RBIs[16]

Year	Total	Player(s)
1979	16	Buddy Bell, Cecil Cooper
1980	30	Eddie Murray...
1996	222	Eddie Murray

Batting Average[17]

Year	Total	Player(s)
1881	.304	Joe Start[18]
1882	.355	Cap Anson...
1886	.347	Cap Anson
1887	.347	Dan Brouthers
1888	.346	Cap Anson
1889	.345	Dan Brouthers
1890	.348	Pete Browning
1891	.345	Pete Browning
1892	.343	Dan Brouthers...
1894	.343	Dan Brouthers
1895	.348	Billy Hamilton
1896	.351	Billy Hamilton

Year	Total	Player(s)
1897	.353	Jesse Burkett
1898	.351	Jesse Burkett
1899	.384	Willie Keeler…
1904	.364	Willie Keeler
1905	.361	Nap Lajoie…
1910	.350	Nap Lajoie
1911	.359	Ty Cobb…
1928	.366	Ty Cobb

Slugging Percentage

Year	Total	Player(s)
1881	.375	Joe Start
1882	.446	Cap Anson…
1886	.464	Cap Anson
1887	.551	Dan Brouthers…
1896	.520	Dan Brouthers
1903	.544	Nap Lajoie…
1906	.529	Nap Lajoie
1907	.519	Dan Brouthers
1916	.522	Joe Jackson
1917	.519	Dan Brouthers[19]
1922	.536	Rogers Hornsby
1923	.708	Babe Ruth…
1935	.690	Babe Ruth

On-Base Percentage

Year	Total	Player(s)
1881	.315	Joe Start
1882	.379	Cap Anson…
1886	.379	Cap Anson
1887	.400	Dan Brouthers…
1893	.423	Dan Brouthers
1894	.449	Billy Hamilton…
1898	.460	Billy Hamilton
1899	.461	John McGraw…
1904	.466	John McGraw
1906	.465	John McGraw
1923	.476	Babe Ruth…
1935	.474	Babe Ruth
1947	.487	Ted Williams…
1960	.482	Ted Williams

Home Runs Per 100 at-bats

Year	Total	Player(s)
1881	0.38	Joe Start
1882	0.72	Jim O'Rourke…
1884	0.71	Jim O'Rourke
1885	1.19	Abner Dalrymple
1886	1.54	Charley Jones
1887	2.15	Dan Brouthers…
1889	2.01	Dan Brouthers
1890	2.03	Harry Stovey
1891	2.12	Harry Stovey
1892	2.10	Jimmy Ryan
1893	2.26	Mike Tiernan
1894	2.14	Mike Tiernan
1895	2.13	Sam Thompson…
1898	2.13	Sam Thompson
1904	2.30	Buck Freeman
1905	2.13	Sam Thompson
1906	2.12	Sam Thompson
1917	3.00	Gavvy Cravath…
1920	3.01	Gavvy Cravath
1923	7.84	Babe Ruth…
1935	8.50	Babe Ruth

Walk Percentage

Year	Total	Player(s)
1881	.016	Joe Start
1882	.041	Jim O'Rourke
1883	.042	Tom York
1884	.047	Tom York
1885	.053	Orator Shaffer
1886	.087	Ned Williamson
1887	.101	George Gore…
1889	.107	George Gore
1890	.120	Paul Radford
1891	.163	Yank Robinson
1892	.162	Yank Robinson
1896	.163	Cupid Childs
1897	.162	Yank Robinson
1898	.179	Bill Joyce
1923	.195	Babe Ruth…
1930	.193	Babe Ruth
1931	.199	Max Bishop…

Year	Total	Player(s)
1935	.204	Max Bishop
1947	.205	Ted Williams
1948	.204	Max Bishop
1949	.207	Ted Williams…
1960	.208	Ted Williams

Strikeouts Per 100 at-bats

Year	Total	Player(s)
1883	6.36	Tom York
1884	7.12	Jack Burdock
1885	11.89	John Morrill…
1888	13.28	John Morrill
1889	15.72	Sam Wise…
1891	14.69	Sam Wise
1892	14.77	Charlie Bennett
1893	15.31	Tom Brown
1894	15.08	Tom Brown
1895	14.97	Charlie Bennett
1923	17.06	Babe Ruth…
1935	15.84	Babe Ruth
1939	18.29	Dolph Camilli…
1942	18.22	Dolph Camilli
1943	21.62	Vince DiMaggio…
1946	21.75	Vince DiMaggio
1961	22.25	Jim Lemon…
1963	22.84	Jim Lemon
1964	23.52	Harmon Killebrew
1965	23.70	Dick Stuart
1966	23.72	Dick Stuart
1967	24.37	Frank Howard
1968	24.26	Frank Howard
1969	26.42	Dick Allen…
1972	25.51	Dick Allen
1973	27.41	Reggie Jackson
1974	26.51	Reggie Jackson
1975	26.15	Nate Colbert
1976	26.36	Nate Colbert
1978	31.59	Dave Kingman…
1983	29.29	Dave Kingman
1984	28.57	Gorman Thomas…
1986	28.63	Gorman Thomas
1992	35.96	Rob Deer
1993	36.00	Rob Deer
1996	36.31	Rob Deer

Notes:

1. This article includes games from the National Association as well as all other leagues traditionally considered major. The primary source for the data was the 1997 *Bill James Electronic Encyclopedia*. I used the 1994 *Total Baseball* CD-Rom for much of the National Association data and used the fifth edition of *Total Baseball* to fill in the RBI data for 1874 and 1875.

2. Part of this was due to the shorter schedules played by the early teams. In Cap Anson's 27 seasons, his teams averaged only 101 games per season. And while it is likely that a longer schedule would've dramatically reduced Anson's durability, simply pro-rating his statistics to 162 game seasons gives him the following career line:

G	AB	R	H	2B	3B	HR	RBI	BB
4047	16479	3202	5478	933	229	157	3330	1578

Even if he had only received half of this boost from an extra 1600 games, his hit total would have reached around 4500, perhaps putting it beyond the reach of Pete Rose and sparing fans the final few years of Rose's career.

3. This article is not the first attempt to provide such information. In the 1980s, John Mercurio wrote a book along similar lines. He did not have access to a computerized data base, however, and in order to make the task manageable decided to ignore all active players. While reducing the work involved, this decision did make much of his work inaccurate.

4. I thought it was curious that Honus Wagner retired tied for the top spot in both hits and stolen bases. This is no doubt only a temporary situation. Statistics from early baseball are continually changing. Anson's hit totals have been variously reported in different editions of *The Baseball Encyclopedia* as 3425 (first), 3471 (sixth), and 3430 (ninth). *Total Baseball* has given him 3425 (first edition), 3413 (second), 3415 (third and fourth), and 3418 (fifth edition). Of course, the tie in hits is also due to my decision to include National Association statistics.

6. RBI data is missing for the 1882 to 1887 and 1890 American Association as well as from the 1884 Union Association seasons.

7. Strikeout data is missing for the 1874 to 1875 National Association, the 1882 to 1888 and 1890 American Association, the 1884 Union Association, the 1897 to 1909 National League, and the 1901 to 1912 American League seasons. Stolen base data is missing for the 1872 to 1875 National Association, the 1876 to 1885 National League, the 1882 to 1885 American Association, and the 1884 Union Association seasons.

8. The definition of a stolen base was changed to its modern one before the 1898 season. Prior to that stolen bases could be awarded, for example, when a base runner advanced from first to third on a single. As a result, I did not include any pre-1898 stolen bases in the career totals from 1898 on. This gives Big Ed Delahanty a brief stay at the top of the list, before being replaced by a man with a nickname ("Little Napoleon") more suited to a base stealer.

9. Complete caught Stealing statistics are available from 1914 to 1915 and from 1920 to the present for the American League as well as for 1915, 1920 to 1925 and from 1951 to the present for the National League. Some incomplete data was also kept during other years (usually only for leaders in stolen bases).

10. Ty Cobb is missing caught stealing data for the following seasons: 1905 to 1911, 1913 and 1917 to 1919. Given that he was successful 64.6 percent of the time for the years we have data, he was likely caught stealing more than 450 times over the course of his career.

11. Sacrifice hit data is missing prior to 1894. From 1894 to 1930 and 1930 to 1953 sacrifice flies were also included in sacrifice hits.

12. Sacrifice fly data is missing prior to 1954.

13. Intentional walk data is missing prior to 1955.

14. Hit by pitch data is available for the 1884 Union Association, 1885 to 1891 for the American Association and for all leagues from 1887 to the present.

15. Grounded into double play data is available from 1933 to the present for the National League and from 1939 to the present in the American League.

16. Game winning RBI data is available from 1979 to the present. It was dropped as an official statistic prior to the 1989 season.

17. A minimum of 3000 at-bats in needed to qualify for any average.

18. Joe Start's leadership here (as well as in the following categories) is by default; he was the only player at the time with 3000 or more at-bats.

19. This is the second time since he retired that Dan Brouthers had retaken the slugging crown. Lajoie dropped back below Brouthers with a sub-par 1907 season; Jackson did the same when he had the worst year of his career in 1917. Brouthers slugging percentage dropped from .520 to .519 in 1904 when he came out of retirement to go hitless in five at-bats for the Giants. His reign as slugging king would end forever in 1922, the year Hornsby finally qualified with 3000 at-bats. Ruth would come of age the following year and end any doubt about the slugging leadership.

Catching A Ball Dropped from A High Place

How hard is it?

Roger J. Hawks

At one time a favored stunt for catchers was to catch a ball dropped (or thrown) from a high place. Pop Schriver (1894), Gabby Street (1908), Billy Sullivan (1910), and perhaps others, all caught baseballs thrown from the Washington Monument, a height of 504 feet. In 1925, Ray Schalk caught a ball dropped 460 feet from the tower of the Chicago Tribune building. The record for balls dropped from structures was set in 1938 when both Frankie Pytlak and Hank Helf caught baseballs thrown from the Terminal Tower in Cleveland, a height eventually determined to be 680 feet.[1] This feat was reenacted in 1980 when professional softballer Mike Zarefoss caught a softball thrown from the Terminal Tower. The most recent attempt at the stunt was in 1982 when Kurt Bevacqua caught five baseballs dropped 390 feet from the Imperial Bank Building in San Diego.

As a prelude to an exhibition game in Los Angeles on April 1, 1930, baseballs were dropped from a blimp hovering over the field. Gabby Hartnett caught two balls dropped from 800 feet and Truck Hannah managed to snag one from an altitude of 650 feet. This stunt was repeated unsuccessfully in 1939 at the San Francisco Golden Gate International Exposition. A baseball was dropped 800 feet from a blimp to Joe Sprinz, a veteran Pacific Coast League catcher who also got into twenty-one games with Cleveland and

the Cards, who muffed the catch losing two teeth in the process. The record for height is thus held by Gabby Hartnett with his 800-foot catch.

The appeal of this feat was the danger inherent in the high speed that a ball would have after falling for such a long distance. When Billy Sullivan made his catch it was estimated that the ball was traveling at 110 miles per hour, though earlier estimates for the speed of baseballs dropped from the Washington Monument were as high as 125 mph. Estimates for the speed of the balls that Bevacqua caught were also 110 mph, even though the height was considerably lower. The estimated speed of the baseball dropped from the Terminal Tower was 138 mph and the ball that knocked out Sprinz's teeth was stated to be traveling 145 mph, this latter estimate being credited to University of California at Berkeley physicists.[°]

Since it was then thought (and later measurements have borne out) that no one could throw a baseball that fast, making the catch was a major achievement. Because the significance of such a catch is directly related to the speed of the ball, it is reasonable to ask what will be the speed of a baseball dropped from a high place will be.

Elementary physics shows that an object dropped from a height of 500 feet, the approximate height of the Washington Monument, will reach the ground with a speed of 122 miles per hour. However, this result assumes that the ball is falling in a vacuum. In actuality, the ball is falling through the air. Air resists this motion by exerting a force called aerodynamic

Roger J. Hawks *is professor and chair of the Department of Mechanical and Aerospace Engineering at Tri-State University. He once was a rocket scientist for NASA.*

drag on the ball.

Terminal velocity—If a ball were allowed to fall "forever" it would eventually reach a constant speed called the terminal velocity. At the terminal velocity the aerodynamic drag is exactly equal to the weight of the ball. A ball dropped or thrown at a speed lower than the terminal velocity will speed up until it reaches terminal velocity. A ball thrown faster than terminal velocity will slow down to terminal velocity.

It is usually reported that the terminal velocity of a baseball is 95 mph. Thus, if Nolan Ryan went up in a blimp to an altitude of 5,000 feet or more and dropped a baseball straight down, it would hit the ground at a speed of 95 mph. Likewise, if he threw it straight down as hard as he could, it would still hit the ground going 95 mph.

A ball dropped from a lower height (such as the Washington Monument) will not have sufficient time or distance to reach terminal velocity before it strikes the ground. When terminal velocity cannot be achieved the actual impact velocity depends on the nature of the aerodynamic drag force and on how this drag changes with the speed of the ball.

Aerodynamic drag—Since all of the balls described previously were effectively dropped (a ball thrown horizontally to clear the building will still fall as if it were simply dropped), all of the estimated impact velocities are clearly too high. They all exceed the terminal velocity by wide margins. In order to obtain more realistic estimates for the impact velocity of a ball dropped from a high place we must know more about the aerodynamic drag force being exerted on a baseball.

The aerodynamic drag on any object depends on the size and shape of the object, its speed squared, and the density of the air. The size effect is determined by the cross-section area and the drag coefficient accounts for the shape. The drag coefficient depends only on the Reynolds number[2] which relates size, speed, and the viscosity (slipperiness or stickiness) of the air. For any object, such as a baseball, a graph of the drag coefficient[3] plotted against the Reynolds number will determine the aerodynamic drag that resists the object's motion.

The aerodynamic drag acting on a smooth sphere is known reasonably well, even though the measurements are difficult to make. For very low speeds—Reynolds number less than two—the drag force is a linear function of velocity. At high speed—Reynolds number greater than 1,000—the drag is

proportional to velocity squared (the drag coefficient is constant). This situation is maintained as long as the flow is smooth and well behaved (what is called laminar). At higher speeds the air becomes turbulent and looses its smoothness to form a large wake behind the ball. For the smooth sphere, transition to turbulence occurs at a Reynolds number of 300,000, precipitating a drop in drag called the drag crisis. During the drag crisis the drag coefficient suddenly drops and becomes a function of Reynolds number. When the Reynolds number increases above 10,000,000 the flow stablizes and the drag coefficient again becomes constant so that drag is once more proportional to velocity squared (ignoring the effects of compressibility).

For a baseball, a Reynolds number of 1,000 is reached at a velocity of 0.45 miles per hour. As a practical matter, then, the drag can be considered to vary with the velocity squared for all speeds lower than the speed which precipitates the drag crisis. The drag coefficient of a smooth sphere under these conditions is about 0.4.

Of course, a baseball is not a smooth sphere. Its shape is more or less spherical,[4] but the seams make it decidedly unsmooth. The special orientation of the seams, in fact, disqualifies the baseball even from being a rough sphere, since that requires the roughness to be evenly distributed over the entire surface.

There have been few actual measurements of the drag on a baseball and this data has not been widely disseminated. We would expect the terminal velocity data to provide some drag information. The widely accepted value of 95 mph for the terminal velocity of a baseball, first published in 1959 by Briggs,[5] was obtained from a "private communication" to him from Hugh Dryden, who reported that a baseball, of unspecified size and origin, placed in the vertical wind tunnel at the National Advisory Committee on Aeronautics at some unknown time, had a terminal velocity of "about 140 feet per second." Watts and Bahill[6] reported a terminal velocity of 150 feet per second, with no citation as to origin or source of this value.

We can interpret "about 140 ft/sec" to mean that the measured terminal velocity is closer to 140 ft/sec than it is to either 130 ft/sec or 150 ft/sec. Thus, the terminal velocity could be anywhere in the range[7] of 135 ft/sec to 145 ft/sec. The size of the baseball is also unspecified. Rule 1.09 states that the circumference of the ball must be between 9 and 9-1/4 inches and the weight must be between 5 and 5-1/4 ounces.[8] In his paper Briggs gives a diameter of 2.88 inches and a weight 5.11 ounces for an "American League" baseball. If this is the baseball that Dryden tested, the drag coefficient at 140 ft/sec would be 0.303. Since the tested baseball is unspecified and the speed has an uncertainty of plus or minus 5 ft/sec, the drag coefficient obtained from the terminal velocity could be as low as 0.264 or as high as 0.338 with the Reynolds number in the range 201,000 to 222,000.

Two sets of experimental data for the drag coefficient of a baseball can be found in the open literature. Watts and Baroni[9] reported wind tunnel measurements made by Gonzalez at Tulane University in 1969. The most extensive drag testing was done in the wind tunnel at Cooper Union by Hollenberg[10] in 1984.

A graph of the available drag data was plotted to show drag coefficient as a function of Reynolds number. The line is the best fit curve to all of the experimental data.

The drag curve[11] shown was used in a numerical integration of the equation of motion. The diameter and weight of the baseball were the values given by Briggs for the "American League" baseball. With this data the terminal velocity of the baseball was calculated to be 95.25 mi/hr.

The impact velocity of baseballs dropped from various high places is given in the table. (The velocity of a softball dropped from the Terminal Tower is also included.) As expected these velocities are much lower than previous estimates. Even though no one has attempted it, the Canadian National Tower in Toronto is also included in the table since it represents the ultimate in what Jack Kavanagh has called "The Heights of Ridiculousness."

The difficulty involved in catching a ball dropped from a great height is not due to the speed of the ball. These balls are traveling no faster than a good major league fastball. (Or a not so good one for the case of the Washington Monument. In fact, Pop Schriver said that the ball dropped from the Washington Monument was not much different than "Wild Bill" Hutchinson's fastball.) The hard part is picking up and tracking the ball, which is probably not visible when it's dropped, and positioning yourself under it as it moves around laterally on its downward path. The smack in the mitt will be less than that of a Randy Johnson fastball.

Impact velocities of dropped baseballs

Location	height	mph
Washington Monument	504	80.1
Terminal Tower (bb)	680	85.4
Terminal Tower (sb)	680	79.1
Blimp	800	87.9
CN Tower	1,465	93.8

Notes:

1. Kavanagh, "The Heights of Ridiculousness," 1993.

2. Unless the speed approaches the speed of sound, then the Mach number must also be included.

3. The drag force on a ball will be $D = 0.0000225C^2U^2C_d$ where D is the drag force in ounces, C is the circumference of the ball in inches, U is the ball's speed in miles per hour, and C_d is the drag coefficient. The Reynolds number can likewise be expressed as $R = 243CU$.

4. Because of the seams, the ratio of the circumference of a baseball to its diameter is larger than pi. Measurements made on a dozen Rawlings "Official NAIA" baseballs indicate that the circumference is 3.193 times the diameter.

5. Briggs, "Effect of Spin and Speed on the Lateral Deflection (Curve) of a Baseball; and the Magnus Effect for Smooth Spheres," *American Journal of Physics*, Vol. 23, No. 8, pp. 589-596, Nov. 1959.

6. Watts and Bahill, *Keep Your Eye on the Ball*, W. H. Freeman and Co., New York, 1990, pg. 24.

7. This is consistent with the precision that can usually be obtained in wind tunnel speed measurements of this type.

8. The measurements on the Rawlings baseballs noted previously gave a circumference of 9.16 inches with a standard deviation of 0.035 in. and a weight of 5.09 ounces with a standard deviation of 0.030 oz.

9. Watts and Baroni, "Baseball-Bat Collisions and the Resulting Trajectories of Spinning Balls," *American Journal of Physics*, Vol. 57, No. 1, pp. 40-45, Jan. 1989.

10. Hollenberg, "Secrets of the Knuckleball," *The Bent of Tau Beta Pi*, Vol. 77, pp. 26-30, Fall 1986.

11. The data from Gonzalez and Hollenberg are for nonspinning baseballs. The spin is unknown for the baseball in the wind tunnel test of terminal velocity reported by Dryden. Hoerner (*Fluid-Dynamic Drag*, Midland Park, NJ, 1958, p. 7-20) reports that a smooth sphere produces induced drag due to the lift force when spinning. This induced drag increases the drag on the smooth sphere by about 20%. Similar results might be expected for the baseball.

One Batter, Three Outs

It's rare. It's embarrassing.

Mark Simon

On June 15, 1997, I went with my dad to the final game of a three-game series between the New York Mets and the Boston Red Sox.

Mets pitcher Bobby Jones cruised through the first two innings and then struck out Shane Mack to begin the third frame. Then Jones ran into trouble. The next eight batters (including pitcher Vaughn Eshelman) reached base. Up stepped Mack again, this time with runners on first and second. Remembering something that Tim McCarver once talked about, I turned to my dad and said, "Shane Mack could be responsible for all three outs in the inning without hitting into a triple play." Before my dad could respond, voilà, a 4-6-3 double play and the inning was over.

Though the Mets lost, 10-1, I left the ballpark convinced that I had seen a baseball rarity. But how rare was it for someone to come up twice in an inning and make three outs? I thought I had seen a first. The next day I called Elias Sports Bureau. It didn't have the answer, but Retrosheet did.

According to Retrosheet, such a scenario has now taken place at least thirteen times since 1973. A rarity indeed. What follows is a recap of the last twelve confirmed occurrences.

Tommy Davis, Orioles
June 14, 1973, Baltimore vs. Kansas City
Kansas City Royals rookie pitcher Mark Littell left in the seventh inning with a lead. Kansas City took a 3-1 lead into the bottom of the eighth. After a Bobby Grich triple, Davis hit a sacrifice fly off Gene Garber. Two walks, three singles, a double and a triple followed. Up stepped Davis again, this time with the Orioles leading, 8-3. He hit into a 5-4-3 double play off Doug Bird to accomplish the distinction.

Rick Burleson, Red Sox
August 7, 1979, Boston vs. Cleveland
In the sixth inning, after a Burleson groundout, the next eight men reached base. In fact, the next four hits (sandwiched around a walk and a hit batsman) were a home run, a double, a single, and a triple. Back-to-back errors gave Burleson his opportunity and he came through with a 1-6-3 double play.

Keith Smith, Cardinals
August 18, 1980, St. Louis vs. Cincinnati
A career .207 hitter who batted .129 in '80, Smith was the only one of twelve men who came to the plate in the second inning to make an out. He hit into a 4-6-3 double play that appeared to thwart a big inning. But that was followed by a walk, a double and six singles before a Smith strikeout ended an eight-run inning.

This feat may have been overshadowed by another rarity. In the fifth inning, Cardinals pitcher Bob

Mark Simon is a sportswriter and sportscaster residing in Yardley, Pennsylvania. He hopes someday to be the radio voice of the New York Mets and New York Knicks.

Forsch induced all three batters to ground out to him.

Fred Lynn, Angels
June 8, 1981, California vs. Cleveland
In the midst of the worst season of his career, Lynn led off a six-run Angels eighth by flying out to left field. He then followed a single, home run, error, and five more singles with a 4-6-3 double play.

Roy Smalley, Yankees
April 16, 1982, New York vs. Detroit
In a five-run Yankees second, Smalley struck out to lead off the frame and lined into a 4-6-3 double play to end it.

Willie Randolph
August 28, 1983, New York vs. California
This one happened in a rare John Montefusco win for the Yankees. In a six-run sixth, Randolph grounded out to shortstop and hit into a 5-4-3 double play.

Lance Parrish, Tigers
April 13, 1984, Detroit vs. Boston
In the midst of their 35-5 start to the '84 season, the Tigers scored eight runs in the first inning of a contest against the Red Sox. Parrish struck out and grounded into a 6-4-3 double play. He atoned later, however, by smashing a home run.

Gary Ward, Rangers
May 25, 1984, Texas vs. Chicago
Charlie Hough dazzled the White Sox with a three-hit shutout to beat Tom Seaver. But Ward made history anyway, in a seven-run third inning, he grounded to third and hit into a 4-3 double play.

Kelly Gruber, Blue Jays
September 14, 1987, Baltimore vs. Toronto
Gruber is the first player I know of to accomplish the feat as a pinch hitter. In the seventh inning of a 17-3 rout, Gruber's 6-4-3 double play preceded a walk, five singles, and two home runs. Gruber then flied to right field to end the inning.

Mike Gallego, A's
September 20, 1988, Minnesota vs. Oakland
En route to knocking off the defending world champions, Gallego grounded to shortstop and hit into a 4-6-3 double play in a five-run eighth inning.

Dan Gladden, Tigers
June 13, 1992, Detroit vs. Baltimore
Gladden was the second to accomplish the mark as a pinch hitter. Mike Flanagan coaxed a 6-4-3 double play and a fly to right field, joining Jones as the only pitchers who stayed in long enough to coax all three outs.

Darren Lewis, Giants
May 5, 1993, San Francisco vs. Philadelphia
Even pitcher Bill Swift got a hit in a seven-run Giants fifth inning in which Lewis popped up to the catcher and hit into a 4-6-3 double play.

The play-by-play information used here was obtained free of charge from and is copyrighted by Retrosheet. Interested parties may contact Retrosheet at 20 Sunset Road, Newark, DE 19711.

Playing right-handed seemed natural for true lefty Kile

Darryl Kile is one of the National League's top righthanded pitchers, even if he struggled last season with the Colorado Rockies—and even if he's truly lefthanded.

Kile throws and bats righthanded, but he writes with is left hand. "I'm really lefthanded, but when I started playing baseball I did it righthanded. I do everything else lefthanded except baseball and golf."

Kile was the oldest of the three children in his family, all boys, and didn't start playing ball fulltime until he was twelve. "Picked up a baseball. Put on a righthanded glove. Started throwing righthanded. Why I did I don't know," he said. "I didn't know any better. Just seemed right, I guess. Maybe I got unlucky and my left arm was better than my right one."

—Joe Naiman

Team Nicknames 1900-1910

It was a whole different ballgame

Marc Okkonen

Having spent countless hours scouring newspaper microfilm from the turn of the century era, I squirm in discomfort every time I see the name "Pilgrims" used by contemporary baseball scholars (including some well-known SABRites) as the official nickname of the pre-1908 Boston Red Sox. Unfortunately, such erroneous usage originated somewhere through some writer's sloppy rush to judgment and the stubborn determination by many baseball scholars that every major league team had to have an official catchy nickname other than something as generic as AMERICANS—consequently many such myths have been exaggerated and perpetuated often enough that they have been accepted as factual. In the interests of historical accuracy and to uphold SABR's reputation as the custodian of the game's history, I hope to set the record straight on many of these early twentieth-century team nicknames.

First, let's try to define what constitutes an "official" or "acceptable" team nickname from this era. Although the clubs themselves seldom used the nickname in letterheads or other official documents even in cases where the name was widely accepted everywhere, the obvious source for locating an accepted nickname is in the newspaper reports of the period. If the nickname is consistently and more or less exclusively used in articles in more than one publication,

Mark Okkonen, a SABRite since 1985, is a semiretired artist, writer, and researcher in Muskegon, Michigan. He is the author of Baseball Uniforms of the 20th Century *and other historical books.*

there is no reason to challenge its claim as the team nickname. On the other hand, if only one newspaper or one writer used the name and other publications never used it at all, it should never be claimed by more contemporary historians as an official team nickname. Such pet names by only one writer or one newspaper were numerous in the 1900-1910 period and I will give examples of this later. Also, many baseball writers used alternate geographic adjectives to describe teams and these were used only to break the monotony and were not intended to suggest an official nickname. Good examples of this would be "Quakers" (either Philadelphia team), "Beaneaters" (either Boston team), or "Rhinelanders" (Cincinnati). In most cases, accepted team nicknames were coined by an individual baseball writer and stuck only if other writers eventually adopted the name in their own write-ups. Examples of inventive nicknames that never caught on with the rest of the baseball media are abundant.

Based on my findings, let's discuss each ML club in the 1900-1910 period in alphabetical order:

BALTIMORE AL 1901-02: ORIOLES—no argument

BOSTON AL 1901-10: from 1901-1907 the AMERICANS is the name used not only in 99 percent of newspaper reports in these years, but the club itself decorated its shirt front on two occasions with BA, signifying BOSTON AMERICANS. As for attempts to identify these teams as "Puritans," "Somersets," or "Pilgrims," the only mention of any of these misnomers I could find were a couple of articles in 1907 in the Boston *Herald* and Boston *Journal* that referred to the home team as "Pilgrims," but also used the correct AMERICANS on the same sports page. Up to 1908 the team wore blue trim and when red was adopted in '08 the RED SOX nickname was universally accepted, although the old name AMERICANS was still used simply out of habit for some years afterward.

BOSTON NL 1900-1910: In 1900 the use of team nicknames seemed unusually rare in newspaper accounts. Despite being known as Red Stockings in the early 1890s, the Boston club was simply referred to as BOSTONS most of the time, except for a very rare mention as "Beaneaters"—not often enough to consider this an accepted nickname. When the AL Boston Americans surfaced in 1901, all newspapers identified the existing NL club as the NATIONALS simply to make a distinction between the two home teams, which at times wore nearly identical uniforms. It was the NATIONALS all the way to 1907, when the name DOVES first appeared, in reference to new owner George Dovey. By 1908, the DOVES name was used freely in all Boston newspapers, and the name stuck through the 1910 season. When the club was sold to William Russell in 1911, the team became the RUSTLERS—another short-lived moniker inspired by the new owner's last name. The club became the BRAVES the following year.

BROOKLYN NL 1900-1910: SUPERBAS—no argument here, although the old familiar "Trolley Dodgers" or "Dodgers" surfaced occasionally—a throwback to a name once used in the 1890s and restored officially in the 1930s after the death of Wilbert Robinson (for whom the name ROBINS was chosen).

CHICAGO AL 1901-1910: In 1900 and 1901 the name WHITE STOCKINGS was used to identify the team. The earliest use I could find of the modified WHITE SOX was in 1902, and it soon became the official team nickname.

CHICAGO NL 1900-1910: ORPHANS was the only nickname I found (besides the CHICAGOS or Chicago NATIONALS) in 1900. In 1901 the name REMNANTS was also used, but not as often as ORPHANS. I found no evidence of the name CUBS in

these two years. In 1902, the team nickname was a free-for-all among Chicago newspapers. Each paper had its own exclusive nickname for the team: The *Daily News* called them CUBS, the *Tribune* REMNANTS or COLTS, the *Inter-Ocean* ORPHANS, and the *Record-Herald* RECRUITS. *The Sporting News* used COLTS while *Sporting Life* referred to them as CUBS—probably because their correspondents were from different Chicago newspapers. This shotgun method of identification continued through 1903. Even in 1905, the *Tribune* continued to use the name COLTS. But by this time the CUBS name was becoming more widely used and was accepted universally by 1906. Once the '06 season was well underway and the Cubs, in their phenomenal record-breaking season, were destined to unseat the haughty reigning champion Giants, the Chicago *Inter-Ocean* consistently referred to the locals as GIANT KILLERS—probably just to rub it in. Despite such journalistic mischief, the Cubs were the CUBS for good by this time.

CINCINNATI NL 1900-1910: REDS—no argument

CLEVELAND AL 1901-1910: BLUEBIRDS or BLUES was the predominant nickname in 1901-02, although the Cleveland *Press* coined the name BRONCHOS in 1902. When superstar Napoleon Lajoie joined the club in 1902, the *Press* soon dropped the Bronchos name in favor of NAPOLEONS, or NAPS for short. In 1905 two events happened which officially established NAPS (or NAPOLEONS) and subsequently shelved the name BLUES. The familiar all navy blue road suits were discontinued for that season and Lajoie's prominence was magnified even more by his appointment as field manager. They were NAPS for the balance of Lajoie's years with Cleveland and became the INDIANS in 1915.

DETROIT AL 1901-1910: TIGERS—no argument

MILWAUKEE AL 1901: BREWERS—no argument

NEW YORK AL 1903-1910: HIGHLANDERS has to be awarded the official nickname during this period but with some reservations. The New York *Times* consistently referred to the AL invaders as AMERICANS or GREATER NEW YORKS in the early years, but HIGHLANDERS was the most commonly used name even then. HILLTOPPERS or INVADERS were sometimes used but not often enough for consideration. As early as 1905 the New York *American* began to use the name YANKEES, and the following year at least six New York papers began to use YANKEES as often as HIGHLANDERS. An argument can be made that both names were used enough by 1906 that neither one could be considered exclusive. This duality continued through 1912. When the AL club abandoned their old Hilltop Park home in 1913 to share the Polo Grounds with the Giants, the HIGHLANDER name lost its meaning and disappeared for good. There is no definitive year in which the New York AL club clearly became the YANKEES, but certainly it became exclusive in 1913.

NEW YORK NL 1900-1910: GIANTS—no argument

PHILADELPHIA AL 1901-1910: the name ATHLETICS is undisputed but its usage is unique compared to other nicknames of the decade. For all other clubs, the nicknames were always more or less "unofficial" and secondary to the city name. But it can be argued that the city name Philadelphia played second fiddle to the traditional team name ATHLETICS, resurrected from an earlier era of professional baseball. Indeed, the name ATHLETICS was very often used in such mundane applications as box scores and standings in place of the city name—a tribute to the impact of that historic nickname.

PHILADELPHIA NL 1900-1910: the name PHILLIES is unchallenged for this period. Surprisingly, the secondary nickname QUAKERS was frequently used in place of Phillies—but not enough to warrant consideration as an alternate nickname.

PITTSBURGH NL 1900-1910: PIRATES—no contest, but BUCCANEERS or BUCS was often substituted, if only to break the monotony. The usage was always an obvious reference to the accepted name PIRATES.

ST. LOUIS AL 1902-1910: BROWNS is the clear choice from the very beginning, but it did not go unchallenged. In 1905, the brown uniform trim was replaced by black. Perhaps inspired by this color change and an eagerness to escape a losing image, the

St. Louis *Post-Dispatch* attempted to identify the locals as RAVENS. The new name never got beyond the pages of the *P-D* and died out in short order.

ST. LOUIS NL 1900-1910: CARDINALS—no argument

WASHINGTON AL 1901-1910: this team identification is one of the more tricky ones to define. Most certainly they were the SENATORS from 1901-1905, but in early 1906 the club itself (not the press) was determined to change their SENATORS identity after five losing seasons. The public was invited to suggest new names, but in the end the club elected to restore one of their old nineteenth-century names, NATIONALS, and even displayed the nickname prominently on the players' shirt fronts. The new name choice was rather curious and ill-advised since the club was now a member of the American League, and several NL clubs already were identified as NATIONALS. In spite of the confusing logic, the ballclub continued to identify itself officially as NATIONALS for decades to come. The newspapers continued to resist the official word, and in most cases would not abandon the SENATORS name. NATIONALS or NATS was also used with frequency, but SENATORS did not disappear and for continuity's sake it is not unreasonable to identify the team as SENATORS even after 1905 because of the continued usage of the name in news reports. This dilemma prevailed all the way into the 1950s, and many baseball reporters were unaware that they were habitually misnaming the Washington team.

In summary, I consider the injection of team nicknames into meaningful historical records as superficial and trivial, especially for nineteenth- and early twentieth-century information. Unlike today, when nicknames are clearly and officially designated as part of the team identification, the practice of arbitrarily attaching the same importance to them in an era that did not always offer the same recognition to nicknames seems to be an exercise in futility. If nicknames are in doubt, we should omit them and not persist in trying to drive a square peg into a round hole. Let's not rewrite history just for the sake of convenience or a misguided sense of consistency.

The Colorado Bullets

Can promotion based on the "battle of the sexes" be successful?

Gai Ingham Berlage, Ph.D.

Nineteen ninety-seven marked the fourth season of operation for the Colorado Silver Bullets, an all-women's professional baseball team. The team is unique in that it is not part of a women's league. The Bullets barnstorm across the country playing only men's professional, semiprofessional, and amateur teams. They have no home field and, therefore, no home town fan base. Promotion for the games is based on the "battle of the sexes." Ticket holders are led to believe that they are seeing history in the making—that women are competing against men in baseball for the first time and that spectators are witnessing the establishment of historic milestones.

The idea for the Colorado Silver Bullets emerged not from women ballplayers clamoring for professional opportunities to play, but from the box office success of the movie, *A League of Their Own*, released by Columbia in 1992.

In the wake of the movie's success, Whittle Communications and Coors Brewing Company announced the formation of an all-women's team on December 10, 1993. For $2.6 million, Coors got brand-name sponsorship, and the team became known as the Colorado Silver Bullets, after its brand of light beer. The company hoped to capitalize on the revived interest in women's baseball created by the

Gai Ingham Berlage, Ph.D. is a professor and chairperson of the Department of Sociology at Iona College, New Rochelle, New York. She is author of Women in Baseball: The Forgotten History, Praeger, 1994 and co-author of Understanding Social Issues: Critical Thinking and Analysis, 5th ed., Allyn & Bacon, 1999.

movie. It hoped that favorable publicity gained from sponsorship would attract more women beer drinkers and increase Coors's market share.

For Bob Hope, president of Whittle Events, the creation of the team was a dream come true. In 1984, he had failed in his bid to win a franchise in the men's Class A Florida State League for the Sun Sox, his proposed all-women's team.[1] His vision for the Silver Bullets was very different from Wrigley's for the AAGBL. Wrigley formed the women's league to keep baseball alive in major league ball parks while the men were off to war. The AAGBL was supposed to be temporary. The Colorado Silver Bullets, on the other hand, were not to be part of a women's league but to play against men's teams. They were to be a permanent barnstorming team.

Hope, the founder of the Silver Bullets, was once described in *Sports Illustrated* as "the most innovative promoter in sports."[2] His experience as public relations and marketing director for the Atlanta Braves and the Atlanta Hawks may have given him experience with creating gimmicks to attract the public to men's baseball games, but it ill-prepared him to deal with marketing women. By having the Silver Bullets play only men's teams, Hope unknowingly doomed them to failure. For the archaic "battle of the sexes" promotion to be successful the women had to be as skilled as the men. They could not be judged on their own merits—the way, say, the 1996 women's Olympic basketball team was—but only in relation to the larger, stronger, and vastly more experienced men they were to play against.

Unlike other sports like basketball, which girls and women play in great and rapidly increasing numbers, few girls or women play baseball. Although Little League Baseball admitted girls in 1974, girls almost always play Little League Softball. Softball is the designated sport for girls at the junior high, high school, and college level. There are no women's baseball teams at the college, high school, or junior high school level. In fact, only four women have played on college men's teams. In 1985 Susan Perabo played one game for Division III Webster College in Missouri. In 1989 Julie Croteau became the first woman to play National Collegiate Athletic Association baseball when she became a member of the St. Mary's College (Maryland) team. In 1990 Jodi Haller pitched for NAIA St. Vincent's College (Pennsylvania). In 1994 Ila Borders became a pitcher for NAIA Southern California College.

So recruitment immediately became a problem. Where were the Silver Bullets going to find women who could play baseball? And if they did find these women, how could they realistically expect women with limited baseball experience to compete against men who had played all their lives? On the movie screen, fantasy sells. On the playing field, reality quickly sets in. How could Hope expect these women to be able to compete against AA players when virtually by definition even most men who grew up playing baseball couldn't handle the competition?

In spite of this, Hope announced that the Silver Bullets would play "approximately 50 exhibition games against men's minor-league, semiprofessional, and college teams," and that it would become " an independent member of the AA Short Season Northern League."[3]

The problem of the women's skills became apparent at the inaugural game, which was played—as might be expected—on Mother's Day, May 8, 1994. The Northern League All-Stars crushed the Silver Bullets, 19-0. The women's fielding was not bad, but pitching and hitting were definite problems. Realizing that the women couldn't successfully compete at this level, management quickly adjusted the schedule to drop some minor league games downward and add more against men's amateur teams.

Even with the adjusted schedule the Bullets won only six games during the season, while losing thirty-eight. On the brighter side, 250,000 people paid to see them play—an average of 5,687 per game, including highs of 33,179, 29,896, and 21,654.[4]

Fans and "firsts"—Even though they were drawing pretty well, the Colorado Silver Bullets had a problem in this area. How could they build a fan base when they were constantly on the road barnstorming? TV could do it, but the few games that were televised on ESPN or Lifetime were often taped and shown days after they were played. It was tough to become a fan.

In an attempt to create media interest, the games were sensationalized. The Silver Bullets's official press kit declared that this was the "first all-women's team recognized for play in the men's minor leagues." Most newspapers omitted the qualifier "recognized for" and merely declared inaccurately that this was the first time a women's team had played against men. Of course, from the 1890s to the 1930s, various Bloomer Girls teams competed against men throughout the United States. As recently as the 1950s, Allington's All-Americans, former AAGBL players, had barnstormed across the country playing local men's teams.[5]

This inaccuracy, though, created the possibility for all kinds of firsts. The implication was that if you went to the games you could see history in the making: the first home run by a woman off a male pitcher or the first woman to shut out a men's team. Bob Hope excelled at this, and would pull off some major coups that involved Silver Bullets players.

In 1994, two Silver Bullets players, pitcher Lee Ketcham and first basewoman Julie Croteau, played in the Class A-AA Hawaii Winter Baseball League. Both played for the Maui Stingrays, though neither distinguished herself.[6]

In 1995, Silver Bullets Shannon Mitchum and Ann Williams tried out for the New York Mets. Neither made the team. In 1996 another Silver Bullets player, Pamela Davis, pitched for a major league farm team in an exhibition game. She tossed a scoreless fifth inning and got the win in the Jacksonville Suns' 7-2 win over the Australian Olympic team.[7]

In 1996 the Silver Bullets were invited to Taiwan to play exhibition games against Taiwan major league men's baseball teams. The tour was hyped as "the first time women have competed with men in the same sport in Taiwan." And Bob Hope declared, "It is really gratifying that the Taiwan major league decided to invite our team. American women playing Chinese men in professional baseball makes a statement that women are accepted as ballplayers…." Unfortunately, the Silver Bullets lost the first five games and the sixth was never played.[8]

Failure—For four seasons, 1994-1997, the Colorado Silver Bullets operated as a barnstorming professional baseball team, backed by Coors's annual $2.6 million sponsorship. Gate receipts for games are split between the sponsoring team and the Bullets. Advertising for the games is the responsibliity of the sponsoring organization.

The team's record improved year by year, and in 1997, the Silver Bullets had a winning season. But attendance began to decline in mid-1996 and lagged disastrously in 1997 as the novelty of women playing baseball against men waned.

(Those poor 1997 attendance numbers were inflated by a turnout of 27,917when the Silver Bullets played the Colorado All-Stars at Coors Field. Attendance at that game may have been helped by another Silver Bullets first—the brawl. On June 11, 1997, Kim Braatz-Voisard, at bat, was told by the catcher of the opposing team that the pitcher was going to hit her with the ball. She got hit by the next pitch and claims she saw the pitcher laughing at her. Incensed, she charged the mound. This resulted in a bench-clearing melee. She and the catcher were both ejected from the game. The media loved it and coverage of the "brawl" appeared on nightly television and in newspapers across the country.)

At the end of the 1997 season, Coors announced that it would no longer be a sponsor. According to Bob Hope, Coors Beer's management from the very beginning had ambivalent feelings about sponsoring the Silver Bullets. On the one hand the company hoped to attract women beer drinkers. On the other, it worried about having their Silver Bullet light beer become identified as a "chick beer." They feared alienating their male drinkers.[9]

The season of 1997 marked the end of play for the Colorado Silver Bullets. Without Coors's backing, Hope-Beckham Inc., which purchased the team from Whittle Communications, found it impossible, in the face of low attendance rates, a loack of media interest, and intense competition from other professional women's sports to find new sponsors.

Competition for sponsors is fierce. Currently, there are two professional women's basketball leagues, the American Basketball League (ABL) and the Women's National Basketball League (WNBA); a professional women's volleyball league; a women's fast pitch softball league, and proposed women's leagues in soccer and ice hockey. All of these sports have greater public recognition than women's baseball. At the summer Olympics in 1996, American women's teams in basketball, softball, and soccer won gold medals. At the winter Olympics in 1998 women's ice hockey won a gold medal. By relying on an outdated gimmick, "the battle of the sexes," the Colorado Silver Bullets never had a chance to develop an identity of their own.

For women to be judged purely on their own merits as athletes, they need their own leagues. Professional women's golf and tennis circuits have already demonstrated that the public will come out to see women play and that women athletes can be accepted for their athleticism. The future success of the newly formed women's basketball, softball, volleyball, ice hockey and soccer leagues will indicate whether or not women's team sports have finally come of age.

What we have learned from the experience of the Colorado Silver Bullets is that the time of the "battle of the sexes" has passed. Women's teams should not be competing against men's. It is a feminist myth that there are no biological differences between the sexes. Men are, on average, physically bigger and stronger than women. In sports in which size and strength are an advantage, women will come out losers if they play against men. The myth of no physical differences not only deceives women, but sets them up for failure. Women's sports need to be accepted in their own right. The only way to do that is to have women's leagues.

Notes

1. "Girls of Summer: An All-Female Lineup for the Sun Sox?" The Sporting News, 1 Oct. 1984.

2. "Colorado Silver Bullets: 1994 souvenir program," p. 2.

3. "Colorado Silver Bullets: 1994souvenir program," p. 6.

4. Statistics supplied by Colorado Silver Bullets organization.

5. Gai Ingham Berlage, Women in Baseball: The Forgotten History, Westport, CT: Praeger, 1994, pp. 30-38, 178-191.

6. Robert Collias, "Hawaiian League Reloads with Pair of Silver Bullets," USA Today Baseball Weekly, Oct. 12-18, 1994, p. 8; "Hawaiian Winter League Final Unofficial Statistics," Howe Sportsdata International, Boston, MA, 1994.

7. Anthony L. Gargano, "Diamonds Are a Girl's Best Friend, Women Players Take Their Swings at Becoming Ms. Met," New York Post, Feb. 2, 1995, p. 82-83; "Minor League Baseball: Davis Lives Out Dream with Scoreless Inning, Win," 1996 Associated Press, 1996 Copyright Nando.net.

8. "Big League Clash of Genders: Bullets Play Six Games in Taiwan," Lifetime on Line, http:/www.lifetimetv.com/sports/ SilverBullets/taiwan.htm; Summer 1996 Taiwan Game Results: 0-5, 11/19/96, http://www-inst.eecs.berkeley.edu/~j-yen/ SilverBullets/taiwan.html.

9. Author's telephone conversation, 29 July 1997, with Bob Hope, president and owner, Hope-Beckham Inc., which owns the Colorado Silver Bullets.

Figure This!

How to compute the change in a player's batting average without a calculator and without knowing much of anything at all

Steve Samuels

On July 15, 1997, Larry Walker of the Colorado Rockies, the major leagues' leading hitter, went 0 for 4. According to the box score in the New York *Times*, his average after the game was .406. Seeing this, I wondered how many points it had dropped just in that one game. To find out, I did the following very simple calculation:

First of all, 0 for 4 is a batting average of .000, which is about 400 points below his season average. Second, July 15 is a little over half the season, so Walker must have played somewhere between 80 and 100 games. Now 400 over 80 is 5, and 400 over 100 is 4, so I concluded that Walker lost 4 or 5 points in that game. His average before the game must have been .410 or .411.

Then I saw that the *Times* had printed a list of the National League's top hitters, as of the day before. Walker was listed as batting .411 in 89 games with 136 hits in 331 at bats. So the July 15 game was his nintieth, and afterward he had 136 hits in 335 at bats, which is indeed a .406 average. Had I seen the list sooner, I obviously wouldn't have needed to do my simple little calculation.

In the same game, Todd Zeile of the Dodgers went 1 for 2, a .500 batting average for the game. How many points did he add to his batting average? Zeile's name was not listed among the NL's top hitters. His postgame average was given as only .243. In that one

game, he'd batted about 260 points above his average, and I reckoned he had somewhere between 200 and 400 at bats coming into the game. Now 200/2 is 100 and 400/2 is 200. I used the 100 and 200 the same way I'd used the 80 and 100 for Larry Walker: I divided the 260 by each, giving me 260/200 = 1.3 and 260/100 = 2.6. So I concluded that Zeile added somewhere between one and three points to his batting average. Had I known that, in fact, Zeile had about 330 at bats coming into the game, I'd have taken 330/2 = 165, and divided 260 by 165, which gives an answer between one and two points.

Can you see what I'm doing here? Suppose it's the 15th of May, and an everyday player with a .300 average has just gotten a hit. How much did that hit raise his average? If you figure he's played about 40 games and had about 150 at bats, then you can compute (1000 - 300)/(150/1) = 700/150 which is between 4 and 5, so that one hit should have raised his batting average by 4 or 5 points. If he had a .200 average, you'd guess 5 or 6 points, because 800/150 is between 5 and 6. And if he also had only about 100 at bats, you'd compute 800/100 = 8, and guess 8 (give or take a point).

If you have enough data, of course, you don't need to do this kind of back-of-the-envelope calculation. But if not, then it comes in real handy. Notice that it works very nicely for estimating the change in batting average after any small number of at bats: one or two or four or whatever.

What's the mathematical basis for my calculation?

Steve Samuels, *born in Brooklyn, teaches statistics and mathematics at Purdue University in West Lafayette, Indiana.*

Just some simple algebraic manipulation. Here it is:

Suppose a player had H hits in (AB) at-bats, and then gets h additional hits in (ab) additional at bats. So his batting average had been H/(AB), and then became [H+h]/(AB)+(ab)]. We're interested in estimating the difference, and you can check that

$$\frac{H+h}{(AB)+(ab)} - \frac{H}{(AB)} = \left[\frac{h}{(ab)} - \frac{H}{(AB)}\right] \times \frac{(ab)}{(AB+ab)} = \frac{\left[\dfrac{h}{(ab)} - \dfrac{H}{(AB)}\right]}{\left[\dfrac{(AB)}{(ab)} + 1\right]}$$

In the Larry Walker example, h/(ab) = 0/4 = .000, H/(AB) is roughly .400, so the difference is roughly 400 points. Also (ab) is about one game's worth of at-bats and we figured (AB) to be between 80 and 100 games worth, so (AB)/(ab) is between 80 and 100, which is a lot bigger than 1, so we ignore the "+1" in the formula. Dividing -400 by 80 or 100 gives us -5 or -4, which represents a drop of 4 or 5 points.

I leave it to you to check the other examples, and to try out the method for yourself. I guarantee that you'll like it!

The "Bizarro" Subway Series

The ultimate dream for any baseball fan in a multiple-team town is to have a "subway series" in the Fall Classic. In many cases, a follower of one the city's clubs abhors the other-league pretender and can't wait for the ultimate, head-to-head bragging rights.

Over the course of the Worlds Series, the New York Yankees faced the Brooklyn Dodgers or the New York Giants thirteen times, by far the dominant matchup. The White Sox beat the Cubs in the 1906 series and the St. Louis Cardinals and Browns squared off in 1944.

But in the "Bizarro" subway series everything is backwards so they take place when the town's teams both finish in last place. During the first half of this century, such coincidences took place on fourteen occasions.

It should not be surprising that the "dynasty of disasters" belongs to Philadelphia. The Athletics and Phillies shared the bottom rung nine times, beginning with a three-year run from 1919-21. They also finished last in 1936, 1938, 1940-42, and 1945.

Boston's teams finished last together three times (1906, 1922, and 1929). The Browns and Cardinals finished in the basement in 1913. In 1948, the Cubs and White Sox became the last pair to have this distinction.

With the rising cost of sports enterprises, the days of one city supporting two teams are most likely over. Since the late '50s, thanks to expansion and franchise shifts, only the New York Mets-Yankees and the Chicago Cubs-White Sox rivalries remain. But as long as they do, "Bizarro" fans still have hope.

—Ron Kaplan

Nineteenth-Century World Series Schedules

Not exactly set in stone

Joseph M. Wayman

Nineteenth-century World Series were not the regularly scheduled annual events we are used to today. They were scheduled year-by-year on a catch-as-catch-can basis between the pennant-winning clubs of the National League and the American Association. The teams negotiated the number of games that would make up the Series. Sometimes they scheduled a Series with an even number of games, with provision for an extra game to decide the championship. As today, the team taking the majority of the games was generally considered the winner. Unlike today, the teams would attempt to play out the full number of games, even after one team had taken the decisive contest. These games, though recognized as World Series games, were, in essence, exhibitions. Not surprisingly, attendance and the champion club's interest waned after a deciding win. Henry Chadwick and others championed a fixed and regulated interleague World Series, but that didn't come about until 1905.

1882: Not a real World Series—Chicago (NL) and Cincinnati (AA) tied 1-1 in games. "Some historians have written that the first World Series took place in 1882 when the Chicago White Stockings, victors in the National League, met the Cincinnati Reds of the American Association. Each team had won once

when that series was abandoned and, although it marked the first postseason meeting of champions, there was no title at stake. The Reds and White Stockings both had numerous postseason games scheduled, and the fact each team had won its respective race was incidental."[1] Cincinnati scheduled postseason exhibition games with the Cleveland, Chicago, and Providence NL clubs. Cleveland topped Cincinnati in games, 2-1, and Chicago tied them, 1-1. Providence, about to engage Chicago in the Philadelphia Agreement games,[2] thereupon cancelled its Cincinnati exhibitions. The Reds then contacted Buffalo (NL) for a series but received a telegram from AA President McKnight, putting an end to their NL exhibition plans.[3]

1883: World Series abrogated—The AA brass hailed their winning Athletics as baseball's best team. Embarrassingly, the Athletics lost the Philadelphia city championship to the last-place NL entry, 1-2. Other exhibition results with NL clubs (0-5) didn't enhance the Athletics's image. Henry Chadwick noted the Athletics "lost the championship of the United States by their failure to play their appointed series of games with the League champions of Boston, though all three games were arranged to be played on the Athletics' own grounds."[4]

1884-1890, AA-NL World Series—The 1885 World Series program called for "a series of seven or more games" to be played. Although an allowance

---

Joe Wayman is a lifelong fan and the self-publisher of his hobby, Grandstand Baseball Annual.

was made for five extra games, "the original conditions were not mandatory beyond seven games."[5] It was mutually agreed and announced that the seventh game would conclude the series, with the results of the forfeited second game being thrown out. Thus, the series was tied, 2-2, with one tie, going into the seventh game. Anson was confident of a Chicago victory, coming off two successive 9-2 wins. St. Louis unexpectedly bashed the Windy City team, 13-4, and the Browns had the championship, 3-2. Anson denied he had made any such commitment. He claimed that, counting the forfeit, the Series was tied 3-3. The public, generally, seemed to agree with him.

The 1890 Series also ended without a winner, due to a combination of cold weather and lack of interest. Most fans felt that the Players' League champion Boston Reds—not invited to participate—was baseball's strongest team.

1891: No World Series—When the Players' League folded after its single season of 1890, its players were supposed to be returned to their former National League and American Association clubs. Bierbauer and Stovey of the AA Athletics were "pirated" away by the NL. This was held legitimate by the Board of Control because the Athletics had forgotten to reserve them. Angrily, the AA withdrew from the National Agreement (baseball's umbrella pact). "Can you imagine," asked the New York *Herald*, "a war over two players when hundreds of thousands of dollars are involved? It was true."[6] King Kelly jumped from the AA to the NL in August, ruining an attempted reconciliation. At season's end, the AA wired the NL a challenge to a three-, five-, or seven-game World Series.[7] The league declined because the Association was no longer a part of the National Agreement, but said it would play if the AA returned to the fold. The AA refused.

The American Association was in sad shape by 1891, but its life might have been prolonged by a Series, since its Boston Reds (former PL champions) were baseball's best team, and a victory might have given the association some credibility. During the Reds's two-year existence in two leagues, the game's best team was denied World Series participation by the politics and disruption of the era.

1892 NL World Series—By 1892, the National League was the only major league left. It contained twelve teams, and it decided to run a split schedule, with the World Series to pit the champion of the first half against the champion of the second half, provided there were two different winners. So in the World Series of 1892, Boston of the National League played Cleveland of the National League.

Notes:

1. *Hot Stove League*, 1955, page 229, by Lee Allen.

2. *Grandstand Baseball Annual 1990*, p. 103

3. *Baseball (1882) From The Newspaper Accounts*, November, 1966, pages 48-50, by Preston D. Orem.

4. *Spalding's Baseball Guide*, 1884, page 54, edited by Henry Chadwick.

5. *New York Clipper*, November 14, 1885.

6. *Baseball—the Early Years*, 1960, page 253, by Dr. Harold Seymour.

7. *Baseball (1891) From The Newspaper Accounts*, September, 1967, page 566, by Preston D. Orem.

8. *The Scrapbook History of Baseball*, 1975, page 21, by Deutsch, Cohen, Johnson, and Neff.

Sources:

Baseball From The Newspaper Accounts (Preston D. Orem), The New York *Times*, The New York *Clipper*, *Sporting Life*, *Spalding Guides* (various), *American Baseball—From Gentleman's Sport to the Commissioner* (David Q. Voigt), *Baseball—The Early Years* (Dr. Harold Seymour), and Bob Davids correspondence.

Suggested Reading:

(1) *Glory Fades Away*, 1991, by Jerry Lansche, and (2) Three *Grandstand Baseball Annual* articles by Frank Williams—(a) "The First League Championship Series-1892," *Grandstand Baseball Annual 1989*; (b) "The Boston Reds, 1890 Champions of the Players' National League," *Grandstand Baseball Annual 1990*; and (c) "The Boston Reds, 1891 Champions of the American Association's Final Season," *Grandstand Baseball Annual 1991*.

World Series, 1882–1892

	Pennant		WS Schedule		Championship			All Games		
Year	NL	AA	Games	W	Winner	Lg	W-L	Winner	Lg	W-L
1882	Chi	Cin	No WS (a)	-	-	-	-	-	-	-
1883	Bos	Ath	3	2	WS abrogated	-	-	-	-	-
1884	Prov	NY	3	2	Prov	NL	2-0	Prov	NL	3-0
1885	Chi	StL	7 (b)	4	Tie	..	3-3+	Tie	..	3-3+
1886	Chi	StL	6 (c)	4	StL	AA	4-2	StL	AA	4-2
1887	Det	StL	15	8	Det	NL	8-3	Det	NL	10-5
1888	NY	StL	10 (c)	6	NY	NL	6-2	NY	NL	6-4
1889	NY	Brk	6 of 11 (d)	6	NY	NL	6-3	NY	NL	6-3
1890	Brk	Lou	8 (c)	5	Tie	..	3-3+	Tie	..	3-3+
1891	Bos	Bos	No WS	-	-	-	-	-	-	-
1892	Bos/Cle	...	5 of 9 (e)	5	Bos	NL	5-0+	Bos	NL	5-0+

Abbreviations: NL—National League pennant winner; AA—American Association pennant winner; Games—Scheduled World Series Games; W—Wins needed to decide championship; Winner—Series winning club; Lg—League affiliationof winning club; W-L—Series won and lost record.

a—Two exhibition games played; b—Seven mandatory games scheduled, with an allowance for five extra games, but by mutual consent the series concluded with the seventh game[8]; c—An extra deciding game was authorized if the scheduled games ended in a tie; d—Series over when the first club won six games of 11 scheduled; e—NL split-season World Series, Boston (1st-half) and Cleveland (2nd-half); +—One tie game.

Place-of-Birth All-Star Teams

Who pitches for New York?

Todd Holcomb

This project began as curiosity about which states in the U.S. could field the best mythical baseball teams determined by place of birth. There is no up-to-date published record of major league players listed by the states or countries in which they were born, which made the task of constructing all-star state and country teams a perpetual search and re-search of baseball encyclopedias. My primary reference books were Thorn and Palmer's *Total Baseball* and Neft and Cohen's *The Sports Encyclopedia: Baseball*.

The result of my research is sixty-two baseball "teams" representing the fifty states, the District of Columbia, seven countries, three cities and one continent (Europe). Each team, when possible, has eleven players who have competed in the major leagues of organized baseball or the Negro major leagues. Each team comprises one player at each of the eight everyday positions, two pitchers and an eleventh man (the best player who didn't make the first ten). Alaska, Hawaii, Montana, Nevada, North Dakota, and Wyoming lack enough major leaguers to field a complete team. A few more states barely sneaked in. Delaware was secured by Charlie Marshall's one game as a catcher for the 1941 St. Louis Cardinals. He never batted, but he did record a putout.

I made a special effort to keep players at the positions they played most frequently in the major leagues. Exceptions are noted with primary positions

in parentheses. Players were placed at less familiar positions within reasonable guidelines. A player "beaten out" at his natural spot could go to a position at which he played primarily for at least one full major league season. Thus, Willie Stargell was placed at first base, where he played 40 percent of his big-league games, because Oklahoma had three other Hall of Fame outfielders. By the same logic, Pete Rose was returned to his rookie position of second base for Ohio. That opened a spot for Al Oliver in the outfield and kept Ron Oester at bay.

A player could go to a position he played occasionally but never primarily if it were required to fill out his team's roster (witness Utah and Hawaii). And a player such as Hall of Fame third baseman George Kell went to a secondary position (first base) when he was far superior to the alternative. Brooks Robinson expedited Kell's move. The case of Phil Garner, Tennessee's shortstop, stretched the limits of common sense, but I attempted to simulate what a manager might do to field a starting nine given those circumstances, and Tennessee has never produced a significant big-league shortstop. Garner, primarily a second baseman, played only forty-two games at short. Tennessee did produce three prominent second basemen and third basemen in Garner, Junior Gilliam, and Bill Madlock.

No player appears at a position he never played in the majors, and no player, even if he was a superstar, was placed at an unnatural position when another quality player was available. Johnny Mize, for ex-

Todd Holcomb is a sportswriter who lives in Marietta, Georgia.

ample, didn't go to Georgia's outfield (Bill Terry beat him out at first base) because Dixie Walker, Ty Cobb and Negro League star Rap Dixon were better "outfielders" than Mize. In fact, Mize was omitted from his team entirely because Frank Thomas (the modern version) was given the nod as Georgia's extra player.

Negro League players were selected conservatively because of the lack of statistics for objective comparison. But to exclude Negro Leaguers would be to suggest Jody Davis and not Josh Gibson is the best catcher ever born in Georgia, orto fail to recognize Cool Papa Bell as Mississippi's greatest baseball player. Despite my conservatism, a few Negro League stars were chosen ahead of more widely known white major leaguers. That list of perennial Negro League all-stars includes Tubby Scales (rather than Ted Sizemore in Alabama), Dobie Moore (rather than Bucky Dent in Georgia), Dixon (rather than Moises Alou, Marquis Grissom, or Wally Moses in Georgia), Frank Wickware and Chet Brewer (rather than Claude Hendrix and Mike Torrez in Kansas), Howard Easterling (rather than Bill Melton in Louisiana), Ben Taylor (rather than Dan Driessen in South Carolina), Spot Poles (rather than Al Bumbry in Virginia) and Cristobal Torriente (rather than Jose Canseco in Cuba). The source of Negro League players' birthplaces, and to a large extent their credentials, was James Riley's *The Biographical Encyclopedia of the Negro Baseball Leagues*.

Not surprisingly, the more populous states field the more powerful teams. New York, with Phil Rizzuto's selection to the Hall of Fame in 1994, became the first state that could comfortably put a Hall of Famer at each position. That distinction requires that first baseman Hank Greenberg go to the outfield, his primary position for three of his 13 seasons, and that outfielder King Kelly play catcher, where he appeared in 583 of 1,455 major league games. Pennsylvania can finagle its lineup in a similar way, putting Honus Wagner in the outfield, his most common position the first five years of his career, and placing Bobby Wallace at shortstop, but that leaves the state a third baseman short of a Hall of Fame starting nine.

Illinois will match New York's achievement if Rickey Henderson, Kirby Puckett, and Robin Yount (as an outfielder) go into the Hall of Fame. California, with everyone at his most natural position, lacks only a Hall of Fame third baseman. (San Francisco-born Tony Lazzeri, a Hall of Fame second baseman, did play 166 big-league games at third.) Ohio, by putting catcher Roger Bresnahan at his frequent position of center field, lacks only a Hall of Fame second

baseman. Perhaps Rose will solve that problem some day.

With last year's induction of Negro League shortstop Willie Wells, Texas has a Hall of Famer at every position but catcher. (Nolan Ryan and Greg Maddux are listed as Texas's pitchers instead of current Hall of Famers Rube and Willie Foster of the Negro Leagues.)

States with middling populations such as Alabama and Oklahoma put out surprisingly crack lineups, as well. Alabama's murderers' row of Billy Williams, Willie Mays, Willie McCovey, and Hank Aaron hit 2,362 home runs and kept Heinie Manush, Monte Irvin, George Foster, Rudy York, and Lee May on the bench. While a state as big as Illinois has no current Hall of Fame outfielders, Oklahoma has four: Lloyd and Paul Waner, Mickey Mantle, and Stargell, plus Johnny Bench behind the plate. Arkansas has four Hall of Famer players on the left side of the infield (Kell, Robinson, Travis Jackson and Arky Vaughan).

Indiana has six Hall of Famers, all in the outfield: Chuck Klein, Oscar Charleston, Sam Rice, Edd Roush, Sam Thompson, and Max Carey. Nebraska may do no better than Otto Miller at catcher, but it has Sam Crawford and Richie Ashburn in the outfield, Wade Boggs at third base, and a pitching staff of "Bob and Pete and pray for sleet." (That's Bob Gibson and Grover Cleveland Alexander.)

Other Hall of Fame trivia came to light through serendipity. For example, six Hall of Famers were born outside the United States, but no two come from the same country. Those six are Ferguson Jenkins (Canada), Martin DiHigo (Cuba), Juan Marichal (Dominican Republic), Rod Carew (Panama), Roberto Clemente (Puerto Rico), and Luis Aparicio (Venezuela). Other Hall trivia: Larry Doby this year became the first South Carolinian to make it into Cooperstown. Next year, George Brett (West Virginia) and Carlton Fisk (Vermont) may be the first players from their states inducted. Massachusetts has nine Hall of Fame players (not counting Leo Durocher and Wilbert Robinson), but none has played a big league game in fifty years.

Hall of Fame players are listed on their teams in bold face. The utility of viewing Hall of Famers by their birthplace persuaded me to favor those in Cooperstown when my personal opinion would have steered me otherwise in a few cases, such as Hal Trosky versus Red Faber as "eleventh man" in Iowa, Wes Ferrell versus Hoyt Wilhelm in North Carolina, and Alex Rodriguez versus Rizzuto in New York. Hall of Famers failed to make their team only when another Hall of Famer or future Hall of Famer was chosen. Mark McGwire, for example, was California's first baseman over George Kelly and Frank Chance.

Needless to say, tough roster cuts were many in a project like this. Many of the hardest "cuts" are evident by the player listed as "eleventh man." Here are some other examples of interesting decisions among top-flight players that can't be discerned by viewing the final state and country teams:

Harry Heilmann, Barry Bonds, Eddie Murray, or Tony Gwynn as "eleventh man" for California? Lazzeri, Joe Gordon, or Bobby Doerr at second base for California? Gary Carter or Ernie Lombardi at catcher for California? Andre Dawson, Tim Raines, Hal McRae, Mickey Rivers, or Gary Sheffield (pick three) in Florida's outfield? Robin Roberts, Red Ruffing, or Joe McGinnity at pitcher for Illinois, with the loser to face Yount for eleventh man? Gil Hodges or Don Mattingly at first for Indiana? Will Clark, Joe Adcock, or "Mule" Suttles at first base and Ron Guidry, Vida Blue, Mel Parnell, Andy Pettitte, or Howie Pollet as pitchers for Louisiana? Warren Spahn, Whitey Ford, Waite Hoyt, Sandy Koufax, or Jim Palmer as lead pitcher for New York? Jimmy Collins, Heinie Groh, John McGraw, or Frankie Frisch (beaten out at second by Eddie Collins) at third base for New York? Buck Ewing, Bresnahan, or Thurman Munson at catcher for Ohio? Phil Niekro, Roger Clemens, Rollie Fingers, or Rube Marquard behind Cy Young as No. 2 pitcher for Ohio? Eddie Plank, Rube Waddell or Big Ed Walsh behind Christy Mathewson as No. 2 pitcher for Pennsylvania? Dave Concepcion, Omar Vizquel, or Aparicio at shortstop for Venezuela?

The kind of problem a manager likes doesn't always apply to researchers.

Place-of-birth all-star teams

	Alabama	Alaska	Arizona	Arkansas
c	Luke Sewell	Tom Sullivan	Ron Hassey	Sherm Lollar
1b	Willie McCovey		Hank Leiber (of)	G. Kell (3b)
2b	Tubby Scales*	Steve Staggs	Eddie Leon (ss)	Aaron Ward
ss	Ozzie Smith		Solly Hemus	A. Vaughan
3b	Joe Sewell (ss)		Jack Howell	B. Robinson
lf	Billy Williams	Scott Loucks	Billy Hatcher	Lou Brock
cf	Willie Mays	Randy Kutcher	Max Venable	Willie Davis
rf	Hank Aaron		Rex Hudler (2b)	Rick Monday
p	Satchel Paige*	Curt Schilling	John Denny	Dizzy Dean
p	Don Sutton		Alex Kellner	Lon Warneke
E	Heinie Manush (lf)		Tom Pagnozzi (c)	T. Jackson

	California	Colorado	Connecticut	Delaware
c	Ernie Lombardi	John Stearns	John Ellis	C. Marshall
1b	Mark McGwire	Buddy Gremp	Roger Connor	John Mabry
2b	Bobby Doerr	Bert Niehoff	Dick McAuliffe	D. DeShields
ss	Joe Cronin	Ike Davis	Tommy Corcoran	Al Cihocki
3b	Stan Hack	Roy Hartzell (of)	Pete Castiglione	Hans Lobert
lf	Ted Williams	Buster Adams	Jim O'Rourke	Randy Bush
cf	Joe DiMaggio	Johnny Frederick	Jimmy Piersall	Dave May
rf	Duke Snider	Johnny Lindell	Johnny Moore	Rube Vinson
p	Tom Seaver	Goose Gossage	Red Donahue	S. McMahon
p	Don Drysdale	Tippy Martinez	Steve Blass	Chris Short
E	Barry Bonds (lf)	Dave LaRoche (p)	Mo Vaughn (1b)	Huck Betts (p)

	Florida	Georgia	Hawaii	Idaho
c	Al Lopez	Josh Gibson*	Tony Rego	Bill Salkeld
1b	Steve Garvey	Bill Terry	Joey Meyer	Kent Hadley
2b	Dave Johnson	Jackie Robinson	Mike Huff (of)	H. Luby (3b)
ss	J. H. Lloyd*	Dobie Moore*	Len Sakata	Pep Goodwin
3b	Larry Parrish	Cecil Travis (ss)		Vance Law
lf	Tim Raines	Rap Dixon*	Jessie Reid	H. K'brew (1b)
cf	Andre Dawson	Ty Cobb	John Matias (1b)	Bob Martyn
rf	Hal McRae	Dixie Walker	Mike Lum	Bob Addy
p	Steve Carlton	Dick Redding*	Charlie Hough	Larry Jackson
p	Dwight Gooden	Kevin Brown	Sid Fernandez	Vernon Law
E	Fred McGriff (1b)	Johnny Mize (1b)	Ron Darling (p)	K. Dayley (p)

	Illinois	Indiana	Iowa	Kansas
c	Ray Schalk	Bubbles Hargrave	Hank Severeid	D. Daulton
1b	Jim Bottomley	Don Mattingly	Cap Anson	G. Grantham
2b	Red Schoendienst	Billy Herman	Bobby Knoop	B. DeMoss*
ss	Lou Boudreau	Donie Bush	Dave Bancroft	Joe Tinker
3b	Fred Lindstrom	Jeff King	Denis Menke (ss)	Bob Horner
lf	R. Henderson	Chuck Klein	George Stone	Duff Cooley
cf	Kirby Puckett	Edd Roush	Fred Clarke	H. Johnson*
rf	Wally Berger	Oscar Charleston*	Bing Miller	Mitch Webster
p	Joe McGinnity	Miner Brown	Bob Feller	W. Johnson
p	Red Ruffing	Amos Rusie	Dazzy Vance	Chet Brewer*
E	Robin Yount (ss)	Sam Rice (cf)	Red Faber (p)	F. Wckwr* (p)

	Kentucky	Louisiana	Maine	Maryland		Massachusetts	Michigan	Minnesota	Mississippi
c	John Grim	Bill Dickey	Bill Carrigan	Bill Holbert	c	Mickey Cochrane	Ted Simmons	Terry Steinbach	Gerry Moses
1b	Dan McGann	Will Clark	Del Bissonette	Jimmie Foxx	1b	Jeff Bagwell	Jack Fournier	Kent Hrbek	George Scott
2b	S. T. Hughes*	D. Malarcher* (3b)	Tom Downey (ss)	Cupid Childs	2b	Jerry Remy	Charlie Gehringer	Jack Crooks	Frank White
ss	Pee Wee Reese	George Strickland	Freddy Parent	Cal Ripken	ss	Rabbit Maranville	Mike Bordick	G. DMonvlle (2b)	B. Myer (2b)
3b	Travis Fryman	Oliver Marcelle*	Harry Lord	J. Johnson*	3b	Pie Traynor	Chris Sabo	Paul Molitor	H. Easterling*
lf	Pete Browning	Albert Belle	Chet Chadbourne	Harold Baines	lf	Joe Kelley	Kirk Gibson	Jim Eisenreich	Chet Lemon
cf	Earle Combs	Reggie Smith	George Gore	Al Kaline	cf	Tommy McCarthy	Ron LeFlore	Roger Maris	C. Papa Bell*
rf	Bobby Veach	Mel Ott	Billy Maloney	Babe Ruth	rf	Tony Conigliaro	Kiki Cuyler	Dave Winfield	Dave Parker
p	Jim Bunning	Ted Lyons	Bill C. Swift	Lefty Grove	p	John Clarkson	Hal Newhouser	Chief Bender	Guy Bush
p	Carl Mays	Vida Blue	Bob Stanley	Vic Willis	p	Tim Keefe	Jim Kaat	Jack Morris	C. Passeau
E	Don Gullett (p)	Ron Guidry (p)	G. Magoon (ss)	F. Baker (3b)	E	Jack Chesbro (p)	Bobby Grich (2b)	Jerry Koosman (p)	Ellis Burks (cf)

	Missouri	Montana	Nebraska	Nevada		New Hampshire	New Jersey	New Mexico	New York
c	Yogi Berra	John Gibbons	Otto Miller	Tyler Houston	c	Tom Padden	Rick Cerone	Al Montgomery	M. Kelly (of)
1b	Jake Beckley	Ed Bouchee	Johnny Hopp (of)		1b	Harry Bemis (c)	Eric Karros	Chuck Stevens	Lou Gehrig
2b	Lonnie Frey	Jeff Doyle	Bob Johnson (ss)	S. Rodriguez	2b	Barney Friberg	Kid Gleason	Fred Haney (3b)	Eddie Collins
ss	Glenn Wright		Ron Hansen	J. Gamble (pr)	ss	Red Rolfe (3b)	Derek Jeter	Vern Stephens	Phil Rizzuto
3b	Ken Boyer	Herb Plews (2b)	Wade Boggs		3b	Arlie Latham	Joe Stripp	Al Clancy	Jimmy Collins
lf	Roy Sievers	Dave Meier	Billy Southworth	Rob Richie	lf	Phil Plantier	Joe Medwick	Ralph Kiner	C. Yaz
cf	G. Van Haltren	John Lowenstein	Richie Ashburn	M. Cordova	cf	Kevin Romine	Billy Hamilton	Joel Hunt	Willie Keeler
rf	Zach Wheat	Jim Tyack	Sam Crawford		rf	Joe Lefebvre	Goose Goslin	Mark Corey	H. Gnbrg (1b)
p	Carl Hubbell	Dave McNally	Pete Alexander	Jim Nash	p	Mike Flanagan	Don Newcombe	Duane Ward	Warren Spahn
p	Clark Griffith	Jeff Ballard	Bob Gibson	Shawn Boskie	p	Lefty Tyler	Andy Messersmith	Steve Ontiveros	Sandy Koufax
E	Pud Galvin (p)	Johnny Couch (p)	Mel Harder (p)	G. Rhodes (p)	E	Bob Tewksbury (p)	Doc Cramer (cf)	W. Blasingame (p)	J. Palmer (p)

	North Carolina	North Dakota	Ohio	Oklahoma		Oregon	Pennsylvania	Rhode Island	S. Carolina
c	Rick Ferrell	Truck Hannah	Buck Ewing	Johnny Bench	c	Mark Parent	Roy Campanella	Gabby Hartnett	A. Robinson
1b	Buck Leonard*		George Sisler	W. St'gell (rf)	1b	Greg Brock	Stan Musial (of)	Johnny Cooney (cf)	Ben Taylor*
2b	Billy Goodman		Pete Rose (of)	Johnny Ray	2b	Harold Reynolds	Nellie Fox	Nap Lajoie	W. Randolph
ss	Luke Appling	Tim Johnson	Barry Larkin	Alvin Dark	ss	Johnny Pesky	Honus Wagner	Bill Almon	Marty Marion
3b	Buddy Lewis		Mike Schmidt	Pepper Martin	3b	Scott Brosius	Dick Allen (1b)	Hobe Ferris (2b)	Al Rosen
lf	Wes Covington		Ed Delahanty	Lloyd Waner	lf	Dave Kingman	Hack Wilson	Davy Lopes (2b)	Jim Rice
cf	Otis Nixon	Ken Hunt	Al Oliver	M. Mantle	cf	Dale Murphy	Ken Griffey Jr.	Hugh Duffy	Larry Doby
rf	Enos Slaughter	Darin Erstad	Elmer Flick	Paul Waner	rf	Ken Williams	Reggie Jackson	Joe Connolly	Joe Jackson
p	Gaylord Perry	Lynn Nelson	Cy Young	Allie Reynolds	p	Mickey Lolich	C. Mathewson	Clem Labine	V. L. Mungo
p	Catfish Hunter	Gary Serum	Phil Niekro	H. Brecheen	p	Larry Jansen	Eddie Plank	Andy Coakley	Bobo Newsom
E	Hoyt Wilhelm (p)	Rick Helling (p)	Roger Clemens (p)	Joe Carter (lf)	E	Larry Andersen (p)	Rube Waddell (p)	Jumbo Brown (p)	C. Smith* (cf)

	South Dakota	Tennessee	Texas	Utah		Vermont	Virginia	Washington	West Virginia
c	Len Rice	Bob Bailey	Biz Mackey*	H. Franks	c	Carlton Fisk	Todd Hundley	Sammy White	A. Seminick
1b	Terry Francona	Dale Alexander	Ernie Banks	Duke Sims (c)	1b	Pat Putnam	Jud Wilson*	John Olerud	D. Hoblitzell
2b	Sparky Anderson	Jim Gilliam	Rogers Hornsby	S. Adams	2b	Amby McConnell	G. Hamner (ss)	R. Sandberg	Bill Mazeroski
ss	Kermit Wahl (3b)	Phil Garner (2b)	Willie Wells	Gordon Slade	ss	Ralph LaPointe	Gene Alley	Kevin Stocker	Jack Glasscock
3b	Scotty Ingerton	Bill Madlock	Eddie Mathews	D. H'w'd (1b)	3b	Larry Gardner	Ray Dandridge*	Ron Santo	George Brett
lf	Kelvin Torve (1b)	Clyde Milan	Ross Youngs	Jay Van Noy	lf	Frank Olin	Willie Horton	Billy North	Greasy Neale
cf	Dave Collins	Vada Pinson	Tris Speaker	G. Theodore	cf	Sun Daly	Spot Poles*	Earl Averill	Jesse Burkett
rf	Carroll Hardy	Turkey Stearnes*	Frank Robinson	B. Mitchell	rf	Fred Mann	Steve Brodie	Woody Jensen	J. Kruk (1b)
p	Floyd Bannister	Tommy Bridges	Greg Maddux	Bruce Hurst	p	Ray Collins	Leon Day*	Randy Myers	Lew Burdette
p	Terry Forster	Claude Osteen	Nolan Ryan	Kelly Downs	p	Ray Fisher	Eppa Rixey (p)	Fred Hutchinson	W. Cooper
E	Jim Scott (p)	Ben Chapman (cf)	Joe Morgan (2b)	E. Heusser (p)	E	Birdie Tebbetts (c)	Deacon Phillippe	Ron Cey (3b)	T. Harrah (3b)

	Wisconsin	Wyoming	District of Columbia
c	Billy Sullivan		Pop Snyder
1b	Ed Konetchy		Lu Blue
2b	Jim Gantner		Bump Wills
ss	George McBride	Mike Lansing	Maury Wills
3b	Lave Cross		Don Money
lf	Al Simmons		Paul Hines
cf	Ginger Beaumont	Rick Sofield	Sonny Jackson (ss)
rf	Harvy Kuenn	Mike Devereaux	Milt Thompson
p	Addie Joss	Tom Browning	Doc White
p	Kid Nichols	Dick Ellsworth	Nip Winters*
E	B. Grimes (p)	Dan Spillner (p)	Johnny Klippstein

Cities

	Greater L. A.	New York City	S. F. Bay
c	Gary Carter	Joe Torre	Ernie Lombardi
1b	Mark McGwire	Lou Gehrig	George Kelly
2b	Joe Gordon	Frankie Frisch	Tony Lazzeri
ss	Alan Trammell	Phil Rizzuto	Joe Cronin
3b	Darrell Evans	H. Zimmerman	Bob Elliott
lf	Darryl Strawberry	H. Greenberg (1b)	Bob Meusel
cf	Duke Snider	Willie Keeler	Joe DiMaggio
rf	Tony Gwynn	Rocky Colavito	Harry Hooper
p	Don Drysdale	Sandy Koufax	Dennis Eckersley
p	Dan Quisenberry	Jim Palmer	Randy Johnson
E	Bobby Doerr (2b)	Whitey Ford (p)	Bill Lange (cf)

Countries

	Canada	Cuba	Dominican Rep.	Mexico
c	George Gibson	Joe Azcue	Tona Pena	Alex Trevino
1b	Larry Walker (rf)	Rafael Palmeiro	Felipe Alou (rf)	Ruben Amaro
2b	Pop Smith	Martin DiHigo*	Juan Samuel	Bobby Avila
ss	Arthur Irwin	Bert Campaneris	Tony Fernandez	C. Carrasquel
3b	Pete Ward	Tony Perez (1b)	P. Guerrero (1b)	Vinny Castilla
lf	Jeff Heath	Minnie Minoso	George Bell	Andres Mora
cf	George Selkirk	C. Torriente*	Cesar Cedeno	Mel Almada
rf	Tip O'Neill	Tony Oliva	Sammy Sosa	J. Orta (2b)
p	Ferguson Jenkins	Mike Cuellar	Juan Marichal	F. Valenzuela
p	John Hiller	Luis Tiant	Ramon Martinez	Aurelio Lopez
E	Terry Puhl (rf)	Jose Canseco (lf)	Rico Carty (lf)	A. R'd'g'z (3b)

	Panama	Puerto Rico	Venezuela	Europe
c	Manny Sanguillen	Benito Santiago	Bo Diaz	Jimmy Archer, Ireland
1b	Rod Carew	Orlando Cepeda	Andres Galarraga	Jack Doyle, Ireland
2b	Rennie Stennett	Roberto Alomar	Manny Trillo	G. Hubbard, Germany
ss	Chico Salmon (2b)	Ivan DeJesus	Luis Aparicio	Steve Jeltz, France
3b	Hector Lopez	Carlos Baerga (2b)	Luis Salazar	Jimmy Austin, Wales
lf	Ben Oglivie	Jose Cruz	Cesar Tovar	J. Anderson, Norway
cf	Omar Moreno	Bernie Williams	Vic Davalillo	P. Donovan, Ireland
rf	Roberto Kelly	Roberto Clemente	Tony Armas	B. Thomson, Scotland
p	Juan Berenguer	Juan Pizarro	Wilson Alvarez	Bert Blyleven, Netherlands
p	Mariano Rivera	Willie Hernandez	Tony Castillo	T. Mullane, Ireland
E	Adolfo Phillips (cf)	Juan Gonzalez (rf)	D. Concepcion (ss)	E. Valo (of), Czech.

Key

Bold: Hall of Fame player

Bold italics: Likely Hall of Fame player

Asterisk: Negro league player

Parentheses: Denotes a player's most frequently played position.

E: Eleventh, or extra, player

On victory and defeat

I asked Frank White if it always felt worse to lose than it felt good to win. Here's what he said:

"I don't agree that defeat always feels worse than victory feels good. When winners say on television, 'I expect it will sink in tomorrow,' they are covering their true feelings, or are unable to express them. Nothing beats that high you get at the moment of clinching that championship win. When you see guys piling up out on the field and swarming all over each other, that's the utmost you can feel in sports. It isn't that good the next morning. It doesn't have to sink in later. That's it. That's the top, right then and there.

"As for losing, it's not that hard to take when you were not expected to win. With Kansas City in 1976 we were a young team. We had never been in the playoffs before. The Yankees had the better team. We weren't expected to win. But by 1978 we felt we were good enough and we expected to win and when we didn't that hurt more, because you knew you were good enough but just didn't do the job. Then when we won against the Yankees in 1980 we know we could win. The same in the World Series in 1980 and 1985.

—Norman Macht

The Great O'Toole

The $22,500 Beauty

Dick Thompson

If Marty O'Toole is remembered at all today, it is as one of baseball's greatest flops; the "$22,500 Beauty" or "Lemon" the Pittsburgh Pirates paid a record price for in 1911. Truth be known, O'Toole was well worth the price. Based on his minor league credentials, Marty could have been one of the game's greatest pitching legends, but by the time Pittsburgh brought him to the major leagues at the age of twenty-two, pieces of his right arm were already strewn across minor league baseball diamonds from Massachusetts to Iowa. I know, countless pitchers have thrown out their arms long before reaching their potential, but few have done it in the meteoric style of Marty O'Toole.

Baseball reference books agree that Marty was born in Pennsylvania on November 27, 1888, but his hometown was Framingham, Massachusetts, where his family moved soon after his birth. The 1900 U.S. census confirms that Marty was born in Pennsylvania in November, 1888. His three younger siblings, including a sister in December, 1889, were born in Massachusetts.

Marty's four brothers all played baseball. Patrick was an outfielder for several New England League teams in the early 1900s. Michael, six years Marty's senior, and twice a minor league 20-game winner, won over 100 career games while pitching in the New England and New York State Leagues, and the American Association. At times, both the Boston Americans and the Detroit Tigers owned his contract. *The Sporting News* obituary on Marty and his contract file card at Cooperstown confuse Michael's minor league stops with Marty's.

After a brief tryout with Providence in the Eastern League in the spring of 1907, Marty joined the Brockton, Massachusetts team in the New England League. The New England League's 1907 pitching averages in the 1908 *Reach Official Baseball Guide* list "M." O'Toole at 11-14 and "J." O'Toole at 20-11. Teammate and brother Mike, the elder O'Toole, was designated "M" in the boxscores. Marty, for his middle name of James, was "J". A 20-game winner as a rookie, Marty completed all twenty-eight of his starts. His nineteenth birthday came two months after the season!

How does a nineteen-year-old pitcher top a 20-win season? How about with a 30-win season. Marty, still with Brockton in 1908, completed thirty-six of his thirty-eight starts, pitching close to 350 innings. He fanned 266 batters, ten or more in a game eight times. His single game high was thirteen, which he did three times. He finished with a 31-11 record, two wins shy of the New England League mark shared by Henry Burns (1887) and Jim McGinley (1904).

Marty joined the Cincinnati Reds after the close of the New England League season and made his major league debut on September 21. His $250-a-month contract earned him a pro-rated $141 for his 1908 major league tenure. That winter the bold youngster wrote to Garry Herrmann requesting the remaining

Dick Thompson's chief interest is collecting biographical data on New England-born players.

$109 he felt he was owed. He quickly found himself back in Brockton.

In 1909 he again led the New England League with twenty-six wins, tossing over 350 innings and fanning 265 batters. He completed thirty-six of his thirty-seven starts, twice striking out fifteen batters in a game. The Boston Red Sox purchased his contract from Brockton in late August, delivery postponed until the end of the season.

Boston owner John I. Taylor released Marty to St. Paul in the American Association early in 1910 as the windup to the deal that sent Charlie Chech, Elmer Steele, and Gulfport Jack Ryan to St. Paul in exchange for Ed Karger and Sea Lion Charley Hall. Mike Kelley, the St. Paul manager, used Marty as a reliever and spot-starter before optioning him to Sioux City in the Western League. Marty made his first Western League appearance on July 4, and from then until the end of the season—now, let me repeat that for effect—from the Fourth of July until the end of the season, O'Toole went 19-5 with 207 strikeouts. Seven times he fanned ten or more batters in a game, including a Western League record eighteen Lincoln batters on July 10—a mark that would stand, to the best of my knowledge, until Cy Blanton fanned twenty Joplin batters in 1933. Marty's 1910 record, St. Paul and Sioux City combined, was 22-8 with 239 strikeouts. He had yet to reach his twenty-second birthday.

If O'Toole felt he was on top of his game in 1910, then 1911 must have felt like he reached the summit of baseball's highest pitching mound. Back with St. Paul, he overwhelmed American Association batters. Reaching double-digit strikeout totals in ten games, he had single game totals of thirteen (twice), fourteen, fifteen, and seventeen. In six consecutive complete-game wins from July 6 to July 30, he fanned ten, seventeen, eleven, ten, fourteen, and fifteen. Despite pitching just three games after July, he won fifteen games and led all American Association pitchers with 199 strikeouts. The seventeen strikeout game stood as the American Association standard until 1915.

By mid-July scouts were following O'Toole like bloodhounds. The Cardinals, Cubs, Giants, Pirates, White Sox, Athletics, and the Cleveland Naps were all interested. The bidding for O'Toole was fast and furious. John McGraw felt he had closed the deal for $15,000 and had a certified check made out as evidence, but the bidding had escalated by the time McGraw's word of approval reached his agent in St. Paul. Charlie Comiskey's offer also came in at $15,000. Roger Bresnahan, the Cardinals manager, offered $16,500. The Cubs raised the ante to $20,000 before Barney Dreyfuss of the Pirates closed the deal with St. Paul for $22,500.

The original check made out for O'Toole can be viewed at the Hall of Fame, but there is evidence to suggest that the price was considerably higher. Several newspaper accounts indicated that an additional $2,500 in "baseball material" was involved. *Sporting Life* reported in February, 1913 that the Pirates had just sent outfielder Ralph Capron to St. Paul because Pittsburgh still owed on the O'Toole deal. O'Toole's batterymate, catcher Bill Kelly, was sold to the Pirates for anywhere from $6,500 to $12,500 and a player, depending on the source. The final tally for the O'Toole-Kelly tandem may have been in excess of $35,000.

O'Toole made his Pirates debut on August 30 with a complete-game, five-hit win versus Boston in which he fanned nine. After two more quick starts Marty was 3-0 with twenty-six K's and just thirteen hits allowed in twenty-seven innings. He had arrived. Unfortunately so had his arm problems. By the middle of September, Marty was in Youngstown, Ohio consulting with "Bonesetter" Reese. Following the season he went back to Massachusetts to see an arm specialist. *Sporting Life* on December 30, 1911, said that Marty was:

> suffering from contracted muscles of the shoulders. Two years ago O'Toole was stricken with rheumatism, but kept on pitching while under treatment. This caused the muscles to become more strained and his arm is in a bad way. Dr. Daniels is of the opinion that the muscles will never reach their normal state.

Spring training in 1912 found O'Toole's "capricious whip" in no better shape. In early April, Pirates manager Fred Clarke reported O'Toole had a lame arm. *Sporting Life* reported that the entire family suffered from "rheumatism of the shoulder." Mike O'Toole, then with St. Paul, was also having arm trouble. As early as May, 1909, after complaining of a sore arm, an examination found Marty's right humerus to be "slightly dislocated" at the shoulder.

Having long been a fan of the book, *The Diamond Appraised*, especially the chapter, *Men-At-Arms Through The Ages*, I presented my research on O'Toole to its author, SABR member Craig R. Wright, and asked for his thoughts:

Cracker Jack
BALL PLAYERS

O'TOOLE, PITTSBURGH - NATIONALS

Transcendental Graphics

As I noted in *The Diamond Appraised*, the style of play in the Dead Ball Era allowed pitchers to throw more innings and go consistently deeper in their starts than pitchers in later eras, but it is fairly easy to see that O'Toole was worked incredibly hard as a young pitcher, even by the standards of his day. By age 22 he had already thrown over 1,500 professional innings and completed 154 of 163 starts.

To put that in perspective for the 1907-1911 period, there was only one big leaguer throwing 150 complete games, Big Ed Walsh with 164. Walsh was a grown man doing it in his physical prime (age 26 to 31), and even then, his arm suddenly blew out shortly thereafter. And while Walsh had more complete games than O'Toole in that period, his 84% CG percentage was well behind O'Toole's mark of 94%, and it would be a reasonable bet

that no pitcher in 1907-1911 in all of organized baseball could match O'Toole's twin feat of 1,500+ innings and a 94% CG rate. That O'Toole did this at age 18 to 22 would certainly make him the most abused young pitcher of that time.

So, given that we know O'Toole was an overhand pitcher who threw a spitter and not a knuckleball, it seems likely to me that his abuse as a young pitcher is primarily responsible for the host of references that you uncovered about his arm miseries.

As it was for Walsh, the spitball was O'Toole's money pitch. In 1907 he read an illustrated newspaper account showing how Jack Chesbro held and threw his spitball. With the aid of those pictures, Marty worked several hours a day until he was able to control the pitch. Chesbro was amused when they met in the spring of 1912 and O'Toole related the story. Bill Kelly, O'Toole's catcher, said that he had never seen another spitball as fast or with as much break to it as O'Toole's. Longtime NL umpire Cy Rigler said he "had no trouble in judging the break on the ball, it being so fast and sharp."

There are several theories why O'Toole's spitter was not successful in the majors. *Low and Inside*, an anecdotal baseball book written in 1949 by Ira L. and H. Allen Smith, said that O'Toole loaded up his spitball by licking the ball like an ice cream cone, and that Fred Luderus of the Phillies applied liniment to the ball causing O'Toole's tongue to swell, driving him from the box. However, in reviewing O'Toole's career, I never found a primary source claiming O'Toole "licked" the ball in that fashion. O'Toole, in six starts, had three complete-game victories against the Phillies in 1912; one, on July 9, a shutout. *Sporting Life*, on July 20, 1912, did report an incident when Luderus indeed was caught applying liniment to the ball but the act was immediately spotted by the umpires, and this was the game O'Toole shutout the Phillies. The more logical and obvious explanation is that O'Toole's spitter broke out of the strike zone, and major league hitters had more control over chasing it than did minor league hitters, thus accounting for his league-leading 159 walks in 1912.

In September, 1911, *Sporting Life* printed a story in which Indianapolis manager Jimmy Burke described both O'Toole's modus operandi and his (Burke's) advice for batters opposing him:

Marty's spitter is started by moistening the side of his third finger of his pitching hand. When he lets go of the ball, one sometimes can hear the finger snap. When hurling his fast one, O'Toole goes through the same stunt of moistening his finger but he doesn't. He merely makes a bluff. Now remember, that O'Toole mixes his spitter and his fast one and that sometimes he won't throw a moist one in an entire inning. Of course, if you can know the fast one is coming along, you can murder the ball, so you must develop all your energy toward this one flaw in Marty's delivery.

Due to the record price Pittsburgh paid for him, O'Toole became a media target and the instant fame was not something he° was well-suited for. In the fall of 1911, he was approached several times by vaudeville agents, and as a Pittsburgh mayoral candidate. Marty laughed off both suggestions but his rookie season seemed jinxed from the start. The *Pittsburgh Post* reported on August 28, 1911:

This high-priced young man appears to pay little attention to the vast amount of publicity that is being heaped upon him. At the same time it must be annoying but Marty takes in the situation sensibly and philosophically, being determined not to allow the limelight to dazzle his eyes. When walking along the street with him or standing about in the hotels, one overhears many a remark referring to none other than this big sunny-haired youth. From newsboy to millionaire, O'Toole's name has become as familiar as though he was the sole owner of the United States, and so frequently has his photograph been reproduced in the newspapers far and wide that he is instantly spotted wherever he goes.

The Pittsburgh sporting pages in the spring of 1912 printed that O'Toole was single and that all interested young ladies should mail their marriage proposals in care of manager Fred Clarke. There were over 100 responses.

On the field O'Toole had mixed success in 1912. He won fifteen games and lost seventeen, holding the opposition to just 7.75 hits per nine innings, second best, according to *Total Baseball*, in the league for pitchers with 200 innings; and a batting average of .241, third best for pitchers with 200 innings. He lost two 1-0 games, one a thirteen-inning affair. On the flip side, he was knocked out of a game against St. Louis after walking five batters in the first inning. By season's end the Pittsburgh papers were referring to him as the "Lemon," one billboard going as far as announcing the batteries for the game as "Pitchers Ames versus Lemon." On August 31, *Sporting Life* stated:

Fan feeling against Marty O'Toole culminated in a big demonstration. It was a distressing moment for O'Toole. The young man hardly deserved the mean flings heaped his way. His work has been most erratic during the year, but there have been numerous games wherein a little batting on the part of his pals would have helped him triumph. O'Toole's wildness is a handicap. Bugs expect too much from Martin. They make the air ring with jeers, hisses and cat calls, 'Take him out,' 'walk everybody,' etc. until Captain Clarke, in sheer pity relieved the New Englander.

Marty was able to stifle the insults somewhat by finishing the season with three consecutive shutouts (although he tossed a league-leading six shutouts in 1912, early editions of *Total Baseball* credited him with just five, failing to recognize an eight inning 0-0 tie). He summed up his feelings in the October 19 issue of *Sporting Life*:

I guess I've lived down that high-priced reputation. The advertising I got through the deal that brought me to Pittsburgh was a handicap that no one but I really understand. The season has been more or less a nightmare to me, and I'm glad it's about to end.

O'Toole's 1913 season was a bust. In late June, *Sporting Life* reported that Marty's wife, Rose Heffernan, whom he had married in Framingham the previous December, was seriously ill following surgery for appendicitis. While his wife was recovering, Marty himself underwent a similar surgical proceedure on July 4. He was released from the hospital two weeks later wearing an abdominal binder. Told not to do anything strenuous, he was back on the hill for Pittsburgh on August 13. He finished the season with just six wins.

1914 was no better than 1913. The trades section of *The Baseball Encyclopedia* states that O'Toole was sold to the New York Giants on August 14, but his last appearance in a Pirates uniform was August 20. John McGraw, finally able to consummate his longstanding desire for Marty, quickly saw enough after O'Toole walked six batters in two September starts in which he didn't make it past the first inning. In October, McGraw, who took O'Toole with the stipulation that he could return him to Pittsburgh if not satisfied, exercised that option. Marty's 1914 record was 2-9.

O'Toole's career was on the decline. He won fourteen games for Columbus in the American Association in 1915, tossing the only no-hitter of his career on July 2.

In 1916 and 1917, Marty won fifteen and nineteen games for Omaha in the Western League. He spent the winter of 1917-18 working in a clothing store in Omaha, by then apparently having abandoned his wife and children. He shifted from the mound to the outfield early in 1918 when the better players marched off to war. In June, *The Sporting News* reported just how far he, and Bill Kelly whom he had

been reunited with, had fallen:

Think of O'Toole and Kelly, former million dollar battery, performing in class A ball before 500 people. When they opened up for Pittsburgh several years ago they were advertised like a circus and drew packed parks.

Because of the war the Western League suspended its season on July 7. Still several months shy of his thirtieth birthday, Marty O'Toole had thrown his last professional pitch.

Marty was sold to San Antonio in the Texas League in the spring of 1919 when the Western League banned the spitball. Marty never reported. Instead, he spent the summer managing an independent team in Omaha.

Members of the O'Toole family can still be found in Framingham, Massachusetts. A grand-nephew, Steve Ryder, played five years of minor league baseball, hitting .346 for Eau Claire in the Northern League in 1959 before a knee injury curtailed his career. Family members report that Marty never came home again. His wife and children, when last heard of, lived in Connecticut, but the Framingham clan has long since lost contact. It's reasonable to assume Marty spent a lot of time dealing with his inner demons. His niece, Maddy Glew, summed it up poignantly:

His life was such a waste and it could have been so different. Imagine having four fine children and never knowing them? I think his pride and low self-esteem after his failing in baseball made him a truly lonely man.

According to *Sporting Life*, O'Toole purchased property in Oregon as early as 1912. He headed west again, as far away from his past, and the major leagues, as he could go. *The Sporting News* reported in December, 1928 that Marty was operating a pool hall in Cosmopolis, Washington. He pitched in semi-pro leagues in the Grays Harbor area until age caught up with him. He later kept in touch with the game as a local umpire. He worked at various times as a salesman and for the Boeing Aircraft Company during World War II.

His last job was as the night dispatcher for a taxi cab company in Aberdeen, Washington. Two local trash collectors, making their morning pick-ups on February 18, 1949, found Marty O'Toole lying dead at the bottom of a flight of stairs.

Long-Service, One-Team Players

At least sixteen years with one—and only one—club

L. Robert Davids

In the long history of major league baseball since 1876, there have been forty-six long-service players who have spent their entire playing careers with only one club. In this study, "entire career" means sixteen or more years. Two active players are on the list—Cal Ripken with eighteen seasons with the Orioles, and Tony Gwynn, seventeen with the Padres. It is likely they will stay with those clubs and move up the longevity ladder headed by Brooks Robinson, who played twenty-three years (1955-77) with the Orioles, and Carl Yastrzemski, the same number with the Red Sox (1961-83).

Cap Anson started the one-team tradition way back when the National League began in 1876 and stayed with Chicago—first called the Colts and later the Cubs—for twenty-two years. No other player came close to that tenure with one team for many years. Walter Johnson joined the Washington Senators in 1907 and was faithful to the Griffith club for twenty-one years. The Big Train closed out in 1927 and remained runner-up to Anson in the one-team saga until Mel Ott passed him in 1947 with twenty-two years with the New York Giants. In 1977 Brooks Robinson reached his milestone with the Orioles. Yastrzemski followed in 1983.

What clubs were best known for hanging onto their prize players? It was the Yankees in the American League with Lou Gehrig, Bill Dickey, Frank Crosetti,

Mickey Mantle, and Whitey Ford. In the Senior Circuit it was the Pirates with Pie Traynor, Willie Stargell, Roberto Clemente, Bill Mazeroski, and Vernon Law. Next in line were the Tigers with four: Charlie Gehringer, Tommy Bridges, and two recent players—Alan Trammell and Lou Whitaker. They set the record for two teammates playing together the longest, nineteen consecutive years, 1977-95, as Detroit's double-play combination. All these players played for their single team for sixteen years or more.

What primary positions did these one-team players field? As might be expected, eleven were pitchers and eleven were outfielders. After that it was eight shortstops, six third basemen, five second basemen, three first basemen, and two catchers. Boston Red Sox outfielder Jim Rice is the only player on the list to play a substantial number of games as Designated Hitter.

Several prominent players, including Hall of Famers, failed to make the list because of a late-career team shift. For example, Christy Mathewson pitched seventeen seasons with the Giants before hurling one final game for the Reds in 1916. Ray Schalk, who spent seventeen seasons behind the bat for the White Sox, played five games for the Giants in 1929. Similarly, Gabby Hartnett, who caught for the Cubs for nineteen years, closed out with the Giants in 1941. His young teammate Phil Cavarretta, who spent twenty years with the Cubs, moved across town for seventy-seven games with the White Sox. Sam Rice, a fixture with the Senators for nineteen seasons, spent a final season with the Indians in 1934. After eigh-

L. Robert Davids is founder of the Society for American Baseball REsearch and author of Baseball Briefs.

teen seasons in Brooklyn, Zack Wheat joined Connie Mack's Athletics in 1927. There he was an outfield teammate of Ty Cobb, who had been with the Tigers for twenty-two years. There have been others. A more recent example was Dwight Evans, the Red Sox outfielder for nineteen years who played a final season with the Orioles in 1991.

Jesse Haines reversed the order, pitching in one game for Cincinnati in 1918 and then hurling eighteen consecutive seasons for the Cardinals. He turned in his toe-plate at age forty-four.

With Ripken and Gwynn being the only current players with lengthy service with one club, what are the prospects for the future of one-team players? Free agency and the availability of big money should affect those numbers adversely. Big name players like Roger Clemens and Mark McGwire have already made their moves. As of this writing, Chuck Finley has spent thirteen years with the California Angels. Tom Glavine has twelve years with Atlanta; Barry Larkin has spent the same time with the Reds, as has Edgar Martinez with Seattle. But that's just over half of the twenty-two Cap Anson spent with Chicago a century ago.

Here is a historical list of the long-service, one-team players. For puristic reasons, Pee Wee Reese is not included on the list because he played fifteen seasons in Brooklyn and one in Los Angeles while wearing a Dodgers' uniform.

The Long-Service, One-Team Players

Yrs.				Yrs.		
23	Brooks Robinson, 3B, Orioles	1955-77		18	Mickey Mantle, OF, Yankees	1951-68
23	Carl Yastrzemski, OF-1B, Red Sox	1961-83		18	Roberto Clemente, OF, Pirates	1955-72
22	Cap Anson, 1B, Cubs (Colts)	1876-97		18	Ed Kranepool, 1B-OF, Mets	1962-79
22	Mel Ott, OF-3B, Giants	1926-47		18	*Cal Ripken, SS-3B, Orioles	1981-97
22	Stan Musial, OF-1B, Cardinals	1941-44; 1946-63		18	Bill Russell, SS-OF, Dodgers	1969-86
22	Al Kaline, OF-1B-DH, Tigers	1953-74		18	Mike Schmidt, 3B-1B, Phillies	1972-89
21	Walter Johnson, P, Senators	1907-27		18	Frank White, 2B, Royals	1973-90
21	Ted Lyons, P, White Sox	1923-42; 1946		17	Pie Traynor, 3B, Pirates	1920-35; 1937
21	Willie Stargell, OF-1B, Pirates	1962-82		17	Lou Gehrig, 1B, Yankees	1923-39
21	George Brett, 3B-1B, Royals	1973-93		17	Bill Dickey, C, Yankees	1928-43; 1946
20	Red Faber, P, White Sox	1914-33		17	Frank Crosetti, SS, Yankees	1932-48
20	Mel Harder, P, Indians	1928-47		17	Bill Mazeroski, 2B, Pirates	1956-72
20	Luke Appling, SS, White Sox	1930-43; 1945-50		17	Bob Gibson, P, Cardinals	1959-75
20	Robin Yount, SS-CF, Brewers	1974-93		17	Johnny Bench, C-3B-1B-OF, Reds	1967-83
20	Alan Trammell, SS, Tigers	1977-96		17	Jim Gantner, 2B-3B, Brewers	1976-92
19	Charlie Gehringer, 2B, Tigers	1924-42		17	*Tony Gwynn, OF, Padres	1982-97
19	Ted Williams, OF, Red Sox	1939-42; 1946-60		16	Clyde Milan, OF, Senators	1907-22
19	Ernie Banks, SS-1B, Cubs	1953-71		16	Carl Hubbell, P, Giants	1928-43
19	Jim Palmer, P, Orioles	1965-67; 1969-84		16	Tommy Bridges, P, Tigers	1930-43; 45-46
19	Dave Concepcion, SS, Reds	1970-88		16	Stan Hack, 3B, Cubs	1932-47
19	Lou Whitaker, 2B, Tigers	1977-95		16	Whitey Ford, P, Yankees	1950; 1953-67
18	Ossie Bluege, 3B, Senators	1922-39		16	Vern Law, P, Pirates	1950-51; 1954-67
18	Bob Feller, P, Indians	1936-41; 45-56		16	Jim Rice, OF-DH, Red Sox	1974-89
					* Still active.	

Sport Stars In The Halls of Fame

Big leaguers who were great at other sports

Stan Grosshandler

In the first six decades of the century the athlete who had starred in baseball and football in college invariably chose the diamond sport when he turned professional. Baseball offered higher salaries, more stability, and a better future.

Bob Reynolds, Stanford All-American tackle (1934-35), a member of the College Football Hall of Fame, and former president of the California Angels, sums up the sentiments of the time. "Pro Football was something you did until you could get a real job. I played two seasons for the Lions and then went into broadcasting."

Seven members of the Baseball Hall of Fame played college football. Frankie Frisch earned his nickname, "the Fordham Flash," as a star halfback at Fordham. Christy Mathewson was considered a fine punter at Bucknell and played for professional teams in the early years of professional football. Lou Gehrig played briefly at Columbia as a guard.

Mickey Cochrane was a star Boston College quarterback. Reggie Jackson (Arizona State), Jackie Robinson (UCLA), and Joe Sewell (Alabama) were halfbacks.

It is not clear if Eddie Collins played for Columbia. A *Colliers* article and another in Cooperstown call him a star quarterback and punter, yet the school has no documentation to prove he played.

Several members of the Professional Football Hall of Fame also played the diamond sport. Greasy Neale who is in both the pro and college halls as a coach was a lefthand hitting outfielder for the Reds for eight years, and had the highest average on his team in the 1919 Series. While Neale was playing college football he was also playing professionally under fictitious names. He coached at six colleges, taking Washington & Jefferson to the 1919 Rose Bowl. He also took the Eagles to the NFL Championship game—the only coach to manage this particular combination.

Jim Thorpe had a six-year baseball career. He was in the 1917 Reds outfield with Neale for the only double no-hit game ever played; Jim's hit finally won it. Thorpe also got into a World Series as a Giant.

Ernie Nevers and Red Badgro, All Americans at Stanford and Southern Cal, respecively, both played briefly with the St. Louis Browns. Ernie once told me about the time he faced Walter Johnson.

"The first two pitches went by me so fast I never saw the ball. Suddenly Walter motioned to his catcher to come to the mound. When he got back the catcher told me Walter was going to let me hit it. I didn't believe him but he said when Walter says something he means it. As Johnson wound up I started swinging and hit the ball against the wall for a double. When I looked at Johnson he was smiling for he had made a raw rookie look good." (This quote appears in the Nevers obituary in the *The Sporting News* and *Walter Johnson: A Life* by SABR member Jack Kavanagh.)

Stan Grosshandler *lives in Raleigh, North Carolina. He and his wife Mary have five children and four grandchildren. He is a physicianj and has taught at the University of South Carolina and North Carolina State University. Stan has published 250 articles on sports history and a dozen medical articles.*

George Halas was briefly a switch-hitting right fielder for the Yankees the year before they acquired Babe Ruth. Paddy Driscoll of Northwestern had a cup of coffee with the Cubs.

Ace Parker, Duke's triple-threat halfback had a brief career with the Philadelphia Athletics. In his first time at bat in the American League, Ace pinch hit for Lynn Nelson against Boston's Wes Ferrell. He hit a home run—the first time in AL history a player had a hit a home run his first time up in a pinch-hitting role. Ace wanted to join the Brooklyn Dodgers of the NFL in 1937, but Connie Mack refused his request. Later Mack relented and Ace went on to a brilliant NFL career with the Dodgers.

Cal Hubbard is the only man in three Halls of Fame. He was a dominating lineman for Centenary and Geneva colleges and then for the Giants, Packers, and Steelers. Later, he umpired in the AL for twenty-three years through 1962.

Many major league players are in the College Football Hall of Fame. This includes Driscoll, Hubbard, Neale, Nevers, Parker, and Thorpe who are also in the Pro Hall.

Harry Agganis was a star quarterback at Boston U. He was drafted by the Cleveland Browns in the early '50s, then included in the largest deal in the history of the league with the Colts. Offered a bonus by the Red Sox, the "Golden Greek" played twenty-five games into his sophomore season before dieing of pneumonia at age twenty-five.

Charlie Berry of Lafayette College was the right end on the last Walter Camp All-American team (1924). He had a long career as a catcher in the AL 1925-38, and played with Pottstown in the NFL in 1925-26, leading the league in scoring. Charlie was a long time AL umpire 1942-63, and NFL head linesman 1940-60. In 1959 he had the unique distinction of officiating in the World Series and in the famous NFL sudden death championship game between the New York Giants and the Baltimore Colts.

Larry Bettencourt of St.Marys was a teammate of Ernie Nevers on the Browns and also played for Green Bay. Paul Desjardien of the University of Chicago briefly played both sports professionally —baseball for Cleveland in 1916, and football for the Chicago Tigers in 1920 and Minneapolis in 1922.

Sam Chapman was a powerful California fullback whom Connie Mack signed for the A's in 1938. Unable to afford an extensive farm system Mack depended heavily on college talent. A hard-hitting outfielder, Sam joined the Navy at the height of his career. Although he managed a long AL career he never regained his prewar form.

Jake Gibbs was a great Mississippi quarterback who caught for the Yankees 1962-71. Paul Giel was a star Minnesota back in the early '50s who pitched in both big leagues and then went into baseball management.

The only Heisman Award winners to play major league baseball and football were Vic Janowicz of Ohio State, who won the award in 1950 and Bo Jackson of Auburn, the 1985 winner. Vic had little success with the Pirates so switched to the Redskins. He was starting to show his Heisman form when an auto accident ended his career. Jackson was well on his way to success in both sports when a severe football injury ended his career on both gridiron and diamond.

Jackie Jensen gained many honors at California in the late '40s, and is the only man to play in a World Series, a Rose Bowl, a College All-Star Game, Baseball's All-Star Game, and to win a MVP award.

Fred Sington won All-American honors as an Alabama tackle 1928-30, then became a major league outfielder. Eric Tipton is still considered one of the best punters in Duke history. After graduation in the late '30s, he became an AL and NL outfielder and later coached baseball at West Point.

Ernie Vick (1918-20) was one of a long line of great Michigan centers who played baseball and football professionally. Another Michigan star Francis Wistert (1931-33) is one of three brothers who made All-American as a tackle for the Wolverines. He pitched briefly for the Reds

Hugo Bezdek is truly a Renaissance man. Born in Czechoslovakia he played football for the U of Chicago. He managed the Pittsburgh Pirates, 1917-19. He also coached four different colleges, taking three—Oregon in 1917, the Mare Island Marines in 1918, and Penn State in 1923—to the Rose Bowl. To top it all off, he coached the Cleveland Rams, 1937-38.

The only member of the Basketball Hall of Fame to play major league baseball is Dave DeBusschere, who pitched briefly for the White Sox. He played seven years with Detroit of the NBA—five as a playing coach—six with the New York Knicks, and was a Commisioner of the American Basketball Association.

The Best Pitcher Ever

Grove? Johnson? Koufax?

Jim Kaplan

In a 1997 poll conducted by the Baseball Writers Association of America, Walter Johnson was named the game's outstanding righthanded pitcher and Sandy Koufax the best lefthander. Historian and statistician Bill James responded that Lefty Grove (who was named the best lefthander in several earlier polls) pitched significantly better than Koufax. Was Grove also, as James has claimed, better than Johnson? Was he the best pitcher ever?

Let's be very clear on one thing before we start. You cannot compare pitchers by matching their numbers. Koufax and Johnson played in pitchers' eras, Grove in the century's hitting paradise (hence, his relative obscurity). Of course Koufax and Johnson have more impressive pure numbers. That doesn't make them better or worse than Grove, just different.

The only objective criterion for judging a pitcher is to compare him with his contemporaries and decide if he was more or less dominant than other pitchers in other eras. That is the basis for this study.

The two most popular standards for judging ballplayers are career value and peak value.

Career value—By definition this measure applies to sustained careers. Since Koufax pitched only twelve seasons and dominated the National League for five, we'll save him for peak value.

Grove and Johnson deserve not just pairing, but poetry. They were the dominant fastball pitchers of their time. They threw almost nothing but heat in their prime. Being forced to swing at them was a crime.

Wins. Johnson won 417 games in 1907-27, Grove 300 in 1925-41. Johnson missed at least half a season with ailments modern medicine could have cured immediately. Grove missed who knows how many starts because he pitched four and one half seasons (1920-24) in a no-draft era for the greatest minor-league team ever, the Baltimore Orioles. He won 108 games before owner Jack Dunn finally sold him to Connie Mack's Philadelphia Athletics. Grove joined the Philadelphia A's in 1925 at age twenty-five. Johnson was a nineteen-year-old rookie in 1907.

Was Grove ready for the majors at twenty? We'll never know. According to one account, the Orioles bought him from the Martinsburg, West Virginia, team of the Blue Ridge League two hours before a telegram arrived from the Giants. According to another story, he was sold four hours before a Dodger offer arrived. If we optimistically prorated his wins over another four and one-half seasons, Grove would move into third place at 379, passing Warren Spahn (363), Christy Mathewson and Pete Alexander (373 each).

In Johnson's mostly dead-ball era, pitchers could pace themselves through games and start often. In Grove's lively-ball era, pitchers had to bear down for most of the game and started less frequently. Johnson averaged thirty-two starts a year, Grove twenty-seven.

Jim Kaplan's book, A Thin White Thread: The Life and Times of Lefty Grove, *will be published by SABR in the spring of 2000, to commemorate the piteher's 100th birthday on March 6 of that year.*

Johnson had more wins, but he also had more opportunities to win.

From 1903 through 1919, there were fifteen 30-win seasons. Between 1920, the start of the hitting era, and today there have been four 30-win[1] seasons. In 1941 Grove became the first 300-game winner since Alexander in 1924, and the last until Warren Spahn won his 300th in 1961. Lefty was the only 300-game winner to pitch his entire career during the offensive explosion between the two world wars.

Grove claimed an unmatched five winning-percentage titles and completed his career with a lifetime percentage of .680, the fourth highest among those with at least 200 decisions.[2] Johnson led the league in winning percentage twice and finished at .599.[3] On the other hand, Grove pitched on only one losing team to Johnson's eleven. Grove's teams averaged 89 wins, Johnson's 74. Certainly, some of Grove's percentage owes to his excellent teams. It is also reasonable to assume that both men would have been big winners for any team. Within the confines of their eras, Grove and Johnson won about as many games as anyone could expect of them.

You pick a winner.

ERA. According to *Total Baseball*, Grove's lifetime ERA of 3.06, when adjusted for league average and parks, tops all others with 148 points. Johnson (2.17) finishes second with 147.[4] Grove won nine ERA titles, the most ever, in seventeen seasons. Think about it: more than half the years he pitched, Grove allowed fewer earned runs per nine innings than anyone in his league. Johnson won five ERA crowns in twenty-one seasons. Grove led the league in ERA and winning percentage four different seasons—twice as often as Johnson or anyone else.

In terms of adjusted ERA, it's virtually a dead heat. In terms of dominance, no one in baseball history matches Grove.

Here are some other criteria to weigh:

Performance under pressure. *Total Baseball* places Grove twenty-ninth in its "clutch pitching index." Johnson, perhaps unfairly, doesn't make the chart. In the 1929-31 World Series Grove had a 4-2 record and two saves, a 1.75 earned-run average, six walks and thirty-six strikeouts in 51-1/3 innings. He won the opening game of the 1930 World Series with a broken blister on his pitching hand. In the 1924 and 1925 Series, Johnson was 3-3, with a 2.16 ERA, fifteen walks and thirty-five strikeouts in fifty innings. Pitching in relief, he won the seventh Series game in 1924

Of course, it is impossible to precisely measure performance under pressure. So much is left to chance:

how many opportunities did the pitcher have? At what point in his career did these opportunities arise? Grove got his chances at his peak. Johnson didn't get his until the twilight of his career. Who would you want on the mound if your life depended on it? A case could be made for either man.

Versatility. Happy to relieve, Grove pitched eight times in ten games over eleven days early in 1933, winning four, saving four. It has been claimed that Johnson was less likely to relieve in his era, when pitchers finished more games. In the lively-ball era, the argument goes, pitchers finished fewer games and therefore were more likely to relieve.

This position doesn't hold up. "Mr. Groves, this ball is yours," A's manager Connie Mack, who always got Lefty's name wrong, told him on the days of his starts. "Pop, this is for nine," Red Sox manager Joe Cronin told an elderly Lefty. In other words, Grove was expected to finish games, lively ball or not. In both 1931 and 1932, he completed twenty-seven of thirty starts. Yet he still pitched out of the bullpen. Grove relieved 159 times, Johnson 136. Grove had fifty-five saves[5] to thirty-four for Johnson.

Pitching strictly in relief during the 1929 Series, Grove had two saves, a 0.00 ERA, and ten K's in 6-1/3 innings.

Grove's relief pitching is worth a longer look. There were virtually no fulltime relievers in his day, and the best starters usually went both ways. Grove had more saves than any Hall of Fame starter this century. Indeed, he may have been a better reliever than starter:

	G	CG/SV	IP	H	H/9	W-L	ERA	BB	BB/9	K	K/9
St	457	298	3563.0	3509	8.9	268-119	3.08	1034	2.61	2023	5.1
Rlf	159	55	377.2	340	8.1	32-22	2.84	153	3.65	243	5.8

Comparing starting and relieving numbers is baseball's ultimate apples-and-oranges game. Wins and losses are terrible stats for relievers, because they're not supposed to get either. (Most top relievers have won-lost relief records around .500.) ERA is equally bad for two reasons. First, relievers rarely continue pitching when they're tired; hence, their ERAs stay down. Second, inherited runners who score don't count against a reliever's ERA. Yet keeping them on base is a prime responsibility.

The area where apples can be compared successfully to oranges is ratio: hits, walks, and strikeouts to innings. Grove had better hit and strikeout ratios as a reliever, and a better walk ratio as a starter. Pitching so late in the day from the bullpen, he was undoubtedly so blinding that hitters took more pitches—hence, more strikeouts and walks. Suffice it to say, Lefty was as effective out of the bullpen as out of the dugout. He shone at both in the Series.

To whom shall we compare him? An obvious match is Dennis Eckersley, who spanned two relief eras: the old one in which pitchers could go for long stretches, and today, when they're rarely expected to pitch more than one and one-third innings. Their relief numbers:

	G	SV	IP	H	H/9	W-L	ERA	BB	BB/9	K	K/9
Gr.	159	55	377.2	340	8.1	32-22	2.84	153	3.65	243	5.8
Eck	710	390	807.1	680	7.6	48-41	2.85	126	1.40	792	8.8

No doubt about it: none finer than the Eck. A better parallel, though, is Rollie Fingers. Like Grove, he was a traditional reliever who might go three innings one day, two more the next.

	G	SV	IP	H	H/9	W-L	ERA	BB	BB/9	K	K/9
Gr.	159	55	377.2	340	8.1	32-22	2.84	153	3.65	243	5.8
Fing.	907	341	1505.1	1275	7.6	107-101	2.72	428	2.56	1184	7.1

One era's fulltime relief ace edges another era's part-timer. In his day, Fingers was incomparable. So was Grove in his.

Durability. Since both Grove and Johnson were asked to pitch complete games, innings per start is a fine measure. Johnson averaged 8.3 (and led the league in innings pitched five times), Grove averaged 7.8. These are both extraordinary feats in any era. To place these numbers in perspective, let's sneak in a Koufax mention. In Sandy's five best years (1962-66) only, he averaged 7.7 innings per start.

Control. Johnson averaged 2.1 walks per game, Grove 2.7. Neither was in the top fifteen for his era.

Strikeouts. Johnson had 3,509 strikeouts in twenty-one seasons to Grove's 2,266 in seventeen (pro-rated to 2,866). Johnson led the league a record twelve times to Lefty's runner-up seven.

Shutouts and complete games. Johnson (110 total) won seven shutout titles, Grove (thirty-five) three. Johnson (531) led the league in complete games six times, Grove (298) thrice.

Fielding and hitting. Johnson was an exceptional fielder; Grove wasn't. Johnson (.235, 24 homers) was a fine hitting pitcher; Grove (.148, 15) a powerful one.

James cites Grove's nine ERA and five winning-percentage titles as proof of Grove's superior career value. Lefty's relief work helps his case further. Johnson was better in other significant categories and pitched four more seasons.

Peak performance—This statistic isolates the time in a player's career when he was at the peak of his powers. Now we can compare all three men.

Single-game dominance? Koufax's four no-hitters begin and end the debate. Johnson threw a sore-armed no-hitter in 1920 and won 1-0 games in 15 (1913) and 20 (1918) innings. Hitters could always anticipate Grove's fastball in his best years. Perhaps that explains the absence of glittery games. He did, however, end the Yankees' 306-game streak of no shutouts when he throttled Ruth & Co., 7-0, on August 3, 1933.

For single-season performance, Grove's 31-4 record in 1931 has the highest (.886) winning percentage. Grove's two-year (59-9) record in 1930-1931, three-year (79-15) record in 1929-31—when he led the majors in winning percentage, ERA, and strikeouts each time—four-year (104-25) record in 1929-32 and five-year (128-33) mark in both 1928-32 and 1929-33 are equally dominant.

In a procedure that has gained much currency of late, researchers examine ERA as a percentage of the league average. Herewith a five-year accounting of Grove, Koufax, and Johnson at their best. It has been asserted time and again that no one was as dominating in his prime as Koufax. Judge for yourself:

_ Grove				Koufax				Johnson			
YR	ERA	AL	%	YR	ERA	NL	%	YR	ERA	AL	%
1928	2.58	4.04	64	1962	2.54	3.94	64	1910	1.36	2.52	54
1929	2.81	4.24	66	1963	1.88	3.29	57	1911	1.90	3.34	57
1930	2.54	4.65	55	1964	1.74	3.54	49	1912	1.39	3.34	42
1931	2.06	4.38	47	1965	2.04	3.54	58	1913	1.14	2.93	39
1932	2.84	4.48	63	1966	1.73	3.61	48	1914	1.72	2.73	63

Boldface—Led league

Johnson (two ERA titles, 51 percent of league average) and Koufax (five and 55 percent) match up well with Grove (four and 59 percent), don't they? But both Grove and Johnson had two periods of peak performance to one for Koufax.

In Grove's second peak period he was playing for the Red Sox. After a sore-armed season in 1934, he became a control pitcher at age thirty-five and won four ERA titles in five years (1935-39). The last came after a dead arm—literally no pulse—shortened the 1938 season. Yes, a lefthander pitching home games in Fenway Park. This was more than a comeback. It was the greatest resurrection in baseball history.

I'm arbitrarily dividing Johnson's ten-year run of greatness into two five-year periods. He was a less effective pitcher in the second half, but those five years would pique anyone's interest.

	Grove				Johnson		
YR	ERA	AL	%	YR	ERA	AL	%
1935	**2.70**	4.46	61	1915	1.55	2.93	53
1936	**2.81**	5.04	56	1916	1.90	2.82	67
1937	3.02	4.62	65	1917	2.21	2.66	83
1938	**3.08**	4.79	64	1918	**1.27**	2.77	46
1939	**2.54**	4.62	55	1919	**1.49**	3.22	46

Johnson averaged 59 percent and Grove 60 percent of the league ERA. Johnson's percentage should actually be higher, since I have given equal weight to the shortened 1918 and 1919 seasons. Grove had four ERA titles and five good percentages, Johnson two and four.

Johnson later staged a comeback that was positively Grovian. Halfway through the 1920 season he went home with an 8-10 record and a sore arm. He struggled (for him) through 1921-23 with records of 17-14, 15-16, and 17-12. Then, as a thirty-six-year-old has-been in 1924, he went 23-7, leading the Senators to a pennant and the league in wins, winning percentage (.767), shutouts (six), strikeouts (158), ERA (2.72), and other categories. In 1925 Johnson was 20-7 and the Senators repeated. This two-year curtain call qualifies as a third, albeit shortened, peak period for the great man.

What, finally, are we to conclude? Grove and Johnson, Johnson and Grove. Let's just link them together forever, the Ruth and Williams of pitching.

Lefty, Walter, and the field

Records of major-league Hall of Fame starters

who pitched primarily in the twentieth century

Pitcher	Yrs	W	L	PCT	ERA	K	BB/G	SV
Grove	17	300(4)	141	.680(5)	3.06(9)	2266(7)	2.7	55(1)
Johnson	21	417(6)	279	.599(2)	2.17(5)	3509(12)	2.1	34
Koufax	12	165(3)	87	.655(2)	2.76(5)	2396(4)	3.2	9
P. Alexander	20	373(6)	208	.642(1)	2.56(5)	2198(6)	1.6	32
Bender	16	212	127	.625(3)	2.46	1711	2.1	34(2)
3-F Brown	14	239(1)	130	.648	2.06(1)	1375	1.9	49(4)
Bunning	17	224(1)	184	.549	3.27	2855(3)	2.4(1)	16
Carlton	24	329(4)	244	.574(1)	3.22(1)	4136(5)	3.2	2
Coveleski	14	215	142	.602(1)	2.89(2)	981(1)	2.3	21
Dean	12	150(2)	83	.644(1)	3.02	1163(4)	2.1(1)	30(1)
Drysdale	14	209(1)	166	.557	2.95	2486(3)	2.2	6
Faber	20	254	213	.544	3.15(2)	1471	2.7	28(1)
Feller	18	266(6)	162	.621(1)	3.25(1)	2581(7)	4.1	21
W. Ford	16	236(3)	106	.690(3)	2.75(2)	1956	3.1	10
B. Gibson	17	251(1)	174	.591(1)	2.91(1)	3117(1)	3.1	6
L. Gomez	14	189(2)	102	.649(2)	3.34(2)	1468(3)	3.9	9
Grimes	19	270(2)	212	.560(1)	3.53	1512	2.8	18(1)
Haines	19	210	158	.571	3.64	981	2.4	10
W. Hoyt	21	237(1)	182	.566(1)	3.59	1206	2.4	52(1)
C. Hubbell	16	253(3)	154	.622(2)	2.98(3)	1677(1)	1.8	33(1)
J. Hunter	15	224(2)	166	.574(2)	3.26(1)	2012	2.5	1
F. Jenkins	19	284(2)	226	.557	3.34	3192(1)	2.0	7
A. Joss	9	160(1)	97	.623	1.89(2)	920	1.4(2)	5
B. Lemon	13	207(3)	128	.618	3.23	1277(1)	4.0	22
T. Lyons	21	260(2)	230	.531	3.67(1)	1073	2.4(4)	23
Marichal	16	243(2)	142	.631(1)	2.89(1)	2303	1.8(4)	2
Marquard	18	201(1)	177	.532(1)	3.08	1593(1)	2.3	19
Mathewson	17	373(4)	188	.665(1)	2.13(5)	2502(5)	1.6(7)	28(1)
M'G'n'ty*	10	246(5)	142	.634(2)	2.66(1)	1068	2.1	24(3)
Newhouser	17	207(4)	150	.580(1)	3.06(2)	1796(2)	3.8	26
P. Niekro	24	318(2)	274	.537(1)	3.35(1)	3342(1)	3.0	29
J. Palmer	19	268(3)	152	.638(2)	2.86(2)	2212	3.0	4
Pennock	22	241	162	.598(1)	3.60	1227	2.3(3)	33
G. Perry	22	314(3)	265	.542(1)	3.11	3534	2.3(1)	11
Eddie Plank	17	326	194	.627(1)	2.35	2246	2.1	23
Rixey	21	266(1)	251	.515	3.15	1350	2.2	14
R. Roberts	19	286(4)	245	.539	3.41	2357(2)	1.7(4)	25
Ruffing	22	273(1)	225	.548(1)	3.80	1987(1)	3.2	16
Seaver	20	311(3)	205	.603(3)	2.86(3)	3640(5)	2.6	1
Spahn	21	363(8)	245	.597(1)	3.09(3)	2583(4)	2.5	29
D. Sutton	23	324	256	.559	3.26(1)	3574	2.3	5
D. Vance	16	197(2)	140	.585	3.24(3)	2045(7)	2.5(1)	11
Waddell	13	193(1)	143	.574(1)	2.16(2)	2316(6)	2.4	5
Ed Walsh	14	195(1)	126	.607(1)	1.82(2)	1736(2)	1.9(1)	34(5)
V. Willis**	13	249	205	.548	2.63	1651(1)	2.7	11
Wynn	23	300(2)	244	.551	3.54	2334(2)	3.5	15
Young***	22	511(5)	316	.618(2)	2.63(2)	2803(2)	1.5	17(2)

Numbers in parentheses = years led league

*Played one season before 1900. **Played two seasons before 1900. *** Played ten seasons before 1900.

Sources: *Total Baseball* fourth and fifth editions.

Notes:

1. Jim Bagby (31-12 in '20), Grove (31-4 in '31), Dizzy Dean (30-7 in '34), Denny McLain (31-6 in '68)

2. Ahead of Grove: Dave Foutz (.690), Whitey Ford (.690), and Bob Caruthers (.688).

3. How did Grove rate against his contemporaries? A telling comparison jumps out at us: Grove pitched for the A's and Red Sox in 1925-41, and Carl Hubbell pitched for the Giants in 1928-43. The A's and Red Sox averaged 89 wins in the seventeen years Grove was pitching for them. The Giants averaged 83 wins in the Hubbell years. The difference in their pitching, however, was far more pronounced: Grove was 300-141, Hubbell 253-154.

4. Benefitting from the Polo Grounds, Carl Hubbell had a lifetime ERA of 2.98 (130 points).

5. The save rule was adopted in 1969 to cover any reliever who finished a game his team won. The rule has since been changed, but pre-1969 saves are calculated using the original rule.

The Most Dominating Starting Pitcher of All Time?

A case for Greg Maddux

John T. Saccoman

Greg Maddux won the National League Cy Young Award for four consecutive years (1992-1995), a feat never duplicated in the forty-year history of the honor. How does his four-year run stack up with stretches of excellence by dominant pitchers from the past?

Several years ago, SABR polled its membership to determine retroactive Cy Young Awards for the years it was not granted in either or both leagues. In that poll, only two other pitchers matched this feat:[1] Christy Mathewson (1907-10) and Sandy Koufax (1963-66). Only one bettered it: Lefty Grove (1928-33).

In Table 1, I present traditional pitching statistics for all four pitchers for the years noted above.

While these are impressive, their league leaderships in five major categories (wins, winning percentage, earned-run average, shutouts, and strikeouts) are especially noteworthy.

Lefty Grove led the league in eighteen major categories during the six years in his run. He was first in wins in '28, '30, '31 and '33; first in winning percentage '29-'31, and in '33, and ERA king '29-'32. He also led the league in shutouts in '31 and '32, and strikeouts from '28-'31. This is an incredibly dominating performance. He led the league in an average of

three major categories per year in the study.

Three decades later Sandy Koufax led the league in ERA every year '63-'66; in wins and strikeouts in all but '64, in shutouts in '63, '64, and '66, and in winning percentage in '64 and '65. This represents an average of almost four of the five categories per year.

Christy Mathewson led the NL in wins in all but 1909, when he nonetheless led the league in winning percentage, ERA in '08 and '09, and shutouts and strikeouts in '07 and '08. This is ten major categories, or an average of 2.5 per year.

Maddux led the league in nine of the categories over the four years, four of them in '95. He never led the league in strikeouts, and his only other league titles were wins in '92 and '94, and ERA in '93 and '94, and Shutouts in '94.

Maddux pitched far fewer innings than Koufax, the pitcher with the next lowest total—almost 250 fewer innings over the four years. This was largely because two of his four seasons were shortened by work stoppages. This should not be held against him, any more than the changes in pitching and batting philosophy should be held against pitchers from the first third of the century, who were schooled to "save their best stuff" for crucial game situations when home runs were not so prevalent. As always, analyzing players from different eras of baseball history requires finer Sabermetric tools to facilitate comparisons.

John T. Saccoman, Ph.D. is an assistant professor of Mathematics and Computer Science at Seton Hall University. He would like to acknowledge the assistance of the Rev. Gabriel Costa, who originated a one-credit course in Sabermetrics and with whom he now team-teaches the course. John lives in New Jersey with his wife Mary, his son Ryan, and dreams of Mets glory.

Table 1. Dominant seasons

Grove

	G	GS	W	L	IP	ER	SO	BB	H	ShO	ERA	Pct.
1928	39	31	24	8	262.0	75	183	64	228	4	2.58	0.750
1929	42	37	20	6	275.3	86	170	81	278	2	2.81	0.769
1930	50	32	28	5	291.0	82	209	60	273	2	2.54	0.848
1931	41	30	31	4	289.0	66	175	62	249	4	2.06	0.886
1932	44	30	25	10	292.0	92	188	79	269	4	2.84	0.714
1933	45	28	24	8	275.0	98	114	83	280	2	3.21	0.750
TOTALS												
	261	188	152	41	1684.3	499	1039	429	1577	18	2.67	0.788

Koufax

	G	GS	W	L	IP	ER	SO	BB	H	ShO	ERA	Pct.
1963	40	40	25	5	311.0	65	306	58	214	11	1.88	0.833
1964	29	28	19	5	223.0	43	223	53	154	7	1.74	0.792
1965	43	41	26	8	336.0	76	382	71	216	8	2.04	0.765
1966	41	41	27	9	323.0	62	317	77	241	5	1.73	0.750
TOTALS												
	153	150	97	27	1193.0	246	1228	259	825	31	1.86	0.782

Mathewson

	G	GS	W	L	IP	ER	SO	BB	H	ShO	ERA	Pct.
1907	41	36	24	13	316.0	70	178	53	250	8	1.99	0.649
1908	56	44	37	11	390.7	62	259	42	285	11	1.43	0.771
1909	37	33	25	6	275.3	35	149	36	192	8	1.14	0.806
1910	38	35	27	9	318.0	67	184	60	292	2	1.90	0.750
TOTALS												
	172	148	113	39	1300.0	234	770	191	1019	29	1.62	0.743

Maddux

	G	GS	W	L	IP	ER	SO	BB	H	ShO	ERA	Pct.
1992	35	35	20	11	268.0	65	199	70	201	4	2.18	0.645
1993	36	36	20	10	267.0	70	197	52	228	1	2.36	0.667
1994	25	25	16	6	202.0	35	156	31	150	3	1.56	0.727
1995	28	28	19	2	209.7	38	181	23	147	3	1.63	0.905
TOTALS												
	124	124	75	29	946.7	208	733	176	726	11	1.98	0.721

In Table 2, I use the Bill James idea of seasonal notation[2] to attempt to address the Innings Pitched discrepancy. In this scheme, a pitcher's "season" consists of forty games, and a relief appearance counts for 6/10 of a start. This way we squeeze each player's statistics for his dominating years into one "season."

Table 2. Seasonal notation.

Matty, 1907-100

ES	GS	W	L	IP	ER	SO	BB	H	ShO	ERA	Pct.
4.06	36	28	10	320.2	58	190	47	251	7	1.62	0.743

Grove, 1928-33

ES	GS	W	L	IP	ER	SO	BB	H	ShO	ERA	Pct.
5.80	32.4	26	7	290.7	86	179	74	272	3	2.67	0.788

Koufax 1963-66

ES	GS	W	L	IP	ER	SO	BB	H	ShO	ERA	Pct.
3.80	40	26	7	314.4	65	324	68	217	8	1.86	0.782

Maddux 1992-95

ES	GS	W	L	IP	ER	SO	BB	H	ShO	ERA	Pct.
3.10	40	24	9	305.4	67	236	57	234	4	1.98	0.721

ES=Equivalent number of Seasons

The identical won-lost records of Koufax and Grove for this "typical season," are a remarkable coincidence. The greatness of all these pitchers is evident when we look at Maddux's composite ERA— an eye-popping 1.98, which is nonetheless third best among the four. However, a four-year ERA under two during the offensive explosion of recent years is itself remarkable. We need this context: How dominating has each of these pitchers been in his own time?

To answer that question, I employed other measures of pitching effectiveness in Table 3. The Winning Percentage Differential (WPD) subtracts each team's winning percentage *without* these four great pitchers from their winning percentages. Palmer and Thorn's Pitching Linear Weights (PLWTS) measures how many more runs than an average pitcher our subjects prevented. I also divided the League's ERA by the pitcher's ERA (LERA/PERA) and divided the sum of hits and walks by innings pitched (Ratio) to obtain a measure of baserunners allowed per inning.

In addition to strikeouts divided by walks (K/W), I include the Park Factor (Park), which measures the effect of each pitcher's home park on his statistics. A factor of 100 indicates a neutral park, a factor over 100 a hitter's park, and a factor under 100 a pitcher's park. Koufax was helped by his park. Maddux and Grove were not helped by theirs.

Adjusted Linear Weights (ADJLW) adapts home and league factors for the given seasons. The Total Pitcher Index (TPI) divides Pitching Runs (and Fielding Runs) by the number of runs prevented required to create a win for the team.[3] Obviously, the larger these factors are, the better the pitcher has performed.

Table 3. Contemporary dominance

Grove

	WPD	PLWTS	LERA/PERA	RATIO	K/W	PARK	ADJ LW	TPI
1928	0.138	42.61	1.568	0.885	2.859	99	42	4.60
1929	0.092	43.71	1.508	1.017	2.099	100	43	3.50
1930	0.237	68.35	1.834	0.945	3.483	101	69	7.30
1931	0.236	74.65	2.131	0.875	2.823	103	78	8.70
1932	0.134	53.35	1.580	0.935	2.380	101	55	5.90
1933	0.288	32.78	1.334	1.025	1.373	101	33	2.90
TOTALS								
	0.188	314.16	1.630	0.947	2.422	101	320	
AVG PER YR	52.36					100.8	53.3	5.48

Koufax

	WPD	PLWTS	LERA/PERA	RATIO	K/W	PARK	ADJ LW	TPI
1963	0.273	48.69	1.749	0.723	5.276	92	39	3.00
1964	0.350	44.71	2.040	0.722	4.208	92	37	3.50
1965	0.210	56.16	1.739	0.667	5.380	92	46	5.00
1966	0.210	67.56	2.090	0.762	4.117	91	56	5.40
TOTALS								
	0.259	217.28	1.883	0.718	4.741	367	178	
AVG PER YR	54.32					91.8	44.5	4.2

Mathewson

	WPD	PLWTS	LERA/PERA	RATIO	K/W	PARK	ADJ LW	TPI
1907	0.149	16.37	1.234	0.816	3.358	100	17	2.50
1908	0.195	40.01	1.645	0.760	6.167	102	43	7.30
1909	0.257	44.23	2.264	0.726	4.139	98	43	7.00
1910	0.208	39.71	1.593	0.921	3.067	98	38	6.00
TOTALS								
	0.202	142.28	1.608	0.806	4.031	398	141	
AVG PER YR	35.57					99.5	35.3	5.7

Maddux

	WPD	PLWTS	LERA/PERA	RATIO	K/W	PARK	ADJ LW	TPI
1992	0.202	48.75	1.750	0.765	2.843	103	42	6.20
1993	0.030	49.85	1.712	0.858	3.788	99	49	6.10
1994	0.162	54.78	2.565	0.743	5.032	101	60	7.30
1995	0.328	59.38	2.563	0.715	7.870	101	61	6.70
TOTALS								
	0.167	213.79	2.028	0.775	4.165	404	212	
AVG PER YR	53.45					101	53	6.6

(Leader underlined)

In context, we can argue, for example, that Grove's 3.21 ERA in 1933 was superior to Mathewson's 1.99 ERA in 1907.

Mathewson, 1907 (16.37 LWT, .149 WPD, 1.234 LERA/PERA)

Grove, 1933 (32.78 LWT, 0.288 WPD, 1.334 LERA/PERA).

Overall, Maddux shines particularly brightly in the LERA/PERA category. His ERAs in 1994 and 1995 are more than two and a half times better than the league average. None of the others in the study approaches that. Out of the five categories, the only one in which he does not place in the top two is in winning percentage differential.

Park adjustment calculations show that Koufax, was aided greatly by his home park. This does not mean his numbers should be discounted. He was one of the greats no matter how you slice it. But pitchers working in less friendly parks and in less friendly times were just as dominant with raw numbers that look a little less impressive.

In Table 4, I apply seasonal notation to some of the non-traditional measures.

Table 4.

	WPD	LWT	LERA/PERA	RATIO	K/W
Grove	0.154	54.21	1.630	0.947	2.422
Koufax	**0.221**	57.25	1.883	**0.718**	**4.741**
Mathewson	0.162	35.04	1.608	0.806	4.031
Maddux	0.137	**68.97**	2.028	0.775	4.165

(Leader in bold)

Maddux holds his own. As commentators and fans have gradually come to understand, we are watching—smack in the middle of an explosive offensive era—one of the great sustained pitching performances of all time.

Notes

1. Alvarez, Mark. *The Perfect Game.* SABR: 1993.

2. James, Bill. *Historical Baseball Abstract.* Villard:1988.

3. Palmer, Pete and Thorn, John. *Total Baseball.* Website:www.totalbaseball.com.

A Conversation with Johnny Vander Meer

"I felt I could strike out anyone on any given day."

Clayton B. Crosley

It was a beautiful day as my friend Peter and I drove the three hours from Chama, Mew Mexico to Nathrop, Colorado to interview Johnny Vander Meer. A sudden thunderstorm interrupted our sojourn as we drove north through the immense and beautiful mountains, which displayed gorgeous purple and blue hues.

At the Deer Valley Lodge I walked down the lush green manicured grass to the front of another building, and found an older gentleman dressed in blue jeans, an Old Milwaukee beer hat, and a Major League Baseball Alumni shirt. Johnny Vander Meer sat there relaxed enjoying the view of the enormous 14,000-foot peaks looming before us. I sat down next to him in a handmade wooden chair that looked as old as the lodge itself. Talk quickly turned to the ballpark and the city he had pitched in for most of his career, and it went on from there.

Clayton Bakewell Crosley *is the great-grandson of Powel Crosley, Jr., former owner of the Cincinnati Reds. He is the proud father of two children, Cassidy Victoria and Christopher Baird. At his residence in Long Beach, California, Clayton continues to create children's stories and works of creative nonfiction.*

Crosley Field sat down a dead end street. It was built below street level, and because of this the outfield had steep eight-foot terraces. On opening day we had such a large crowd that additional seating was brought in and put in the outfield. Any ball hit into the additional seating was an automatic two-base hit.

Another thing about Crosley Field was that Matty Schwabb, who was the groundskeeper, kept as fine a field as there was in the major leagues. There was not a bad hop on the whole field.

Cincinnati was a great place to play professional baseball. I'll give you an example. In New York and New Jersey they have a combined population of fourteen million people and drew about two-and-a-half million. Cincinnati, which had a population of about a million people, had an annual attendance of about a million. Heck, you weren't part of the population in Cincinnati if you didn't attend the games at Crosley Field. If I had to do it all over again, I would definitely play baseball in Cincinnati for the Reds.

Crosley Field was the first major league park to install lights. I was just breaking into the minor leagues when lights came in. We played at night, so I had some experience at night pitching before going to the majors. The lighting was fine for me as a pitcher, but I was told that the outfielders had a little more difficulty in running down their balls. We played one night game with each team during the regular season. There were not that many night games at first.

Let me tell you, the big joke was that if they put the games on the radio no one would physically come to the games and that would make the attendance suffer. Powel Crosley, Jr., the owner of the Reds, was also the largest manufacturer of radios and owned the largest broadcasting station in the world. He was ahead of his time in many ways. It turns out that broadcasting was the largest developer of baseball. It definitely increased its popularity.

The Reds games were carried on all of Mr. Crosley's radio stations, but it wasn't until he hired a broadcaster named Red Barber that he realized the impact of broadcasting on pro ball. Red became a very popular sportscaster and carried a radio backpack that allowed him to interview the fans prior to the start of each game. He left to call games in Brooklyn.

I'll tell you this much, the Dodger fans are the most loyal fans and I bet my second no-hitter was the only time that they ever cheered for a player from another team. You know, Brooklyn was a great place for that team, I never understood why they moved the team to the West Coast.

Next to the consecutive no-hitters, the thing I remember best is that I pitched in the longest scoreless game—it was against the Dodgers. I pitched fifteen scoreless innings and was pulled from the game when I was thrown out at home plate. Harry Gumbert pitched three more scoreless innings. Eventually the game was called off on account of night

I was a hardball thrower and only threw fast balls and curves. I kept them guessing by throwing high, low, behind, and inside. I felt that I could strike out anyone on any given day. That's what you call having a positive winning attitude.

The 1938 All-Star Game was quite memorable in the fact that it was probably the two greatest baseball teams ever put on one field. Bill Terry, who was the manager for the Giants, was the NL manager. He took pitchers in the clubhouse and we went over all of the batters on the AL roster as was typical before a game—all strong batters with lots of power. Bill Terry was telling me that I needed to pitch high inside and low outside, on and on until we got to Earl Averill. Then he said, "Hey, Johnny, why don't you just throw the ball straight down the middle, no one will be looking for it." Lots of laughter started up and it became a big joke on how we were pitching the game.

We lost the 1939 Series to the Yankees four games to none. I didn't play because of an injury. The Yanks were heavily favored because of all their big sluggers, but they had some of the best pitchers in the league, too. The 1940 Series, which was against Detroit, went the full seven games. We were down three games to two going into Game 6 of the Series. Bucky Walters hit a homer in Game 6 and we ended up winning, 4-0. That seemed to be the straw that broke the Tigers' back.

You know, I've always hunted or fished my whole life. Me and Babe [Ruth] would go duck hunting and we would be sitting behind our duck blind. A duck would fly over and Babe would tell me to shoot it. I'd take a shot and miss, but Babe would shoot after me and nail the duck. He was a hell of a good shot. He could make a Christian out of a person with that rifle. We never drank while we hunted, either. Babe had a hell of a personality.

Mr. Branch Rickey, the Cardinals business manager, pretty much set the standard for the National League players. Most players started at $3,200 per year and received a $125 increase each year thereafter. In 1936, I was voted Outstanding Minor League Player of the Year, so when I came to the majors, I made $500 a month, about $3,500 a year. My third year I got a raise to $12,000 a year. That was unheard-of for most third-year players. You could count on one hand the number of players making $25,000 a year in both leagues.

Back when I played, I feel we were more dedicated because baseball was our livelihood. Jobs were scarce; we never took that for granted. People need food, clothing, shelter, and water; those are necessities. People don't need baseball and somewhere along the way we forgot that principle. Strike is the dirtiest word in baseball and hopefully I will not witness another one during my lifetime. The strike hurt baseball and the sport is just now beginning to recover and get over it. On top of all that, we didn't know what dope was. No one ever used drugs back when I played baseball.

SABR's Sherlock Holmes

Bill Haber and the search for "Walsh, J.G."

Cappy Gagnon

In the most recent issue of *The National Pastime*, Dick Thompson wrote an outstanding biography of Tom Shea, whom he described as one of baseball's four greatest biographical researchers. All of us fortunate enough to have met with Tom over the years would readily agree. Dick mentioned Bill Haber as another member of this research quartet.

I met Haber after writing him a fan letter, more than twenty years ago, for his *Baseball Research Journal* article "A Favorite Paige of Mine." Beginning biographical researchers would do well to read that story.

Sadly, Bill is no longer with us, but in one of his letters to me, he left the contents of another research article. I am offering his April 24, 1989, letter to me as the basis for this biographical sketch on both John Gabriel Walsh and Haber himself.

By way of background, I had been searching for information about "Walsh, J. G.," a one-gamer with the 1903 Philadelphia Phillies. An obscure clue I found in the musty files of the Notre Dame Sports Information Department suggested that a "Walsh" from early Notre Dame baseball had played in the major leagues. Unfortunately, all the other clues were in error. The time period was too early for Ed Walsh, Jr., son of the White Sox Hall of Famer, who pitched for Notre Dame in the '20s before joining his dad's former team.

I began by checking for players named Walsh in the Notre Dame lettermen lists, while also checking for players named Walsh in the *Baseball Encyclopedia*. Nothing matched. I asked Notre Dame Archives to see if any Walsh from the *Encyclopedia* had ever enrolled at ND. Back came a "hit", on "Walsh, J. G.," a major leaguer with scant biographical information, and no death date.

I then checked microfilm of the South Bend *Tribune* and the Notre Dame *Scholastic* (the student newspaper) to see if I could find Walsh, J. G. in a box score. Sure enough, there he was as Notre Dame's second baseman in 1901. He was not only a starting player, he was one of the top hitters on the team, with an average around .400 (box score records are incomplete). On May 3, 1901, Walsh scored five runs in a rout of Purdue. This remains the Notre Dame record for runs scored in a single game, having been duplicated only once in the university's 107 years.

Despite his fine playing record, Walsh did not earn a Notre Dame monogram. This happened several times in the first two decades of Notre Dame baseball, usually because the player signed a pro contract before completing an academic year, or because there were allegations about—or proof of—professionalism.

Having found out a little bit about Walsh, J. G., I wrote to Haber and asked if he had any new leads. Prodded by my letter, Haber went to work, and wrote me a year or two later that he had found our man. I was disappointed with his reply, because the person Haber located, even though he fit several necessary

Cappy Gagnon owes a great debt to many SABR researchers named Bob: Davids, Hoie, McConnell, Lindsey, Richardson, Tholkes, and Bailey—as well as many others with a variey of first names.

categories, would have been way too young to have played at Notre Dame in 1901. In any case, the misidentified Walsh entered at least one of the baseball encyclopedias.

Haber was nothing if not thorough and precise. Stung by my refusal to accept his newly found Walsh, he got back on the case. The final part of the Walsh saga is in Haber's own words, along with a letter from Jack Walsh, son of J. G. It gives you a taste of Haber the man as well as Haber the researcher.

Tom Shea, S. C. Thompson, Lee Allen, and Bill Haber are all gone now, probably tracking down baseball biographical leads with Ernie Lanigan and John Tattersall, but fortunately there are some outstanding biographical researchers still carrying on this painstaking research. Someday a SABR researcher will be adequately recognizing Dick Thompson, Bill Carle, Bob Hoie, and some of the rest of SABR's research stars.

April 24, 1989
Dear Cappy,

As you must have surmised by now, I found John Gabriel Walsh in early-March....

The bottom line here is that John Gabriel Walsh was born in Wilkes-Barre, Pennsylvania, March 25, 1879 (which you knew). What you didn't know is that he died in Jamaica, New York, April 25, 1947 (42 years ago tomorrow as I write this letter).

The key to finding our man was locating the deed to the Walsh property at 248 Hazle Avenue. During my inquiries, I learned that the office of the Recorder of Deeds of Luzerne County, Pennsylvania permits the public to request a trace of property records. Inasmuch as the family residence was known, I made such a request. This resulted in the location of the deed dated February 21, 1924, a copy of which I sent you on April 10th.

In addition to establishing the fact that our man was still alive as of that date and a resident of New York City, the deed revealed the fact that the Walsh family head at that time was the ballplayer's mother (listed as a widow) and that she had been preparing for her death.

Armed with this information, I wrote to the Luzerne County Register of Wills to request a search for a probated will for John G. Walsh, Jr. (who died prior to 1924) and for Mary E. Walsh (who died subsequent to February 21, 1924). My purpose here was to establish the exact date of death for either the ballplayer's father or mother. The exact date of either death would lead to a newspaper obituary and/or death notice which, in turn, would reveal the identity of <u>a cemetery containing a Walsh family plot</u>.

(I was ultimately hopeful of ascertaining the identity of such a cemetery. Those records would reveal subsequent deaths in the Walsh family and would likely lead to the identity of a surviving relative. This was the approach I chose to take, the same approach which has served me well in numerous other searches I've conducted.)

Sure enough, I was able to locate a probated will for Mary E. Walsh, the ballplayer's mother. (She died January 29, 1926.) I was disappointed to find that there was no mention of a cemetery in newspaper accounts of her death. However, when I obtained a copy of the will, I found mention of <u>St. Mary's Cemetery, Hanover Township, Luzerne County, Pennsylvania</u>.

Upon discovering the identity of this cemetery, I immediately called there and reached a woman named Marguerite. Marguerite said she'd check for the Walsh family information I requested and I should call her back in an hour. When I called her back an hour later, she stunned me by saying that she knows THIS Walsh family, that she's a distant relative....

Marguerite suggested I call a Mr. Johnson. This man turned out to be a nephew of the ballplayer, a son of John's sister, Mary Walsh Johnson. He told me he had an uncle, John Walsh, who was a minor league umpire. I told him that this was my man, that he had gotten into one game with the Philadelphia Phillies in 1903. (He didn't know of the one major league playing appearance.) In any event, he told me that the man I should speak with is the Walsh family genealogist, a Mr. Rowan who lives in Baltimore. This man turned out to be a son of John's sister, Catherine Walsh Rowan. I then called this man in Baltimore. He seemed a bit hesitant at first to provide me with any information, perhaps, as it turned out, because I happened to reach him at an inconvenient time. I called him on a Tuesday, and he then suggested I call him back on Friday to give him some time to investigate as to the information I was requesting. I should call him on Friday at 11 AM, the Friday was February 24th.

Well, I called him back on Friday at precisely 11 AM, on the button, which is my nature. He even commented that I'm so punctual, and I told him that it drives my wife "nuts." At that point Mr. Rowan told me that John Walsh died in New York City in April of 1947. He didn't have the exact date but as a result of making a series of telephone calls to Pennsylvania, Florida and elsewhere, he had located the last surviving child of John Walsh. He gave me the man's name, and when he told me the man's address, I was stunned once again. Cappy, THE GUY LIVES RIGHT IN MY NEIGHBORHOOD, SOME TEN MINUTES FROM HERE AT THE MOST. HE HAS LIVED RIGHT HERE FOR YEARS AND IS RIGHT THERE IN THE PHONE BOOK.

Well, of course I then made a local call to John F.

Walsh of 1411 Avenue N, Brooklyn. He told me that his father's middle name was Gabriel, and kidded that his grandmother wanted her son to be an angel. (A real nice guy with a good sense of humor.) He didn't know the exact date of his father's death but told me that his father died in Queens General Hospital, Jamaica. After completing our telephone conversation (and alerting him that I'd be sending him a Baseball Questionnaire), I called the hospital for the exact date of the death. They do not maintain records more than twenty years, thus I had to send for the death certificate in order to verify the date of death.

When the DC arrived, I learned that the death occurred April 25, 1947. The son told me there was no obituary or death notice in New York or Pennsylvania but I checked out the possibility just the same. True, there was no mention of the death in New York but there was brief coverage in Pennsylvania, likely due to the fact that the body was returned to Wilkes-Barre for burial in the same family plot in which his mother was interred.

That's pretty much the story, Cap....

I wanted you to know the methods by which this death record was ascertained. Inasmuch as the name "WALSH" is so common, I really couldn't trace family members through Wilkes-Barre City Directories with any certainty. There was a time that I began making other efforts. One such effort resulted in the discovery that a brother of the ballplayer, Charles A. Walsh, had graduated from the University of Pennsylvania School of Dentistry in 1910 and had died May 13, 1962. (It was at this point that I had learned his middle name was Aloysius and I wrote you about ascertaining the middle name of a brother of John Walsh.) This was a secondary trail to pursue and as it turned out, proved to be unnecessary. Once I learned that the office of the Recorder of Deeds could trace the property record, everything fell into place.

Enclosed please find a copy of the death certificate, the newspaper coverage of the death, the Questionnaire completed by the son and the accompanying letter written by the son. I found the letter most interesting and hope that you do also. Let me know what you think of all this.

Sincerely,

B

Here is the letter Bill enclosed.

J. Walsh

Mr. Bill Haber—This will give you a little of my father's background. He was a very wonderful man - but unfortunately he couldn't control a drinking problem. He wouldn't touch a drink for a six-month period, but when he started - he was good for a few weeks.

He never completed any of the colleges he attended. He played football at Notre Dame—until he suffered a broken shoulder, and his mother forbid him to play football. He excelled at baseball and track at the various colleges. He won so many medals, plaques and awards at track meets.

As I explained to you on the phone, my mother threw them all away. My father used to take these tokens to different "bars" to promote drinks—and it angered my mother.

He was a personal friend of John McGraw, Hughie Jennings, Bill Klem, Connie Mack, Ed Barrow and too many, many more to enumerate.

A little more his anecdotes: He was umpiring in the Texas League. A couple of days running he made some close "calls" against the home club. The fans and players got on him—so about the third day, he showed at park drunk, wearing two exposed guns.

He naturally was escorted off the playing field - When asked why he had two guns, he replied, everyone in Texas has one gun—being an umpire, I figured I needed two. That ended his career in Texas.

He also umpired in the old Piedmont League, the Sally League, the Mid-Atlantic League—I really don't know if he ever completed a season. In later years he worked the old Negro Leagues—the Lincoln Giants, Homestead Grays, etc.

He also was a personal friend of Andy Coakley, coach of the Columbia Univ. baseball team. One of the players at that time was the great Lou Gehrig—My father was umpiring the college games—he, also was a personal friend of a Yankee scout—his name escapes me. He recommended Gehrig to this scout—telling he never seen a kid who could hit a ball so far—you know the rest.

He was umpiring in the mid-Atlantic League—One of the teams had a big raw-boned farmer pitcher, named Wilcy Moore, who had a fabulous sinker ball. In 1927, the Yankees where[sic] in a heated pennant race. My father recommended to the Yankee scout—that this said Wilcy, can shut-out any team for 2 or three innings. The rest is history—the Yankees signed him and won the pennant—Moore was sensational for a couple of late innings.

Jack W.

The Ill-Fated Rookie Class of 1964

A fast start and a quick finish

Rick Swaine

The 1964 season featured two of the more excit-ing pennant races in baseball history. In the National League, the surprising Philadelphia Phillies led by 6-1/2 games with only twelve to go when their over-worked pitching staff collapsed. The last week of the season saw four teams still in the race and when the dust settled the St. Louis Cardinals were in first place with only five games separating the top five teams. In the American League, the New York Yankees lan-guished in third place most of the season, but woke up after the infamous Yogi Berra-Phil Linz harmonica episode to capture their final pennant of the "Mantle era." Only two games separated the top three teams at the end of the season.

An outstanding group of rookie stars had a dramatic impact. Slugging third baseman Richie Allen, the National League Rookie of the Year, kept the youth-ful Phillies in the lead most of the season with his sensational hitting. Right fielder Mike Shannon helped spark the Cardinals to the pennant and World Championship after a midseason call-up. The Cincin-nati Reds tied for second place with rookie aces Sammy Ellis and Billy McCool in the bullpen. Jim Ray Hart of San Francisco led NL rookies with 31 homers as the Giants finished in fourth place, and outfielder Rico Carty hit .330 for the fifth-place Mil-waukee Braves.

In the American League, Rookie of the Year Tony Oliva enjoyed one of the greatest freshman seasons of all time for the Minnesota Twins. Mel Stottlemyre was a major contributor to the Yankees' September surge after joining the Bombers in August. The third-place Baltimore Orioles won 97 games with rifle-armed Sam Bowens patrolling right field and a pitching staff led by nineteen-year-old Wally Bunker. In Boston nineteen-year-old Tony Conigliaro set a teenage home run record and became the idol of Red Sox fans. The Cleveland Indians' future looked solid with youngsters Luis Tiant on the mound and Bob Chance at first base, while first-year man Bob Lee took over as the Los Angeles Angels' bullpen stopper.

Based on their freshman performances, the Rookie Class of '64 promised several future Hall of Famers, but the group was destined for disappointment. A staggering number of career-altering injuries, as well as unusual illnesses, emotional problems, personal tragedies, and scandals took their toll. The result is an incredible story of shattered careers and premature retirements. Many of the rookie stars of 1964 enjoyed successful careers, but none fully realized their poten-tial.

Richie Allen—In 1972, at the age of thirty, Allen was named the American League Most Valuable Player. Richie (Dick, later in his career) was one of the most controversial players in his era—constantly at odds with management, feuding with fans and the press, and fighting with teammates. He quit the team in

---

Rick Swaine is a CPA with the State of Florida and a sore-armed third baseman in the Tallahassee adult baseball league. He is forty-eight years old and expects to sign with the Atlanta Braves imminently.

mid-season several times, suffered injuries that some managers and teammates considered suspicious, and was frequently fined or suspended. Following his sensational MVP campaign he missed half of the next season with an injury and then quit with a month to go the following year. He returned to play parts of three more seasons for various teams before retiring for good. Over a fifteen-year career he posted a .292 average and belted 351 homers, but missed more than 400 games due to holdouts, retirements, suspensions, and injuries.

Tony Oliva—This wonderful young hitter is a classic example of the injury jinx that plagued the Class of '64. At the age of thirty-one he suffered a severe knee injury which robbed him of his speed and power, and ended his outfield career. He is the only player to win the batting title his first two years, and he captured a third title in 1971, the year he was injured. He missed most of the 1972 campaign but returned as a designated hitter and hung on for four more years, while his lifetime average dropped to .304.

Tony Conigliaro—The greatest tragedy of the class of '64 was Conigliaro's. At twenty-two he was the youngest home run champ in major league history. He had already slammed 104 homers when he was hit in the face by a wild pitch which destroyed his vision. After sitting out a year, his eyesight miraculously improved and he returned to win the Comeback of the Year award in 1969. However, his vision began to deteriorate again and he was forced to retire midway through the 1971 campaign, still only twenty-six years old. Subsequent comeback attempts failed and at the age of thirty-seven he suffered a serious heart attack that left him severely incapacitated. Tony C died in 1990, age forty-five. His teenage home run record still stands.

Rico Carty—At the age of twenty-nine, Carty had just won the National League batting title and his career average stood at .322 when he shattered his leg playing winter ball. He missed the entire 1971 season and was never the same player. As a rookie in 1964, he outhit everyone in the majors except Roberto Clemente, and, after missing half of 1965 with injuries, he finished third in the league in 1966. Tuberculosis hampered him in 1967 and forced him to sit out all of 1968, but he rebounded to hit .342 in 1969 despite seven shoulder dislocations. He led the league with a .366 average in 1970. However, his comeback from the broken leg was less successful. After limping through two part-time seasons he drifted down to the Mexican League in 1974, then came back for five years in the American League as a designated hitter. He closed out his career with a solid .299 average, but what kind of numbers would a healthy Rico Carty have put up?

Transcendental Graphics

Tony Oliva

Rico Carty

National League record for most games in a single season by a teenage hurler. But after two years as the Reds bullpen ace his arm went bad. Like Bunker, he was through at the age of twenty-six.

Sammy Ellis—McCool's partner in the Cincinnati bullpen, Ellis, suffered a similar fate. Following a brilliant rookie season he was converted to a starter and recorded 22 wins in 1965. Arm trouble soon ruined his career effectiveness and he was out of the majors at the age of twenty-eight.

Wade Blasingame—Blasingame was another young pitching star from the Class of '64 whose career was over before he turned thirty. The southpaw posted a promising 9-5 record as a twenty-year-old rookie for the Braves and won 16 games in 1965. A sore arm reduced his effectiveness and he never had another winning season. His major league career ended when he was twenty-eight.

Mel Stottlemyre—Stottlemyre was only thirty-two years old and the ace of the Yankee staff when his career came to a premature end. In midsummer 1964, Stottlemyre was called up from Richmond and quickly established himself as a star. He won 20 games in 1965, but the Yankee dynasty was crumbling around him and in the ensuing years the hard luck workhorse led the league in losses twice despite excellent pitching. A torn rotator cuff ended his career just as the Yanks were re-emerging as contenders. The unfortunate injury and poor support cost Mel a place among Yankee legends.

Luis Tiant—An arm injury may have cost "El Tiante" a spot in the Hall of Fame. He burst on the major league scene in midseason 1964 with a 10-4 record and won 21 games with a 1.60 ERA in 1968. But he was back in the minors after fracturing his pitching arm in 1970. His career appeared over at the age of thirty when he was released by the Braves' Richmond farm club, but he fought his way back to the majors with the Boston Red Sox. In 1972 he went 15-6 with a league leading 1.91 ERA and captured the Comeback Player of the Year award. Tiant registered three

Jim Ray Hart—A shoulder injury reduced Hart to a part-timer at age twenty-seven after he had averaged 28 homers a year over his first five seasons. He hit only 31 more over the next six seasons and was through by the age of thirty-two. Hart's misfortune actually started before his outstanding rookie year. In his first game after being called up in 1963, Bob Gibson initiated him into the big leagues by breaking his shoulder blade with a fastball. He played only six more games upon his return before he was beaned by Curt Simmons and missed the rest of the season.

Sam Bowens—Poor Bowens didn't even make it out of spring training his sophomore year before suffering the leg injury that ruined his career. He lost his spot in the Orioles outfield to 1965 Rookie of the Year Curt Blefary, and never regained a regular job. Bowens was back in the minors at the age of thirty.

Bunker and McCool—The rookie pitching stars were just as unlucky. *The Sporting News* selected teenagers Wally Bunker of Baltimore and Billy McCool of Cincinnati the top rookie pitchers of their respective leagues. Only five years later both were attempting comebacks with expansion teams. Bunker set the twentieth-century major league record for wins by a teenage pitcher with 19, but was out of the majors at the age of twenty-six. McCool didn't turn twenty until late in the 1964 season and is credited with the more twenty-win seasons and continued pitching into his forties before finishing his major league career with 229 major league victories, 147 of them after returning from the minors.

Mike Shannon—A kidney disorder forced Mike Shannon's premature retirement during the 1970 season at the age of thirty-one. The midseason acquisition of Lou Brock received most of the credit for the Cardinals 1964 championship season, but the emergence of Shannon as a solid everyday right fielder was also a critical element of the Cards success. He moved to third base before the 1967 season to make room for Roger Maris in right and was a major factor in the Cardinals' pennant winning 1967 and 1968 seasons.

Rich Reichardt—Oddly enough, a kidney ailment also tragically affected the career of another promising young player who made his debut in 1964. The California Angels' signing of Reichardt for the biggest bonus in baseball history at the time was the story of the year. The young outfielder was rushed to the majors, but batted only 37 times. By 1966 Reichardt was showing signs of developing into a superstar when illness felled him and necessitated the removal of a kidney. Reichardt returned the following year, but never lived up to expectations. Over the next seven seasons he bounced from team to team and was barely thirty-one years old when released.

Bob Chance—Chance's appetite cost him a successful career. He hit .279 with power as Cleveland's regular first baseman in 1964, but the Indians worried about his tendency to gain weight. In a rare display of good judgment, they shipped him to the Senators in the off-season where he ate his way back to the minors before the season ended. Big Bob received several more big league opportunities but never regained his rookie form.

Bob Lee—At 6'3" and about 240 pounds, Lee had already gained nicknames such as Horse and Moose as well as a reputation as a troublemaker in eight minor league seasons. When given a chance by the 1964 Angels he became the ace of their bullpen, ranked among the league leaders in saves, and racked up impressive strikeout totals. However, his off-field behavior soon proved to be his undoing. His performance deteriorated and he was hustled out of the big time by the end of 1968 at the age of thirty.

Late bloomers—The stars of the Rookie Class of 1964 weren't the only ones to experience career disappointments. The class included many late bloomers who suffered similar fates.

Tommy John of the Indians endured a disappointing rookie season, but wound up the most successful of the 1964 rookies. However, his career was not without adversity. John flourished after a trade to the White Sox and was eventually swapped to the Dodgers for fellow Class of '64 alumnus Richie Allen. In 1974 the thirty-one-year-old starter was off to a 13-3 start when his elbow blew out, ending his season and apparently his career. However, after revolutionary surgery in which a tendon was transplanted to his damaged elbow, he returned to the mound in 1976 and earned the Comeback Player of the Year award. He went on to record three 20-win seasons and retired with 288 lifetime victories. The year and a half he missed for surgery and rehab certainly cost him a spot in the exclusive 300 victory club.

One of the more mysterious psychological afflictions in baseball history involved a member of the 1964 rookie class. Despite a modest start, **Steve Blass** gradually developed into one of the top hurlers in the game with the Pittsburgh Pirates. But he developed a debilitating mental block after enjoying a career best 19-8 record in 1972, and totally lost control of his pitches. Although he still looked great on the sidelines he simply couldn't get the ball over the plate during the game. Blass tried psychotherapy, hypnosis, transcendental meditation, and various mechanical experiments without success. His 1973 season was a disaster and he pitched only once in 1974 before leaving the majors for good at the age of thirty-one.

Tony Horton, who broke in with the Red Sox in 1964, was another whose career was ruined by psychological problems. After being traded to the Indians, Horton developed into a solid power-hitting first baseman slamming 27 homers in 1969. But in 1970, he was institutionalized after suffering a nervous breakdown in a late-season game. He never took the field again, his promising career over at the age of twenty-five.

Outfielder **Alex Johnson**, who hit .303 as a rookie part-timer for the 1964 Phillies, actually went to court later in his career to prove his strange behavior was due to an emotional disorder. Early in his career, the dangerous righthanded hitter earned a reputation as clubhouse dissident and habitual loafer. After three trades he captured the 1970 AL batting championship at the age of twenty-seven with the California Angels. But he played only sixty-five games in a turbulent 1971 season despite perfect health. He was benched four times, fined twenty-nine times, and finally suspended without pay "for failure to give his best efforts to the winning of games." However, Alex and his psychiatrist convinced an arbitration board that his problems were psychological and he was reinstated. After playing for four more teams over the next five seasons he was cut loose at the age of thirty-three despite a .288 lifetime batting mark. His admitted refusal to give 100 percent kept him from taking full advantage of his tremendous talent.

One of the more bizarre incidents in Johnson's troubled 1971 season was his assertion that former rookie classmate, **Chico Ruiz**, had pulled a gun on him (twice) in the Angels locker room. Ruiz was another victim of the 1964 rookie hex. After winning the Cincinnati third base job and enjoying a productive rookie season, he missed most of 1965 with injuries, and spent the rest of his career as a utility infielder—a career which ended at age thirty-two when he was killed in an automobile crash.

No discussion of wasted baseball careers would be complete without mention of **Denny McLain**, baseball's last 30-game winner, who was a Detroit Tiger rookie in 1964. After winning the Cy Young award in 1968 with 31 victories and sharing the award with Mike Cuellar in 1969, the twenty-five-year-old hurler's career quickly fizzled out when he was implicated in a gambling scandal.

Denny infuriated the baseball establishment. He was an accomplished organ player with a lounge act in Vegas, who flew his own plane, promoted rock concerts, hustled golf, and stayed in shape by partying constantly. He spent a quiet first year working his way into the starting rotation, but blossomed in 1965. Denny suffered a mysterious foot injury in the closing weeks of the 1967 pennant race which might have cost the Tigers the pennant. A February 1970 *Sports Illustrated* article tied the injury to gambling activities. After serving a suspension he returned to action in July, but was soon suspended again for the rest of the 1970 season. He was traded to the Washington Senators in the off-season and led the league with 22 losses in 1971. A year later, after trials with Oakland and Atlanta, he was out of the majors for good at the age of twenty-eight.

McLain's problems were just beginning, however. He declared bankruptcy and suffered a heart attack after his weight ballooned to more than 300 pounds. In 1984, he was found guilty of racketeering, extortion, and possession of cocaine, and sentenced to twenty-three years in prison. The conviction was overturned on a technicality in 1987 and he managed to plea-bargain for his freedom. However, Denny was recently in the news again when he was sentenced to eight years in prison for stealing from the pension plan of a company that went bankrupt shortly after he bought it.

Not all of the 1964 rookies were victims of injuries, psychological disorders, or other calamities. Bert Campaneris and Dick Green of the Kansas City Athletics both broke in with modest rookie efforts in '64 and enjoyed long, successful careers, although they did suffer the misfortune of playing for Charlie O. Finley. In fact, Campy ended his career as a utility infielder for George Steinbrenner's Yankees so he could justifiably be added to the "bad luck" list despite his nineteen years as a star shortstop and base stealer.

Other 1964 rookies who went on to successful major league careers after unremarkable rookie seasons were Gene Alley, Don Buford, Jerry Grote, Jesus Alou, Willie Smith, Sonny Siebert, Wes Parker, Hal Lanier, Bobby Knoop, and Woody Woodward.

In the final analysis, the Class of '64 was far from a flop. Collectively they won five batting titles (Oliva [3], Carty, and Johnson) and three home run crowns (Allen [2] and Conigliaro); led the league in slugging four times (Allen [3] and Oliva), wins twice (McLain), ERA twice (Tiant), and winning percentage five times (Bunker, Blass, John, McLain, and Siebert). Allen was named MVP and McLain captured the Cy Young award two years in a row. However, the four Comeback Player of the Year awards (Conigliaro, Johnson, Tiant, and John) might be the most telling statistic.

With the exception of Oliva, none of the 1964 rookies has received more than token support for the Hall of Fame.

In contrast the 1965 class featured two of the weakest Rookie of the Year award winners in history. In the American League, the aforementioed Curt Blefary's award winning stats (.260, 22 HR, 70 RBI), were almost identical to his predecessor Sam Bowens's 1964 rookie marks (.263, 22 HR and 71 RBI) although Sam didn't receive a single vote for Rookie of the Year. In the National League, Jim Lefebvre hit only .250 with 12 homers as the Los Angeles Dodgers second baseman. Yet the 1965 class eventually sent four of its members to the Hall of Fame: Catfish Hunter, Joe Morgan, Jim Palmer, and Phil Niekro.

Harry the Horse

One of the last pre-war Giants

Barry Schweid

Harry Danning says his knees still hurt.

He says it with a soft smile as he pads through the rooms at the Baseball Hall of Fame a few days before the induction ceremonies. Bill Lohrman is at his side. Batterymates on the New York Giants, they seem inseparable.

Almost nobody notices them. Two old sports writers, Bob Broeg and Jerry Holtzman, stop for a few pleasantries. Danning and Lohrman seem pleased with the attention, but soft-spoken and modest.

Harry Danning came home from World War II with bad knees. He never played another game for the Giants. He was, by then, nearly thirty-five years old. And, if truth be told, the Giants had other plans, having paid the St. Louis Cardinals $175,000 for Walker Cooper, nearly five years younger than Danning, but at thirty, old enough to be dealt for the

Harry Danning

cash Branch Rickey treasured as much as pennants.

As it turned out, the Cardinals won without Cooper in 1946, the first postwar season. Rookie Joe Garagiola, Del Rice, Clyde Kluttz, Ken O'Dea, and Del Wilber shared the catching.

The Giants, to the despair of their fans who had hoped with the return of Johnny Mize, Willard Marshall, Sid Gordon, and Babe Young for a revival of the McGraw-Terry glory days, finished dead last. Cooper caught only seventy-three games.

Danning and Cooper finished with matching .285 lifetime batting averages. That's a whopping thirty-two points above Ray Schalk's .253, but Harry the Horse and Walker Cooper aren't even remotely candidates for enshrinement in the Hall.

There's no way of knowing what heights Danning might have reached if he had not lost three years to World War II. There is no point in speculating, anymore than there is in imagining the victories and strikeouts Bob Feller and

Barry Schweid *travels the world as AP's diplomatic correspondent but has never found a place as happy as the Polo Grounds.*

Warren Spahn would have recorded, the home runs Hank Greenberg and Ted Williams would have bashed, the fame emerging stars like Pete Reiser would have enjoyed, if their careers had not been interrupted.

Danning had joined the Giants in 1933, a pennant-winning year, appearing in just three games. He was twenty-one years old, from Los Angeles and the younger brother of Ike Danning, who played in two games for the St. Louis Cardinals in 1928.

It took the 6-foot-1, 190-pounder more than three years to win the top catcher's job from Gus Mancuso. An injury to Mancuso in the 1937 season gave the once-aspiring rug salesman the chance he needed. Playing in ninety-three games, he hit .288 and the Giants were able to rally in midsummer and drive on to the pennant.

John Carmichael, in *Who's Who in the Major Leagues*, praised Danning as "one of the big reasons" the Giants won the National League flag. The 1940 Danning Play Ball bubble-gum card paid tribute to Harry as "one of the best handlers of pitchers in the league and a master strategist." In the 1941 *Who's Who*, Carmichael hailed Danning's "deadly throwing accuracy and speed on defense."

Danning's three best years were 1938, 1939, and 1940. He hit .306, .313, and .300. In all, he played in 890 games over ten years, six of them catching Bill Lohrman, his Brooklyn-born sidekick, who was traded to St. Louis with cash and O'Dea in a 1941 deal for Mize, only to return to the Giants in 1942 to win thirteen games and lose only four. Overall, Lohrman won sixty games, all but one of them for his hometown Gi-ants. In 1940, he tied for the National League lead in shutouts with five.

Lohrman pitched in four games for the 1934 Philadelphia Phillies, returning to the majors with the Giants in 1937 after winning twenty games for the Baltimore Orioles of the International League. Playing in a tiny home ballpark, he went the distance in twelve of his twenty victories. The age of relief pitchers had barely dawned.

To a Bronx youngster like me, taken by his father to the Polo Grounds even before the first grade, the fading of the Giants' glory was a sad ordeal that lasted an eternity—until 1951 when a very different kind of Giants, led by a very different, down-and-dirty sort of manager, Leo Durocher, and not the gentlemanly, legendary Mel Ott, won the pennant. And again in 1954, before disappearing forever in 1957, as Horace Stoneham was seduced by the siren song of Walter O'Malley, who was taking the Dodgers from Brooklyn to Los Angeles.

The lore of McGraw, Mathewson, Ott, Terry, and Hubbell could not be transported to San Francisco, no matter how hard the publicists tried.

Danning was a small part of that legend. But important enough, and remembered enough, to be asked for his autograph. He obliged, with a smile, signing the Hall of Fame *Guide to Exhibits* "Harry the Horse Danning." Bill Lohrman signed alongside Harry.

"You know," Danning said, referring to the pre-war Giants, "there are only four of us left." Joe Moore, the star left fielder, who is eighty-nine; Ray Hayworth, a backup catcher who will be ninety-five next January; Danning, eighty-seven, and Lohrman, eighty-five.

Harry "The Horse" Danning will never be voted into the Hall of Fame. But for those who like to dream up all-what-ever teams, he belongs in any Jewish Hall of Fame as the catcher, over the celebrated Moe Berg, who could speak at least a half-dozen languages and hit in none of them, and the cerebral but weak-hitting Norm Sherry. (Johnny Kling, of the turn-of-the-century Chicago Cubs, has often been considered the greatest Jewish catcher, but there is serious doubt that he was, in fact, Jewish.)

The New York Giants, either fortuitously or by design, gathered Jewish ball players far more than any other team. Playing with Danning at times in the most populous Jewish city in the world were Morrie Arnovich, Sid Gordon, Harry Feldman and Phil Weintraub.

—Barry Schweid

Late-Season Acquisitions by Pennant Contenders

Recent novelty or long standing practice?

Guy Waterman

Like many older fans, perhaps, I've been dismayed by what seems like a much greater proclivity for unseemly late-season pennant-race horse-trading. Each pennant contender strives to tilt the level playing field by adding a major player or two as August and September roll around. The also-rans happily unload high-salaried stars.

But general impressions often turn out to be wrong when the factual record is carefully examined. Am I really correct in regarding this as a recent phenomenon? Haven't contenders always beefed up their rosters in late season? Didn't the Yankees of the Stengel-Weiss era do this every year? Didn't Lincoln bring in Grant for the stretch drive? Didn't Agamemnon pick up Achilles in late season—no, actually he was on the Greek bench the whole campaign.

So I undertook to analyze the historical record. What follows is a decade-by-decade listing of late-season acquisitions by contenders, together with an evaluation of their qualitative significance in pennant races.

Ground rules: Include only acquisitions in August and September. A contender is defined as a second-place team that finished within ten games of the top, a third-place team that finished within nine, or a fourth-place team that finished within eight. (It must be harder to overtake two or three rivals than one.)

First, the overall trend. I broke these data into half decades, partly because the 1990s aren't complete and I wanted comparable units of time, and partly because free agency (sometimes identified as one cause of recent trades) arguably dates from the mid-1970s, about halfway through that decade. Using *The Baseball Encyclopedia*, 10th Edition, and Joe Reichler's *Baseball Trade Register*, I've come up with the results below.

Half-decade	No. of contenders	Transactions	Players moved	T/C	PM/C
1901-1905	24	7	8	.292	.333
1906-1910	22	13	14	.591	.636
1911-1915	16	8	9	.500	.563
1916-1920	26	16	17	.615	.654
1921-1925	25	3	3	.120	.120
1926-1930	25	5	5	.200	.200
1931-1935	21	6	6	.316	.316
1936-1940	23	9	13	.391	.565
1941-1945	19	6	6	.316	.316
1946-1950	26	4	4	.154	.154
1951-1955	21	9	10	.429	.471
1956-1960	23	14	14	.609	.609
1961-1965	28	17	19	.607	.679
1966-1970	30	23	23	.767	.767
1971-1975	44	47	48	1.068	1.091
1976-1980	47	33	34	.702	.723
1981-1985	44	46	50	1.045	1.136
1986-1990	52	59	63	1.135	1.212
1991-1995	54	50	54	.926	1.000

Guy Waterman *lives off the grid, writing on a manual typewriter and computing baseball stats with pencil and grade school math. He also contributes to* The National Pastime, Baseball Digest, *and* NINE.

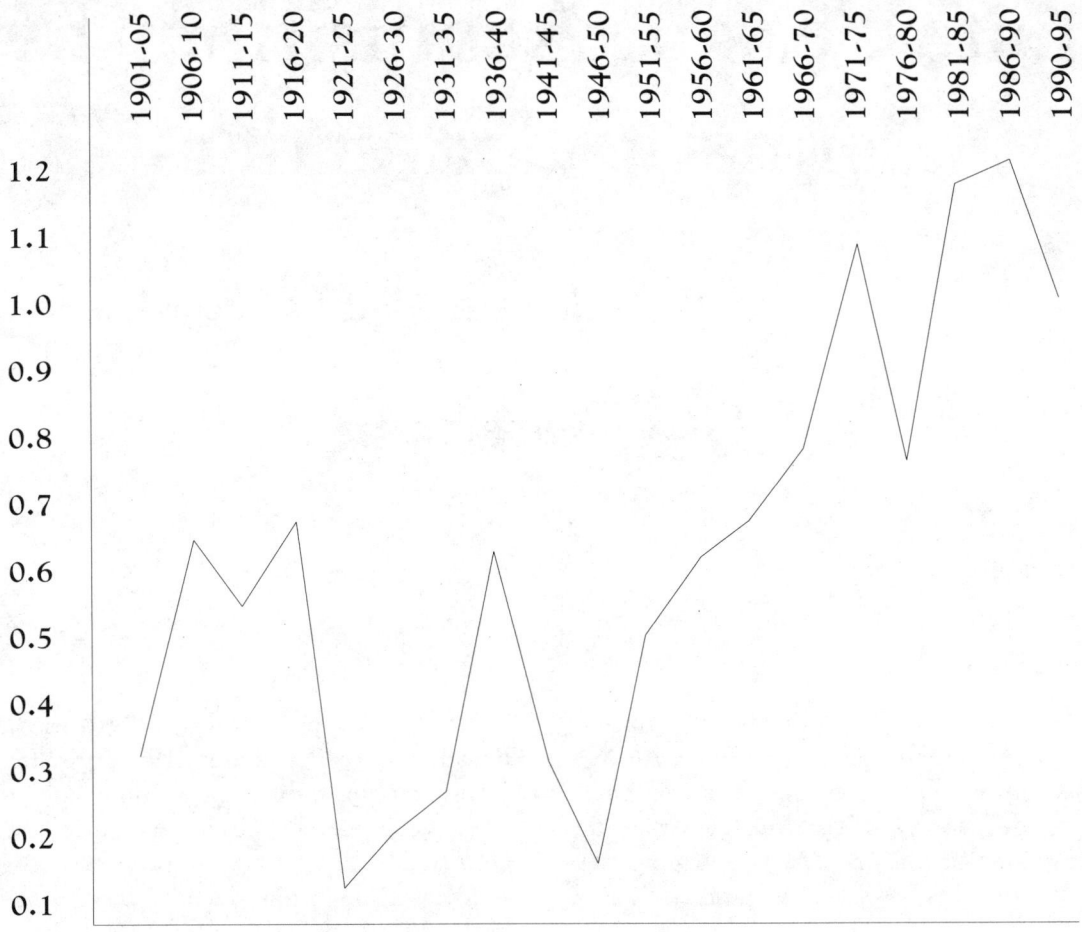

Number of late-season player acquisitions per pennant contender, 5-year intervals.

In short the trend is demonstrably toward more late-season acquisitions by contenders, but the phenomenon is by no means unprecedented. The table is shown in graph form above. The 1920s certainly saw the lowest level of late-season shifting of personnel; the 1950s definitely began the upward trend, and activity since the 1970s is on the whole about four times more common than the 1920s-30s-40s.

Now about the quality of players acquired. The following is a complete list of late-season deals, by decade, and also grouped by their significance. Group A includes only players truly dominant in the game during the two or three years preceding their acquisition. For others I took a ten-year overall career as indication of a quality player. But within that I sorted out players in their prime at the time of the trade—not necessarily at their peak, but still performing well—and called them Group B. Then I separated out ten-year players who were either over the hill (Group D) or so new as to be unproven (Group E), and created a separate category for those acquired so late in the year that they weren't used by the acquiring club

during that season (Group F). Lesser players went into a large Group G, but I also set up Group C to accommodate players with less than ten-year careers but who, at the moment they were acquired, gave immense promise. Under "Type of transaction," c=cash, w=waiver, p=player deal. Here are the results.

The 1900s

Players Acquired	Acquired by	Acquired from	Date	Type of transaction
A: Dominant players of past 2-3 years				
None				
B: 10-year players in their prime				
Piano Legs Hickman	Chicago AL	Washington	Aug. 1, 1907	c
Cy Falkenberg	Cleveland	Washington	Aug. 1908	c
Jim Delahanty	Detroit	Washington	Aug. 13, 1909	p
C: Lesser players showing promise				
None				
D: 10-year players over the hill				
Malachi Kittridge	Cleveland	Washington	Aug. 15, 1906	c
Deacon McGuire	Cleveland	Boston AL	Aug. 1908	c

E: 10-year players not yet proven

Gavvy Cravath	Chicago AL	Boston AL	Aug. 1908	c
Bobby Byrne	Pittsburgh	St. Louis NL	Aug. 19, 1909	p

F: 10-year players acquired but not used

George Browne	Chicago NL	Boston NL	Sep. 1908	c

G: Lesser players

Jimmy Burke	Pittsburgh	Chicago AL	Sep. 1901	c
Pop Foster	Chicago AL	Washington	Sep. 1901	c
Charlie Shields	St. Louis AL	Baltimore	Sep. 1902	c
Charlie Carr &				
Fritz Buelow	Cleveland	Detroit	Aug. 7, 1904	p
Claude Elliott	New York NL	Cincinnati	Aug. 1904	c
Ned Garvin	New York AL	Brooklyn	Sep. 1904	w
Mike Powers	Phil. AL	New York AL	Aug. 7, 1905	c
Rabbit Nill	Cleveland	Washington	Aug. 11, 1907	p
Charles Armbruster	Chicago AL	Boston AL	Sep. 1, 1907	c
Dave Altizer	Cleveland	Washington	Aug. 1908	c
Andy Coakley	Chicago NL	Cincinnati	Sep. 1908	c
Denny Sullivan	Cleveland	Boston AL	Sep. 1908	c
Tom Jones	Detroit	St. Louis AL	Aug. 20, 1909	p

Of note in the 1900s—None of the three most significant transactions paid good dividends for the acquiring contender. Hickman, hitherto one of the more powerful sluggers of the early AL, batted only .261, mostly in pinch-hit assignments, with no home runs, and muffed one of the three balls he got to in the field. Delahanty, coming off a .317 season in 1908, hit only .253 for the Tigers in 1909. Falkenberg went 2-4 with a high ERA (3.88) in seven games for Cleveland.

A footnote to these comments on the performance of players acquired: John Sasman's excellent article on pennant-run trades in the free agent era ("One Player Away," *BRJ*, 1997, pp. 80-84) makes the point that a full evaluation of such trades should compare the acquired player's performance with that of any player or players surrendered to acquire him. My comments here are not attempting any such overall evaluation, merely observing the short-run pennant-drive results. But Sasman's point is entirely valid for the full picture.

Note that Washington was most often the club from which players were acquired, including all three of the most important deals. This was the decade when Washington earned its reputation as "first in war, first in peace, and last in the American League."

The 1910s

Players Acquired	Acquired by	Acquired from	Date	Type of transaction
Dominant players of past 2-3 years				

None

B: 10-year players in their prime

Vean Gregg	Boston AL	Cleveland	Aug. 20, 1914	p
Fred Snodgrass	Boston NL	New York NL	Aug. 1915	c
Fred Merkle	Brooklyn	New York NL	Aug. 20, 1916	p
Heinie Zimmerman	New York NL	Chicago NL	Aug. 28, 1916	p
Art Nehf	New York NL	Boston NL	Aug. 15, 1919	p
Slim Sallee	New York NL	Cincinnati	Sep. 5, 1920	w

C: Lesser players showing promise

Al Demaree	New York NL	Chicago NL	Aug. 15, 1917	p
Erskine Mayer	Chicago AL	Pittsburgh	Aug. 1919	w

10-year players over the hill

Kitty Bransfield	Chicago NL	Phil. NL	Aug. 9, 1911	c
Mickey Doolan	New York NL	Chicago NL	Aug. 28, 1916	p
Bobby Byrne	Chicago AL	Phil. NL	Sep. 17, 1917	w
Pat Ragan	Chicago AL	New York NL	Aug. 1919	w

E: 10-year players not yet proven

Doc Lavan	Phil. AL	St. Louis AL	Aug. 24, 1913	c
George Kelly	New York NL	Pittsburgh	Aug. 4, 1917	w
Joe Wilhoit	New York NL	Pittsburgh	Aug. 5, 1917	w

F: 10-year players acquired but not used

George Gibson	New York NL	Pittsburgh	Aug. 5, 1916	w

G: Lesser players

Jack Rowan	Chicago NL	Phil. NL	Aug. 1911	p
Bert Humphries	Phil. NL	Chicago NL	Aug. 8, 1915	c
Bill James &				
Grover Lowdermilk	Detroit	St. Louis AL	Aug. 18, 1915	p
Zip Collins	Boston NL	Pittsburgh	Sep. 3, 1915	c
Lew McCarty	New York NL	Brooklyn	Aug. 20, 1916	p
Erv Kantlehner	Phil. NL	Pittsburgh	Sep. 2, 1916	c
Jimmy Walsh	Boston AL	Phil. AL	Sep. 2, 1916	p
Bill James	Chicago AL	Boston AL	Aug. 1919	c
Wynn Noyes	Chicago AL	Phil. AL	Aug. 1919	w

Of note in the 1910s—The three most prominent non-pitchers of this decade share the unfortunate fate of bad reputations: Merkle and Snodgrass for supposedly having cost championships by calamitous misplays, Zimmerman for unsavory connections to gambling. In fact, all three were solid performers with proven records at the time they were acquired by contenders.

Of the pitchers—all three lefthanders—Nehf especially came through, going 9-2 with an ERA of 1.50 in the last six weeks of 1919, in a fruitless effort to help McGraw's second-place Giants try to catch the pennant-bound Reds.

About Al Demaree and Erskine Mayer: both were promising young pitchers, giving every reason to expect better careers than in fact they achieved. Demaree had won nineteen games in 1916, his fourth campaign in a row at ten or more wins. He was thirty-two years old when acquired by the Giants. But he proved a disappointment in 1917 and 1918, moved to Boston for an even drearier year, and then was gone from the majors. Mayer had put together two twenty-one-win seasons for the Phils in 1914-1915, but struggled in 1916, only to come back to winning form again. So in 1919, still just thirty years old when acquired, Mayer could have been perceived as a major catch. In fact he did poorly (1-3 in six games) and never pitched again in the majors.

Bobby Byrne, dealt previously in 1909 early in his career, and Bill James (Big Bill, not Seattle Bill of the 1914 Miracle Braves) share the distinction of being the first to be sought by contenders twice.

The other notable observation about this decade is the role of John McGraw. Eleven of the sixteen significant late-season trades were arranged by the Giants manager. He made eight acquisitions and three disposals. So credit McGraw with a pioneering role in the art of late-season horse-trading. Had it not been for Little Napoleon, this decade would have seen no more late-season changes than other decades of the first half of the century.

The 1920s

Players Acquired	Acquired by	Acquired from	Date	Type of transaction
A: Dominant players of past 2-3 years				
None				
B: 10-year players in their prime				
Alex Ferguson	Washington	New York AL	Aug. 19, 1925	c
Dutch Ruether	New York AL	Washington	Aug. 27, 1926	p
Tony Kaufmann	St. Louis NL	Phil. NL	Sep. 10, 1927	c
Tom Zachary	New York AL	Washington	Aug. 23, 1928	p
Pinky Hargrave	Washington	Detroit	Sep. 10, 1930	c
C: Lesser players showing promise				
None				
D: 10-year players over the hill				
Eddie Foster	St. Louis AL	Boston AL	Aug. 15, 1922	w
Bobby Veach	Washington	New York AL	Aug. 17, 1925	w
E: 10-year players not yet proven				
None				
F: 10-year players acquired but not used				
None				
G: Lesser players				
Jesse Petty	Chicago NL	Pittsburgh	Aug. 24, 1930	c

Of note in the 1920s—While four pitchers technically make the grade as ten-year players in their prime, only two of the four are fully deserving. Ferguson and Kaufmann barely lasted ten seasons in the majors, never winning big. Ruether and Zachary

were good ones, though. Again, both these men were southpaws. Is it a coincidence that the five best pitchers acquired in late season between 1910 and 1930 were all portsiders? Or were good lefties harder to come by in those days?

The 1930s

Players Acquired	Acquired by	Acquired from	Date	Type of transaction
A: Dominant players of the past 2-3 years				
Al Crowder	Detroit	Washington	Aug. 4, 1934	
B: 10-year players in their prime				
Si Johnson	St. Louis NL	Cincinnati	Aug. 6, 1936	p
Joe Heving	Boston AL	Cleveland	Aug. 1938	c
C: Lesser players showing promise				
None				
D: 10-year players over the hill				
Lyn Lary	St. Louis NL	Brooklyn	Aug. 14, 1939	w
Al Simmons	Cincinnati	Boston NL	Aug. 31, 1939	c
E: 10-year players acquired but not used				
Dick Coffman	New York NL	St. Louis AL	Sep. 24, 1935	c
G: Lesser players				
Red Worthington	St. Louis NL	Boston NL	Sep. 11, 1934	w
Spike Merena	Detroit	Boston AL	Sep. 24, 1934	c
Euel Moore	New York NL	Phil. NL	Aug. 2, 1935	c
Blondy Ryan	New York AL	Phil. NL	Aug. 6, 1935	c
Ivy Andrews	New York AL	Cleveland	Aug. 14, 1937	c
Johnny Babich &				
Gil English &				
Bobby Reis &				
Johnny Riddle	Cincinnati	Boston NL	Aug. 10, 1938	p
Milt Shoffner	Cincinnati	Boston NL	Aug. 19, 1939	w
Jimmy Ripple	Cincinnati	Brooklyn	Aug. 23, 1940	w
Charley Gelbert	Boston AL	Washington	Aug. 30, 1940	w

Of note in the 1930s—In 1934 the Tigers made a Grade A late-season move to help secure the pennant that year. They picked up "General" Al Crowder, who had won twenty-four games for the pennant-winning Senators the year before, and twenty-six the year before that—the winningest pitcher in baseball in those years. Washington was now slipping to seventh place and Crowder had a dismal 4-10 record and 6.79 ERA. So they waived him to Detroit, where he proceeded to win five games, including one shutout, during the final run for the flag.

Until the Yankees of 1949 and thereafter, the Crowder case stands as the most significant, if not the only, truly major instance of tying down a pennant through a player deal in August or September.

That multiplayer grab by Cincinnati in late 1938 was in exchange for twenty-one-year-old shortstop

Eddie Miller, regarded as the coming superstar of defense, the heralded Ozzie Smith of his day.

The 1940s

Players Acquired	Acquired by	Acquired from	Date	Type of transaction
A: Dominant players of past 2-3 years				
John Mize	New York AL	New York NL	Aug. 33, 1949	c
B: 10-year players in their prime				
Bobo Newsom	Brooklyn	Washington	Aug. 30, 1942	c
Roy Cullenbine	New York AL	Washington	Aug. 31, 1942	w
Hank Borowy	Detroit	Pittsburgh	Aug. 3, 1950	c
Johnny Hopp	New York AL	Pittsburgh	Sep. 5, 1950	c
C: Lesser players showing promise				
None				
D: 10-year players over the hill				
Larry French	Brooklyn	Chicago NL	Aug. 20, 1941	w
George Caster	Detroit	St. Louis AL	Aug. 8, 1945	w
E: 10-year players not yet proven				
Hank Majeski	New York AL	Boston NL	Sep. 25, 1942	c
F: 10-year players acquired but not used				
None				
G: Lesser players				
Jim Tobin	Detroit	Boston NL	Aug. 1945	c
Mickey Haefner	Boston NL	Chicago AL	Aug. 8, 1950	c

Of note in the 1940s—At the end of this decade, the New York Yankees, embarking on that string of fourteen pennants in sixteen years, initiated their nearly annual fall rite of acquiring a major figure in late season. During this sixteen-year period they averaged at least one significant acquisition each fall.

In 1949 it was no less than Hall of Famer John Mize, age thirty-six, who had tied Ralph Kiner for NL home run leadership during the immediately preceding two years. This deal was fully as significant as the Crowder one of the 1930s.

In 1950 it was thirty-four-year-old Johnny Hopp, speedy outfielder-first baseman, who laced out nine hits in twenty-seven at-bats, four of them for extra bases, after being acquired in September—and drew eight walks while striking out but once.

Four of the ten late-season acquisitions of this decade were by the Yanks, a mode of operating that continued into the next decade.

I put Haefner and Tobin in the category of lesser players only because they failed to stick in the majors for ten seasons. Actually both these knuckleball artists were effective pitchers for several seasons, though their best years came during World War II's watered-down competition.

Also worthy of note: for three decades now, pitchers have slightly outnumbered non-pitchers as late-season pickups.

The 1950s

Players Acquired	Acquired by	Acquired from	Date	Type of transaction
A: Dominant players of past 2-3 years				
Johnny Sain	New York AL	Boston NL	Aug. 30, 1951	p
B: 10-year players in their prime				
Johnny Schmitz	New York AL	Brooklyn	Aug. 1, 1952	w
Wally Westlake	Cleveland	Cincinncti	Aug. 7, 1952	c
Ted Wilks	Cleveland	Pittsburgh	Aug. 18, 1952	p
Ray Scarborough	New York AL	Boston AL	Aug. 22, 1952	c
Jim Konstanty	New York AL	Phil. NL	Aug. 22, 1954	c
Gerry Staley	New York AL	Cincinnati	Sep. 11, 1955	w
Enos Slaughter	New York AL	Kansas City	Aug. 25, 1956	w
Russ Meyer	Cincinnati	Chicago NL	Sep. 1, 1956	w
Irv Noren	St. Louis NL	Kansas City	Aug. 31, 1957	w
Sal Maglie	New York AL	Brooklyn	Sep. 1, 1957	w
Ted Kluszewski	Chicago AL	Pittsburgh	Aug. 25, 1959	p
Dale Long	New York AL	San Francisco	Aug. 22, 1960	c
Rocky Bridges	St. Louis NL	Cleveland	Sep. 2, 1960	c
C: Lesser players showing promise				
None				
D: 10-year players over the hill				
Ewell Blackwell	New York AL	Cincinnati	Aug. 28, 1952	p
Murry Dickson	New York AL	Kansas City	Aug. 22, 1958	p
Ray Boone	Milwaukee	Kansas City	Aug. 20, 1959	w
Enos Slaughter	Milwaukee	New York AL	Sep. 12, 1959	w
Dave Philley	Baltimore	San Francisco	Sep. 1, 1960	c
Del Rice	Baltimore	St. Louis NL	Sep. 7, 1960	c
E: 10-year players not yet proven				
George Strickland	Cleveland	Pittsburgh	Aug. 18, 1952	p
F: 10-year players acquired but not used				
None				
G: Lesser players				
Joe Garagiola	New York NL	Chicago NL	Sep. 8, 1954	w
Ted Wilson	New York AL	New York NL	Aug. 22, 1956	w
Bobby Del Greco	New York AL	Chicago NL	Sep. 10, 1957	c

Of note in the 1950s—Obviously, the most prominent features are:

(1) More significant deals. Although the total number of late-season transactions in the decade of the 1910s was actually higher, the quality of player involved makes the 1950s more impressive:

	1910s	1950s
Group A and B	6	14
Groups C, D, E	9	7
Group F and G	11	3
Total	26	24

(2) New York Yankees domination. Fully half of all late-season pennant-contender acquisitions in the 1950s were by the Yanks. So that impression we all had *is* correct. These deals include no fewer than eight front-line pitchers, one almost every year. They missed 1953, 1959, and 1960, but landed two in 1952.

Johnny Sain was clearly a dominating pitcher when acquired in 1951. He had won twenty games or more in four of the preceding five seasons and was only thirty-three years old.

After Sain, I had trouble sorting out which could be described as in their prime and which over the hill. None was far over. Readers may reasonably disagree with my describing, for example, Maglie as still in his prime in 1957, or Blackwell as over the hill in 1952. Not one of the eight was an insignificant prize. And besides the pitchers, the Yanks picked up Slaughter in 1956 and Dale Long in 1960.

A further word on Slaughter: the first time the Yanks got him he was arguably a Group A player—but that deal was in April 1954. I decided to call him still in his prime the second time (August 1956) and over the hill the time they dispatched him to the Braves (September 1959).

The 1960s

Players Acquired	Acquired by	Acquired from	Date	Type of transaction
A: Dominant players of past 2-3 years				
None				
B: 10-year players in their prime				
Reno Bertoia	Detroit	Kansas City	Aug. 2, 1961	p
Ron Kline	Detroit	LA AL	Aug. 10, 1961	w
Lenny Green	Baltimore	LA AL	Sep. 5, 1964	c
Pedro Ramos	New York AL	Cleveland	Sep. 5, 1964	p
Don McMahon	San Francisco	Detroit	Aug. 9, 1969	c
Tommy Davis	Chicago NL	Oakland	Sep. 16, 1970	c
C: Lesser players showing promise				
None				
D: 10-year players over the hill				
Gerry Staley	Detroit	Kansas City	Aug. 2, 1961	p
Vic Wertz	Detroit	Boston AL	Sep. 8, 1961	w
Ruben Gomez	Minnesota	Cleveland	Aug. 20, 1962	p
Hal Brown	New York AL	Baltimore	Sep. 7, 1962	c
Frank Thomas	Phil. NL	Minnesota	Aug. 7, 1964	p
Frank Lary	Milwaukee	New York NL	Aug. 8, 1964	p
Bobby Shantz	Phil. NL	Chicago NL	Aug. 15, 1964	c
Vic Power	Phil. NL	LA AL	Sep. 9, 1964	c
Smoky Burgess	Chicago AL	Pittsburgh	Sep. 12, 1964	w
Gene Freese	Chicago AL	Pittsburgh	Aug. 25, 1965	c
Dick Schofield	LA NL	New York AL	Sep. 10, 1966	p
Elston Howard	Boston AL	New York AL	Aug. 3, 1967	p
Eddie Mathews	Detroit	Houston	Aug. 17, 1967	p
Roy Face	Detroit	Pittsburgh	Aug. 31, 1968	c
Ken Johnson	Chicago NL	New York AL	Aug. 11, 1969	c
Jim Bunning	LA NL	Pittsburgh	Aug. 15, 1969	p
Tito Francona	Oakland	Atlanta	Aug. 22, 1969	c
Hoyt Wilhelm	Atlanta	California	Sep. 8, 1969	c
Juan Pizarro	Oakland	Cleveland	Sep. 21, 1969	c
George Brunet	Pittsburgh	Washington	Aug. 31, 1970	p
Mudcat Grant	Pittsburgh	Oakland	Sep.1 4, 1970	p
Dean Chance	New York NL	Cleveland	Sep. 18, 1970	c
Hoyt Wilhelm	Chicago NL	Atlanta	Sep. 21, 1970	c
E: 10-year players not yet proven				
Sandy Alomar	Chicago AL	New York NL	Aug. 15, 1967	c
F: 10-year players acquired but not used				
None				
G: Lesser players				
Darrell Johnson	Cincinnati	Phil. NL	Aug. 14, 1961	c
Dave Sisler	Cincinnati	Washington	Aug. 14, 1961	p
Ken MacKenzie	St. Louis NL	New York NL	Aug. 5, 1963	p
Wayne Graham	Phil. NL	Minnesota	Aug. 7, 1964	p
Ken Rowe	Baltimore	LA NL	Sep. 10, 1964	c
Dave Roberts	Baltimore	Pittsburgh	Sep. 12, 1966	c
Fred Talbot	Oakland	Seattle	Aug. 29, 1969	p
Jack Jenkins	LA NL	Washington	Sep. 1, 1969	c
Bob Priddy	Atlanta	California	Sep. 9, 1969	c
Jimmie Hall	Chicago NL	New York AL	Sep. 11, 1969	p
Ron Herbel	New York NL	San Diego	Sep. 1, 1970	p
Angel Mangual	Oakland	Pittsburgh	Sep. 14, 1970	p

Of note in the 1960s—Two clear trends. First, more transactions—forty-two for this decade, versus a previous high of twenty-six. Second, fewer real prize catches—no dominant players, and the six listed as in their prime include no one really good, except maybe Tommy Davis and the relief pitchers, but they were close to being over the hill. The Hall of Famers of the decade—Mathews, Bunning, Wilhelm—were all elder statesmen by the time these deals were made.

Those who remember this decade may grumble over Reno Bertoia being given a higher classification than Jimmie Hall. For his first three seasons, Hall was terrific, but by the time he was picked up by the Cubs in 1969, he had long since cooled off. Bertoia did at least last ten years in the bigs, and, at the time the Tigers recalled him from exile in 1961, he was only 26 years old and coming off his strongest season. No way to know he'd soon be through.

The 1970s

Players Acquired	Acquired by	Acquired from	Date	Type of transaction
A: Dominant players of the past 2-3 years				
None				
B: 10-year players in their prime				
Woody Fryman	Detroit	Phil. NL	Aug. 2, 1972	c
Eddie Fisher	Chicago AL	California	Aug. 17, 1972	p
Tommy Davis	Baltimore	Chicago NL	Aug. 18, 1972	p
Matty Alou	Oakland	St. Louis	Aug. 27, 1972	p
Dal Maxvill	Oakland	St. Louis	Aug. 30, 1972	p
Frank Howard	Detroit	Texas	Aug. 31, 1972	c
Rico Carty	Chicago NL	Texas	Aug. 13, 1973	c
Matty Alou	St. Louis	New York AL	Sep. 6, 1973	c
Rico Carty	Oakland	Chicago NL	Sep. 11, 1973	c
Claude Osteen	St. Louis	Houston	Aug. 15, 1974	p
Alex Johnson	New York AL	Texas	Sep. 9, 1974	c
Dave Kingman	New York AL	California	Sep. 15, 1977	c
Johnny Grubb	Texas	Cleveland	Aug. 31, 1978	p
Mickey Rivers	Texas	New York AL	Aug. 1, 1979	p
Willie Montanez	Texas	New York AL	Aug. 12, 1979	p
Dale Murray	Montreal	New York NL	Aug. 30, 1979	c
Aurelio Rodriguez	New York AL	San Diego	Aug. 4, 1980	c
Kurt Bevacqua	Pittsburgh	San Diego	Aug. 5, 1980	p
Sparky Lyle	Phil. NL	Texas	Sep. 13, 1980	p
C: Lesser players showing promise				
None				
D: 10-year players over the hill				
Mudcat Grant	Oakland	Pittsburgh	Aug. 10, 1971	c
Bob Miller	Pittsburgh	San Diego	Aug. 10, 1971	p
Stan Williams	St. Louis	Minnesota	Sep. 1, 1971	p
Andy Kosco	Boston	California	Aug. 15, 1972	p
Bob Veale	Boston	Pittsburgh	Sep. 2, 1972	c
Bernie Allen	Montreal	New York AL	Aug. 13, 1973	c
Tommie Agee	St. Oouis	Houston	Aug. 18, 1973	p
Eddie Fisher	St. Louis	Chicago AL	Aug. 29, 1973	c
Lew Krausse	St. Louis	Oakland	Sep. 1, 1973	c
Felipe Alou	Montreal	New York AL	Sep. 6, 1973	c
Bob Miller	New York NL	Detroit	Sep. 23, 1973	c
Tim McCarver	Boston	St. Louis	Sep. 1, 1974	c
Deron Johnson	Boston	Milwaukee	Sep. 7, 1974	c
Bill Hands	Texas	Minnesota	Sep. 9, 1974	c
Jim Northrup	Baltimore	Montreal	Sep. 16, 1974	c
Tommy Harper	Oakland	California	Aug. 31, 1975	c
Ron Hunt	St. Louis	Montreal	Sep. 5, 1974	c
Cesar Tovar	Oakland	Texas	Aug. 31, 1975	c
Deron Johnson	Boston	Chicago AL	Sep. 22, 1975	p
Willie McCovey	Oakland	San Diego	Aug. 30, 1976	c
Ron Fairly	Oakland	St. Louis	Sep. 14, 1976	c
Ken Sanders	Kansas City	New York NL	Sep. 17, 1976	c
Tommy Davis	Kansas City	California	Sep. 20, 1976	c
Bob Bailey	Boston	Cincinnati	Sep. 19, 1977	p
Nelson Briles	Baltimore	Texas	Sep. 19, 1977	c
Dave May	Pittsburgh	Milwaukee	Sep. 13, 1978	c
Cito Gaston	Pittsburgh	Atlanta	Sep. 22, 1978	c
Ralph Garr	California	Chicago AL	Sep. 20, 1979	c
Dock Ellis	Pittsburgh	New York NL	Sep. 27, 1979	c
John D'Acquisto	Montreal	San Diego	Aug. 11, 1980	p
Gaylord Perry	New York AL	Texas	Aug. 14, 1980	p
Willie Montanez	Montreal	San Diego	Aug. 31, 1980	p
E: 10-year players not yet proven				
Larry Haney	Oakland	San Diego	Sep. 6, 1972	c
Larry Haney	St. Louis	Oakland	Sep. 1, 1973	c
Jose Morales	Montreal	Oakland	Sep. 18, 1973	c
Jamie Quirk	Kansas City	Milwaukee	Aug. 3, 1978	p
F: 10-year players acquired but not used				
Gorman Thomas	Texas	Milwaukee	Aug. 30, 2977	p
G: Lesser players				
Tony LaRussa	Atlanta	Oakland	Aug. 14, 1971	c
Adrian Garrett	Oakland	Chicago NL	Aug. 31, 1971	p
Carl Taylor	Pittsburgh	Kansas City	Sep. 3, 1971	c
Mike Jackson	St. Louis	Kansas City	Sep. 13, 1971	c
Steve Blateric	New York AL	Cincinnati	Sep. 16, 1972	c
Steve Kealey	Cincinnati	Chicago AL	Aug. 29, 1973	p
Gonzalo Marquez	Chicago NL	Oakland	Aug. 29, 1973	p
Mike Paul	Chicago NL	Texas	Aug. 31, 1973	p
Dick Billings	St. Louis	Texas	Aug. 12, 1974	c
Barry Lersch	St. Louis	Atlanta	Sep. 4, 1974	c
Richie Scheinblum	St. Louis	Kansas City	Aug. 5, 1974	c
Pat Bourque	Minnesota	Oakland	Aug. 19, 1974	p
Jim Holt	Oakland	Minnesota	Aug. 19, 1974	p
Bob Oliver	Baltimore	California	Sep. 11, 1974	p
John Montague	Phil. NL	Montreal	Sep. 2, 1975	c
Stan Thomas	New York AL	Seattle	Aug. 2, 1977	c
Jim Umbarger	Texas	Oakland	Aug. 25, 1977	c
Paul Lindblad	New York AL	Texas	Aug. 2, 1978	c
Larry Anderson	Phil. NL	Chicago NL	Aug. 6, 1978	p
Steve Foucault	Kansas City	Detroit	Aug. 16, 1978	c
Pete Mackanin	Phil. NL	Montreal	Sep. 5, 1978	c
John Montague	California	Seattle	Aug. 29, 1979	p
Bob Molinaro	Baltimore	Chicago AL	Aug. 30, 1979	c
Mark Lee	Pittsburgh	San Diego	Aug. 5, 1980	p
Jesse Jefferson	Pittsburgh	Toronto	Sep. 11, 1980	c
Dennis Lewallyn	Los Angeles	Texas	Sep. 13, 1980	p

Of note in the 1970s—A big jump in overall activity: Eighty late-season deals, versus the previous high of forty-two (1970). Also more significant players involved: nineteen in their primes, versus the previous high of fourteen (1950s). Of course, with the full effects of expansion, there were also a great many more contending teams, so the latter figure is not especially remarkable.

Some notable firsts: Unless I missed someone earlier, Tommy Davis here becomes the first player in history to be acquired by a contender after August 1 on three separate occasions. Rico Carty was picked up by two different contenders in the same year (1973), both after August 1.

The 1980s

Players Acquired	Acquired by	Acquired from	Date	Type of transaction
A: Dominant players of past 2-3 years				
None				
B: 10-year players in their prime				
John Milner	Montreal	Pittsburgh	Aug. 20, 1981	p
Phil Garner	Houston	Pittsburgh	Aug. 31, 1981	p
Doug Blair	St. Louis	Cincinnati	Sep. 19, 1981	p
Doug Flynn	Montreal	Texas	Aug. 2, 1982	c
Joel Youngblood	Montreal	New York NL	Aug. 4, 1982	p
Randy Lerch	Montreal	Milwaukee	Aug. 14, 1982	c
Don Sutton	Milwaukee	Houston	Aug. 30, 1982	p
Tommy John	California	New York AL	Aug. 31, 1982	p
John Denny	Phil. NL	Cleveland	Sep. 12, 1982	p
Manny Trillo	Montreal	Cleveland	Aug. 17, 1983	p
Sixto Lezcano	Phil. NL	San Diego	Aug. 31, 1983	p
Omar Moreno	New York AL	Houston	Aug. 10, 1983	p
Glenn Abbott	Detroit	Seattle	Aug. 23, 1983	c
John Montefusco	New York AL	San Diego	Aug. 26, 1983	p
Miguel Dilone	Pittsburgh	Chicago AL	Sep. 7, 1983	p
Chris Speier	Detroit	Cincinnati	Aug. 27, 1984	p
Ray Knight	New York NL	Houston	Aug. 28, 1984	p
John Candelaria	California	Pittsburgh	Aug. 2, 1985	p
Bo Diaz	Cincinnati	Phil. NL	Aug. 8, 1985	p
Bill Madlock	Los Angeles	Pittsburgh	Aug. 31, 1985	p
Don Sutton	California	Oakland	Sep. 10, 1985	p
Joe Niekro	New York AL	Houston	Sep. 15, 1985	p
Mike Heath	Detroit	St. Louis	Aug. 10, 1986	p
Danny Darwin	Houston	Milwaukee	Aug. 19, 1986	p
Dave Henderson &				
Spike Owen	Boston	Seattle	Aug. 19, 1986	
Jim Morrison	Detroit	Pittsburgh	Aug. 7, 1987	p
Rick Reuschel	San Francisco	Pittsburgh	Aug. 12, 1987	p
Dennis Rasmussen	Cincinnati	New York AL	Aug. 26, 1987	p
Rick Honeycutt	Oakland	Los Angeles	Aug. 29, 1987	p
Storm Davis	Oakland	San Diego	Aug. 30, 1987	p
Don Baylor	Minnesota	Boston	Aug. 31, 1987	p
Dave Henderson	San Francisco	Boston	Sep. 1, 1987	p
John Candelaria	New York NL	California	Sep. 15, 1987	p
John Tudor	Los Angeles	St. Louis	Aug. 16, 1988	p
Ted Power	Detroit	Kansas City	Aug. 31, 1988	p
Greg Harris	Boston	Phil. NL	Aug. 7, 1989	w
Glenn Wilson	Houston	Pittsburgh	Aug. 18, 1989	p
Jim Acker	Toronto	Atlanta	Aug. 24, 1989	p
Ken Phelps	Oakland	New York AL	Aug. 30, 1989	p

Players Acquired	Acquired by	Acquired from	Date	Type of transaction
Luis Salazar	Chicago NL	San Diego	Aug. 30, 1989	p
Zane Smith	Pittsburgh	Montreal	Aug. 8, 1990	p
Harold Baines	Oakland	Texas	Aug. 29, 1990	p
Willie McGee	Oakland	St. Louis	Aug. 29, 1990	p
Pat Tabler	New York NL	Kansas City	Aug. 30, 1990	p
Larry Andersen	Boston	Houston	Aug. 31, 1990	p
Bill Doran	Cincinnati	Houston	Aug. 31, 1990	p
Tommy Herr	New York NL	Phil. NL	Aug. 31, 1990	p
Bud Black	Toronto	Cleveland	Sep. 16, 1990	p
C: Lesser players showing promise				
None				
D: 10-year players over the hill				
Grant Jackson	Montreal	Pittsburgh	Sep. 1, 1981	c
Doc Medich	Milwaukee	Texas	Aug. 11, 1982	c
Richie Hebner	Pittsburgh	Detroit	Aug. 16, 1982	c
Sparky Lyle	Chicago Al	Phil. NL	Aug. 21, 1982	c
Jim Kern	Chicago AL	Cincinnati	Aug. 23, 1982	p
John Curtis	California	San Diego	Aug. 31, 1982	c
Dave Tomlin	Montreal	Cincinnati	Sep. 8, 1982	c
Dave Tomlin	Pittsburgh	Montreal	Aug. 2, 1983	c
Milt May	Pittsburgh	San Francisco	Aug. 19, 1983	c
Miguel Dilone	Chicago AL	Cleveland	Aug. 25, 1983	p
Derrel Thomas	California	Montreal	Sept. 5, 1984	c
George Hendrick &				
Al Holland	California	Pittsburgh	Aug. 2, 1985	p
Cliff Johnson	Toronto	Texas	Aug. 28, 1985	p
Cesar Cedeno	St. Louis	Cincinnati	Aug. 29, 1985	p
Phil Niekro	Toronto	Cleveland	Aug. 7, 1987	p
Doyle Alexander	Detroit	Altanta	Aug. 12, 1987	p
Mike Flanagan	Toronto	Baltimore	Aug. 31, 1987	p
Gene Garber	Kansas City	Atlanta	Aug. 31, 1987	p
Dickie Noles	Detroit	Chicago NL	Sep. 22, 1987	p
Fred Lynn	Detroit	Baltimore	Aug. 31, 1988	p
Lee Mazzilli	Toronto	New York NL	Aug. 2, 1989	w
Ed Romero	Milwaukee	Atlanta	Aug. 23, 1989	p
Larry McWilliams	Kansas City	Phil. NL	Sep. 2, 1989	p
Alex Trevino	Cincinnati	New York NL	Sep. 7, 1990	w
Dan Schatzeder	New York NL	Houston	Sep. 10, 1990	p
E: 10-year players not yet proven				
Greg Harris	Montreal	Cincinnati	Sep. 27, 1983	c
Juan Guzman	Toronto	Los Angeles	Sep. 22, 1987	p
Paul Assenmacher	Chicago NL	Atlanta	Aug. 29, 1989	p
Darrin Jackson	San Diego	Chicago NL	Aug. 30, 1989	p
Charlie O'Brien	New York NL	Milwaukee	Aug. 31, 1990	p
Dennis Cook	Los Angeles	Phil. NL	Sep. 13, 1990	p
F: 10-year players acquired but not used				
None				
G: Lesser players				
Joe Edelen &	Cincinnati	St. Louis	Sep. 19, 1981	p
Neil Fiala	Cincinnati	St. Louis	Sep. 19, 1981	p
Warren Brusstar	Chicago AL	Phil. NL	Aug. 30, 1982	c
Bob Molinaro	Phil. NL	Chicago NL	Sep. 1, 1982	c

Tom Hausman	Atlanta	New York NL	Sep. 10, 1982	p
John Martin	Detroit	St. Louis	Aug. 4, 1983	c
Steve Fireovia	Phil. NL	San Diego	Aug. 31, 1983	p
Randy Niemann	Chicago AL	Pittsburgh	Sep. 7, 1983	p
Gene Roof	Montreal	St. Louis	Sep. 16, 1983	c
Bill Scherrer	Detroit	Cincinnati	Aug. 27, 1984	p
Pat Putnam	Minnesota	Seattle	Aug. 29, 1984	c
Rod Scurry	New York AL	Pittsburgh	Aug. 14, 1985	c
Jeff Zaske	Texas	Pittsburgh	Sep. 30, 1986	p
Dave Owen	Kansas City	Texas	Aug. 1, 1987	p
Nelson Simmons	Seattle	Baltimore	Aug. 11, 1987	p
Pat Perry	Cincinnati	St. Louis	Aug. 31, 1987	p
Scott Terry	St. Louis	Cincinnati	Aug. 31, 1987	p
Julio Solano	Seattle	Houston	Sep. 30, 1987	p
Mike Maksudian	New York NL	Chicago AL	Aug. 4, 1988	p
Mike Young	Milwaukee	Phil. NL	Aug. 24, 1988	p
Ricky Horton	Los Angeles	Chicago AL	Aug. 30, 1988	p
Dale Mohoric	New York AL	Texas	Aug. 30, 1988	p
Manny Hernandez	New York NL	Minnesota	Aug. 1, 1989	c
Ray Chadwick	Boston	Chicago AL	Aug. 2, 1989	p
Phil Stephenson &				
Calvin Schiraldi	San Diego	Chicago NL	Aug. 30, 1989	p
Marvel Wynne	Chicago NL	San Diego	Aug. 30, 1989	p
Ron Tingley	California	Cleveland	Sep. 6, 1989	p
Carmelo Martinez	Pittsburgh	Phil. NL	Aug. 30, 1990	p
Lloyd McClendon	Pittsburgh	Chicago NL	Sep. 7, 1990	p
Rick Luecken	Toronto	Atlanta	Sep. 24, 1990	c
Mike Munoz	Detroit	Los Angeles	Sep. 30, 1990	p

Of note in the 1980s—Another big surge in late-season activity, confirming the impression many have, that far more players shuffle around in August and September in this first full decade of free agency's effects. Overall, there were 113 player moves, versus the previous high of eighty-two (1970s) and forty-two (1960s). The quality of player shuffled is up to forty-nine players in their prime, or more than 40 percent of the total acquired.

I still identify no truly dominant player being moved since Johnny Sain way back in 1951. This period includes the year (1990) when Willie McGee was en route to a NL batting crown when he was traded right out of the league on August 29, so he has to come close. But if you look at his performance during the preceding two-three years, you see McGee was a good player, but in no way was he a dominant one.

The 1990s

Players Acquired	Acquired by	Acquired from	Date	Type of transaction
A: Dominant players of past 2-3 years				
Lee Smith	New York AL	St. Louis	Aug. 31, 1993	p
B: 10-year players in their prime				
Alejandro Pena	Atlanta	New York NL	Aug. 28, 1991	p
Steve Buechele	Pittsburgh	Texas	Aug. 30, 1991	p
Mike Bielecki	Atlanta	Chicago NL	Sep. 29, 1991	p
David Cone	Toronto	New York NL	Aug. 27, 1992	p
Jeff Reardon	Atlanta	Boston	Aug. 30, 1992	p
Bill Krueger	Montreal	Minnesota	Aug. 31, 1992	p
Craig Lefferts	Baltimore	San Diego	Aug. 31, 1992	p
Jeff Russell &				
Ruben Sierra &				
Bobby Witt	Oakland	Texas	Aug. 31, 1992	p
Scott Sanderson	San Francisco	California	Aug. 3, 1993	w
Bobby Thigpen	Phil. NL	Chicago AL	Aug. 10, 1993	p
Jim Deshaies	San Francisco	Minnesota	Aug. 28, 1993	p
Chris James	Texas	Houston	Sep. 17, 1993	p
Rob Murphy	New York AL	St. Louis	Sep. 3, 1994	w
Mariano Duncan	Cincinnati	Phil. NL	Aug. 8, 1995	p
Bobby Witt	Texas	Florida	Aug. 8, 1995	p
Pat Borders	Houston	Kansas City	Aug. 11, 1995	p
Luis Polonia	Atlanta	New York AL	Aug. 11, 1995	p
Brett Butler	Los Angeles	New York NL	Aug. 18, 1995	p
Mike Devereaux	Atlanta	Chicago AL	Aug. 25, 1995	p
C: Lesser players showing promies				
None				
D: 10-year players over the hill				
Candy Maldonado	Toronto	Milwaukee	Aug. 9, 1991	p
Dan Petry	Boston	Atlanta	Aug. 16, 1991	p
Jose DeLeon	Chicago AL	Phil. NL	Aug. 10, 1993	p
Frank Tanana	New York AL	New York NL	Sep. 17, 1993	p
Dave Winfield	Cleveland	Minnesota	Aug. 31, 1994	c
Mike Henneman	Houston	Detroit	Aug. 8, 1995	p
Chris James	Boston	Kansas City	Aug. 14, 1995	p
Vince Coleman	Seattle	Kansas City	Aug. 15, 1995	p
Mike Aldrete	California	Oakland	Aug. 24, 1995	p
Rick Honeycutt	New York AL	Oakland	Sep. 25, 1995	c
Candy Maldonado	Texas	Toronto	Aug. 31, 1995	c
Alejandro Pena	Atlanta	Florida	Aug. 31, 1995	p
E: 10-year players not yet proven				
Steve Scarsone	Baltimore	Phil. NL	Aug. 11, 1992	p
Sean Berry	Montreal	Kansas City	Aug. 29, 1992	p
F: 10-year players acquired but not used				
Scott Bankhead	New York AL	Boston	Sep. 1, 1994	p
G: Lesser players				
William Suero	Milwaukee	Toronto	Aug. 9, 1991	p
Steve Wilson	Los Angeles	Chicago NL	Sep. 6, 1991	p
Damon Berryhill	Atlanta	Chicago NL	Sep. 29, 1991	p
Gil Heredia	Montreal	San Francisco	Aug. 18, 1992	p
Archie Corbin	Montreal	Kansas City	Aug. 29, 1992	p
Darren Reed	Minnesota	Montreal	Aug. 31, 1992	p
Dave Eiland	Texas	Cleveland	Aug. 4, 1993	p
Doug Lindsey	Chicago AL	Phil. NL	Sep. 1, 1993	p
Donn Paul	Phil. NL	Chicago AL	Sep. 1, 1993	p

Eric Gunderson	Seattle	New York NL	Aug. 4, 1995	w
Dave Gallagher	California	Phil. NL	Aug. 8, 1995	p
Eric Gunderson	Boston	Seattle	Aug. 10, 1995	w
Craig Worthington	Texas	Cincinnati	Aug. 16, 1995	p
Dwayne Hosey	Boston	Kansas City	Aug. 31, 1995	w
Chris Howard	Texas	Boston	Aug. 31, 1995	p
Domingo Jean	Cincinnati	Texas	Aug. 31, 1995	w
Jack Voigt	Boston	Texas	Aug. 31, 1995	p

Of note in the 1990s—The overall level of activity shows a slight decrease for the first half of this decade, more marked when you note the greater number of contenders. The quality of players moved also slipped very slightly.

But we finally have a fourth player who can probably be ranked as dominant. Lee Smith led the league in saves during the two years before his late-season acquisition by the Yanks in 1993—and again led the league the year after.

Although several players moved a second time during the 1990s (Gunderson, Honeycutt, James, Maldonado, Pena, Witt), no one has yet matched Tommy Davis's feat of being sought after by contend-

ers three times in late-season shifts.

Of note overall—The overall conclusions I see in all these data is that there has unquestionably been a trend to more late-season player deals, especially since the late 1950s, most especially since 1969. Within this trend, there is also a pronounced shift toward more significant players being sought. See the chart on the next page.

A curious piece of trivia: Using the criteria I set out at the beginning of this study, precisely 400 players have been acquired by pennant contenders in August or September—and precisely half (200 of the 400) have been pitchers. Thus pitchers are proportionately more sought-after than the other position players, but not by an overwhelming margin.

In the foregoing pages, no attempt has been made to evaluate the results of these acquisitions. My sole purpose has been to determine with some precision the trend in their frequency and in the quality of the players as perceived at the time of acquisition, not as later evaluated with benefit of hindsight. That too would make an interesting study, some other time.

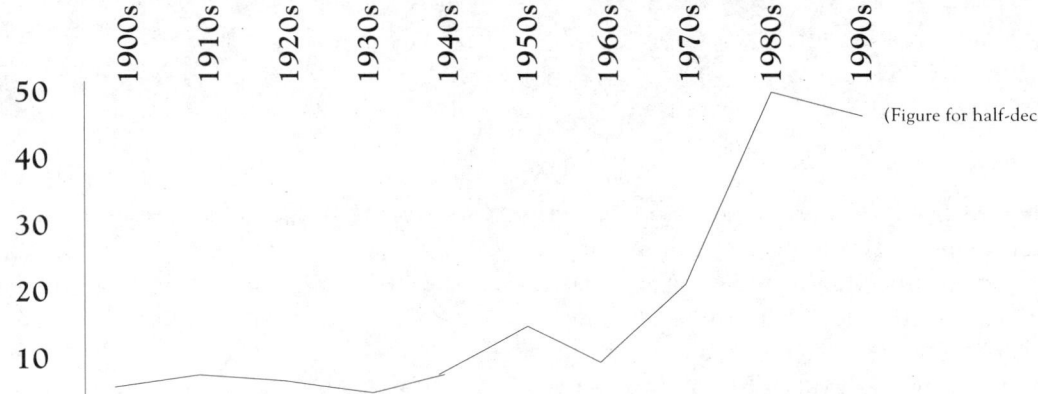

Total number of significant late-season acquisitions by decade. (Significant means 10-year career players in their prime.)

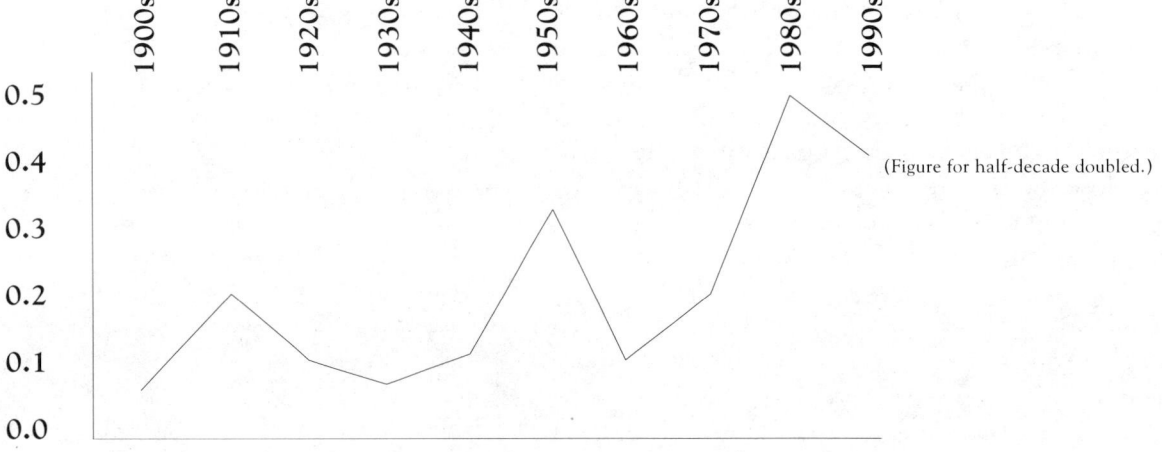

Total number of significant late-season acquisitions per pennant contender, by decade.

Family Values

Kin hitting and pitching leaders

Albey Reiner and Biff Brecher

In 1997, baseball fans were reminded in dramatic fashion that baseball is a family game. We were treated to the sight of a smiling Bobby Bonds giving son Barry high fives from the first base coaching box as he circled the bases forty times during the Giants' exciting pennant run. Cleveland's Sandy Alomar, Jr., enjoying a career year, beat his brother, Robby, and the Orioles in the playoffs. Then during the World Series, the cameras were often trained on the tense faces of Felipe Alou and Sandy Alomar Sr. as their sons went down to the wire in one of the most exciting postseasons ever witnessed. Young Pete Rose Jr., wearing the familiar Reds uniform, got his first two major league hits, putting him only 4,254 behind the great Charlie Hustle. The '97 Reds boasted another scion of the Big Red Machine, Eduardo Perez, son of the redoubtable RBI man Tony. The same team also featured a third-generation player, Bret Boone. Grandfather Ray, father Bob, and Bret, with 3,670 hits, are currently in eighth place on the all-time list of family hitters.

Baseball history is replete with examples of fathers, sons, and brothers playing in the big leagues. More than a quarter century before Kitty Hawk, the *first* Wright Brothers, George, Harry, and Sam, all played for Boston in the National League in 1876. Together, they amassed a grand total of 388 NL hits, all but five by George. (The brothers totaled 1,121, including their National Association days.) George and Harry went on to the Hall of Fame.

The Wrights were quickly succeeded by the Clapps, Aaron, and John, and the Gleasons, Bill and Jack. The turn of the century saw the five Delahanty brothers amass 4,217 hits among them, the higest total generated to that time, and still good enough for sixth place on the all-time list.

The tradition of family play has continued and, in fact, accelerated in the twentieth century. Table 1 lists the twenty-four families that have amassed at least 3,000 hits through the end of the 1997 season. At the head of the pack are the Alous. The first generation of brothers—Felipe, Mateo, and Jesus (who once played together in the Giants outfield)—plus rising star Moises, have collected 5,878 hits.[1] They will surely be the first group to pass the 6,000 hit mark and their record appears safe for the foreseeable future.

It is interesting to note that almost forty percent of the combinations shown here have a currently active member. They include the Alou, Rose, Boone, Bonds, Griffey, Alomar, Ripken, McRae, and Gwynn families. We don't know of any other record category that contains such a high ratio of active players.

Some of the combinations are statistical oddities, dominated by one great player, whose relative is merely a footnote in baseball history. Thus, Pete has 99.5 percent of the Rose family hits. On the other hand, some groupings consist of players whose statistics are virtually equal, such as Barry and Bobby

---

Albey Reiner and *Biff Brecher* are Brooklyn Dodger fans who have not yet recovered from the blow.

Bonds: Bobby has 51.9 percent of the hits and Barry 48.1 percent.

There are illustrious pitching families, too. Table 3 presents those that have won 200 or more games.[10] Unlike the hitters groups, none of the leading pitching families is currently active in the majors. Two recent brother acts, the Niekros and the Perrys, are far ahead of their nearest competitors. Is it a mere coincidence that all four of them have been accused of occasionally applying foreign substances to the baseball? These two brother acts are also one-two in lifetime strikeouts, with the order reversed—the Perrys had 5,110, the Niekros, 5,082.

In addition to the groups listed here, several other baseball families are worthy of attention. They include some noted for their humorous names—Tookie Gilbert and his dad and brother, Larry and Charlie; Heinie and Frank Manush. Others are remembered for their spectacular lack of ability—Marvelous Marv and Faye Throneberry. And who can forget the fabulous Peploski Brothers, Henry and Pepper, who collected a total of four hits between them?

As excellent players such as Ken Griffey Jr., Barry Bonds, Moisés Alou, Tony Gwynn, and the Alomars roll along, these standings will be altered. It will be interesting to revisit this topic in a decade or so to see whether the numbers have changed significantly.

Table 1
Families with at least 3,000 hits (through 1997)

Family	Hits	Player	Hits		Family	Hits	Player	Hits
Alou[2]	5878	Felipe	2101		Sisler	3557	George	2812
		Mateo	1777				Dick	720
		Jesús	1216				Dave	25
		Moisés	784		Alomar*	3534	Roberto	1659
Waner[3]	5611	Paul	3152				Sandy, Sr.	1168
		Lloyd	2549				Sandy, Jr.	707
DiMaggio[4]	4853	Joe	2214		Griffey*[6]	3552	Ken, Sr.	2143
		Dom	1680				Ken, Jr.	1389
		Vince	959		Wagner	3489	Honus	3430
Bell*[5]	4434	Buddy	2514				Butts	59
		Gus	1823		Collins	3377	Eddie	3311
		David	97				Eddie, Jr.	66
Rose*	4258	Pete	4256		Ripken*	3369	Cal, Jr.	2715
		Pete, Jr.	2				Billy	654
Delahanty	4211	Ed	2591		Johnson	3343	Bob	2051
		Jim	1159				Roy	1292
		Frank	223		Brett	3254	George	3154
		Joe	222				Ken	91
		Tom	16		Meusel	3214	Bob	1693
Aaron	3987	Hank	3771				Irish	1521
		Tommie	216		McRae*	3193	Hal	2091
Boone*	3670	Bob	1838				Brian	1102
		Ray	1260		Murray	3297	Eddie	3253
		Bret	572				Rich	44
Bonds*	3636	Bobby	1886		May	3158	Lee	2031
		Barry	1750				Carlos	1127
Sewell	3619	Joe	2226		Gwynn*[7]	3043	Tony	2780
		Luke	1393				Chris	263
Boyer	3559	Ken	2143					
		Cletes	1396					
		Cloyd	20					

Table 2
Families with at least 400 home runs (through 1997)

Family	Hits	Players	HR	Family	Hits	Players	HR
Aaron	768	Hank	755	Murray	509	Eddie	504
		Tommie	13			Rich	4
Bonds[8]	706	Barry	374	May	444	Lee	354
		Bobby	332			Carlos	90
DiMaggio[9]	573	Joe	361	Boyer	444	Ken	282
		Vince	125			Cletes	162
		Dom	87	Bell	410	Gus	206
Griffey	546	Ken, Jr.	294			Buddy	201
		Ken, Sr.	152			David	3
				Berra	407	Yogi	358
						Dale	49

Table 3
Families with at least 200 wins (through 1997)

Family	Wins	Names	Wins	Family	Wins	Names	Wins
Niekro[11]	539	Phil	318	Trout	258	Dizzy	170
		Joe	221			Steve	88
Perry	529	Gaylord	314	Bagby	224	Jim, Sr.	127
		Jim	215			Jim, Jr.	97
Radbourne	309	Old Hoss	308	Reuschel	230	Rick	214
		George	1			Paul	16
Coveleski[12]	296	Stan	215	Barnes	214	Jesse	153
		Harry	81			Virgil	61
Forsch[13]	282	Bob	168	Walsh	206	Big Ed	195
		Ken	114			Ed, Jr.	11
Weyhing	267	Gus	264	Dean[14]	200	Dizzy	150
		John	3			Paul	50

Notes:

1. The rumored fourth Alou brother, Roberto, is best known for his rhumba music.

2. This is the only family grouping with at least 3 men who had at least 1,000 hits. The Alomars and Boones will almost certainly join them, but by then, Moises will have enough hits to assure that there will be four Alous with at least 1,000 hits.

3. The Waners are the only family with more than one man with 2,000 hits. The Griffeys are a lock to equal this record.

4. Joe and Dom each missed three seasons during World War II, when they were at their peak. If they had maintained their pre- and post-war paces, they would have added at least another 1,000 hits to their total, putting them in first place. The Alous would be passing them in 1998, but they then would have been Number One for forty-five years, longer than any other family group, by far.

5. Three generations of Bells and Boones have played in the majors.

6. The Griffeys are the only father-son combination we have found who played in the majors concurrently. This is a very unusual feat, which occurred because Ken, Jr. was born when Ken, Sr. was only nineteen years old, and Ken, Jr. arrived in the bigs at the same age. Also, Ken, Sr. was able to play through age forty-one.

It is also notable that the two Griffeys played for the same team, Seattle, for a season and a half. Compare this situation to that of the Wakefield father-son duo of Howard and Dick. The latter broke into the majors in 1941, thirty-four years after his dad left the game, and four months before he died.

7. The Gwynns have the highest lifetime family batting average, .331. Next in order are Collins (.330), Manush (.328072), Sisler (.328069), and Wagner (.327)

8. The Bonds family could easily take the lead by the end of the millenium.

9. This was the first family with more than 500 home runs.

10. Both Christy Mathewson (373 wins) and Will White (229 wins) had brothers who pitched in the majors, but won no games. Therefore they are not listed in this Table.

11. The Niekros were in the majors together for 21 seasons, the longest time for any family group.

12. Together, the Coveleskis had eight 20-game seasons, the most of any family grouping. Amazingly, Harry had three 20-game seasons, yet won a total of only 81 games!

13. Each brother pitched a no-hitter.

14. The Deans had the most combined wins in a season, 49 in 1934. They also put together a total of 47 in 1935.

Notice on Nat Peeples

The only African American in the Southern Association

Kenneth R. Fenster

Just as Jackie Robinson integrated major league baseball, Nat Peeples integrated the Class AA Southern Association in 1954 when he played in two games for the Atlanta Crackers. In those games, Peeples went hitless in four at bats and failed to hit the ball out of the infield. A few days later, Earl Mann, the owner of the Crackers, demoted him to Class A Jacksonville of the Sally League.

In the politically correct world in which we live, the knee-jerk reaction would be to conclude that Mann demoted Peeples because of discrimination and racism. But, according to Peeples: "I really don't think that had anything to do with it. Mr. Mann told me the [Milwaukee] Braves thought I ought to play every day so I needed to go to Jacksonville."[1] In 1954, Peeples, an outfielder, would have played rarely for the Crackers. The team boasted a starting outfield of Bob Montag, Chuck Tanner, and Pete Whisenant. That year, Montag set a franchise record of 39 home runs. He also batted .305 and knocked in over 100 runs. Tanner batted over .320, had over 100 RBIs, and hit 20 home runs. Whisenant belted 20 homers. Moreover, Montag was one of the most popular players ever to wear an Atlanta uniform: "I used to get a bigger hand for popping up or striking out than some guys got for getting base hits," he remembered. "I could do no wrong here."[2]

With their slugging outfielders, the 1954 Crackers won more than 90 games and were one of the best teams ever to play in Atlanta. They were the only team in Southern Association history to win the midseason All-Star Game, the Southern Association pennant, the Shaughnessy playoffs (beating the second-, third-, and fourth-place teams in a tournament), and the Dixie Series against the Texas League champion.

Nat Peeples was demoted for strictly baseball reasons. On the 1954 Crackers, he would have sat on the bench and contributed little to the team's tremendous success. According to Montag: "He just wasn't ready for the league is what it amounted to. He was like the lamb going to the slaughter is what it amounted to. They [Crackers' management] wanted a black player, and Nat was the best one at that time in the organization that they could use...He was in the wrong place at the right time."[3]

At Jacksonville, Peeples played in 94 games and batted a respectable .288. As of 1985, he harbored no bitterness and no resentment about his quick departure from the Crackers and the Southern Association. In an interview with the Atlanta *Journal-Constitution*, he insisted that the people of Atlanta and especially Earl Mann treated him cordially and fairly.[4]

Notes

1. Interview with Nat Peeples, Atlanta *Journal-Constitution*, September 1, 1985.

23. Interview with Bob Montag, Atlanta Historical Society, MSS. 735, Southern Bases Collection, folder 48.

3. Ibid., folder 47.

4. Interview with Nat Peeples, Atlanta *Journal-Constitution*, September 1, 1985.

Kenneth R. Fenster is assistant professor of history at DeKalb College, Central Campus, Clarkston, Georgia.

The Eastern League's Only .400 Hitter

"'The American League ball,' I thought. 'Oh, boy!'"

Gerald Tomlinson

In 1947 the Eastern League put out a small, spiral-bound record book entitled *Silver Anniversary, 1923-1947*. The league had incorporated the New York-Pennsylvania League in 1932, and the book included combined NYP-Eastern League statistics for those twenty-five years, complete through the 1946 season. Using the combined statistics, the only .400 hitter the league had ever produced was Joe Munson, who batted an even .400 for the NYP Harrisburg Senators in 1925. After 1997, the Eastern League's seventy-fifth season, Munson's record still stood.

The hitter who came the closest to matching it was player-manager James "Rip" Collins of the Albany Senators. In 1944, in the middle of World War II, the Ripper, a forty-year-old former first baseman for the St. Louis Cardinals' Gashouse Gang, batted .396 in 100 games. Collins had been a bona-fide major league star. Munson reached the majors but not for long. He spent most of his fifteen-year career in the minors.

Joe Munson was born Joseph Martin Napoleon Carlson in Renovo, Pennsylvania, on November 6, 1899, and died on February 24, 1991, at his home in Upper Darby, Pennsylvania. For all of his ninety-one years he was known by the name of Carlson, usually Butch Carlson, although he never played a day of professional baseball under that name.

A catcher as a youngster, he switched to the out-

field as a pro. Munson was a stocky, righthanded thrower who batted left. After starring in football, basketball, and baseball at Perkiomen School in Pennsburg, Pennsylvania, he entered Lehigh University. The summer before he entered college he received an offer to play professional baseball for Martinsburg, West Virginia, of the Class D Blue Ridge League. The pro offer was irresistible. To preserve his college eligibility, he played for Martinsburg in 1918 under the name of Joe Martin. It was a brief stint. The season ended after three weeks because of America's involvement in World War I.

Next year, 1919, he played for Suffolk, Virginia, of the Class C Virginia League under the same assumed name. Before the 1920 season began he dropped out of college because "the urge and offers of baseball were too strong" and signed on with Raleigh, North Carolina, of the then-new Class D Piedmont League. This time he took the name Joe Munson, the surname coming from that of a close friend of his mother's. He retained the Munson name throughout the rest of his baseball career. Off the field, however, he was Butch Carlson.

Joe Munson had a fine year in 1920, hitting .304 in 120 games. His play earned him a promotion not just out of the Piedmont League but straight into spring training with the New York Yankees, where a photo of him at a table with Babe Ruth became one of his prized possessions. The Yankees, after a brief look, shipped Joe off to the Dallas club of the Texas League, a Class A circuit in those days. Munson put in a good

Gerald Tomlinson, who has followed the Eastern League for more than half a century, is probably the only SABR member who saw Don Zimmer get married at home plate. Zimmer, then a star shortstop for the Elmira Pioneers, was wed at Elmira's Dunn Field in 1951.

year with the Dallas Marines, batting .298, with 169 hits, including forty doubles, eleven triples, and eight home runs.

Next season the Yankees sold Joe to Galveston, also of the Texas League. After hitting .310 in 102 games for the Crabs, Munson stayed in Galveston for the winter, working on the docks and "counting bales of cotton until I couldn't see straight."

In 1923 he was back with Galveston, hitting .281 for the season. He started the '24 season there, too, but fate intervened. Galveston had hired a new manager, Paddy Baumann, and "the first thing I know, Baumann said to me, 'Munson, we're not going to take you on the road with us. We want to take a look at someone else.' He chose George Whiteman, who had done well for the Red Sox in the World Series of 1918. He decided to keep Whiteman and send me down to Marlin."

The move was a bitter disappointment for Joe. Marlin, Texas, a little town southwest of Waco, fielded a team in the lowly Class D Texas Association. At that less challenging level of competition Munson hit .346.

Over the winter he was sold to Waco of the Texas League and looked forward to a return to the high minors. But before the season started, "Del Pratt decided to break up the club, get rid of the older fellows. Older fellows? I was twenty-five at the time." They sold him to Harrisburg, Pennsylvania, of the Class B New York-Pennsylvania League, which would later be incorporated into the Eastern League. Although Joe had done well up to that time, and was a veteran outfielder, there was little to suggest the remarkable season he was about to have.

Munson joined the Harrisburg club in Shippensburg, Pennsylvania, at the end of spring training. "I remember that first batting practice. I was hitting the ball well. The ball would just jump off the bat. I was hitting long drives.

"I said to one of the boys, 'What ball are you using here?'

"He said, 'Joe, it's the American League ball.'

"'The American League ball,' I thought. 'Oh, boy!'"

On opening day Munson, the cleanup hitter, went 0 for 3 against minor-league legend Lefty George of the York White Roses. Harrisburg lost the game, 7-0. Two days later in their home opener the Harrisburg Senators edged York, 5-4, as Joe Munson, playing his first game at West End Field, lined a homer over the right field wall.

"Everything, it seemed, went my way in 1925," said Munson. "Every ball I hit was between somebody. I

changed my style, got down on the end of the bat. I used a Frank Schulte model bat with a Sam Crawford knob. The Schulte model was a thin bat; the diameter wasn't more than two and a half inches. I could really pull an outside pitch with it…I hit lots of hard drives, lots of them over the fence."

He certainly did. For Harrisburg in 1925 he not only batted .400, he also hit a record-setting thirty-three home runs, a mark surpassed five years later by Ken Strong, an outfielder for Hazleton, and a future National Football League Hall of Famer. Strong, although a spectacularly powerful slugger, hit many of his forty-one homers at Hazleton's bandbox Buhler Stadium.

In 1925 Munson drove in 129 runs, a record subsequently recognized by the Eastern League that held until 1950 when Dale Long collected 134 for Binghamton. Two of Joe's other marks that year stand to this day. His 355 total bases have never been topped, and his seventeen times being hit by a pitch tied a mark set by Lee Kelley of Elmira in 1923.

Here are Joe Munson's 1925 totals, an asterisk indicating that he led what was then the New York-Pennsylvania League in that category.

G	AB	R	H	2B	3B	HR	RBI	BB	SB	BA
131	470	132*	188*	34	17*	33*	129*	88*	29	.400*

Even in the categories where he failed to lead the league, he turned in impressive numbers. Del Bissonette of York, a future Brooklyn Dodgers star, led the league in two-base hits with forty-six to Joe's thirty-four. Harry Topel of Elmira, a swift runner but going nowhere, stole thirty-seven bases to Joe's twenty-nine.

Despite having Joe Munson in the lineup, the Harrisburg Senators under manager Rankin Johnson had a so-so season, winning sixty-one and losing sixty-nine to finish in sixth place. But Munson made headlines. From York's Eagle Park, which had a hill in right field that Joe didn't care for, to Binghamton's Johnson Field (located in Johnson City), which he considered the best ballpark in the league, he stayed consistently around the .400 mark. "They always say you have to have a lot of luck to hit .400," he said, "and I probably had some. But I was hitting the ball good, hitting it hard."

There was no night baseball in 1925, but the daytime fans showed up in sizable numbers to watch the close pennant race that year, won by York in a playoff against Williamsport. Joe found the crowds friendly and enthusiastic, though a bit less knowledgeable than fans in the television era. Solid newspaper coverage helped sustain local interest in the club. The Harrisburg newspapers, the *Patriot* and the *Telegraph*, carried full accounts of the Senators' games.

Since the New York-Penn league was only in the third season of its existence, the sportswriters had no inkling that they were watching what would be a combined circuit's only .400 hitter in three-quarters of a century, perhaps ever. Their stories reflected this. They knew Joe was good and predicted he would finish the season in the majors (which he did, batting .371 for the Chicago Cubs in thirty-five times at bat), yet there was no press frenzy over his stats, and his "day" at Harrisburg came only on the final home date of the season.

Munson played briefly for the Chicago Cubs in 1926, batting .257 in 101 plate appearances. After being traded during the season for the formidable Riggs Stephenson, Joe dropped back into the minors. He played mainly for Tulsa of the Class A Western League, batting .383 in 1927, .385 in 1928, and .369 in 1929. He made no repeat appearances in the NYP or Eastern League. He put in just one season at West End Field, Harrisburg, then moved on.

But what a season it was.

Shoeless Joe in the Hall of Fame?

Does he have the numbers?

Michael Hoban, Ph.D.

In early 1998, Hall of Famers Ted Williams and Bob Feller reopened the question of whether the ban of Shoeless Joe Jackson should be lifted and he should be made eligible for consideration for induction into the Hall of Fame. Jackson has been banned from consideration for the Hall because of his role in the infamous Black Sox scandal of 1919.

My concern about this question has nothing to do with the scandal of 1919. My view is that baseball decided to ban him, so baseball can also decide to lift the ban if circumstances appear to warrant this. What I fear is that if the ban is lifted, there may be a rush to judgment and an assumption that Jackson belongs in the Hall. It seems fair to say that there are few figures in baseball history more surrounded by myth and hype than "Say it ain't so, Joe" Jackson.

My point is that if the ban is lifted, we have to step back and examine Jackson's career and his numbers carefully and ask ourselves whether he truly has Hall of Fame numbers, or whether another Chick Hafey is about to go into the Hall. In fact, given that he has been banned for so long, some may argue that he would need truly outstanding numbers in order to be admitted.

Put simply, I believe that Joe Jackson's statistical record is not good enough for him to be elected to the Hall of Fame.

Mike Hoban is a professor of mathematics at Monmouth University in New Jersey. He has spent the last three years creating and perfecting his rating system. His book, Baseball's Complete Players: The HEQ Rating System, *will be published by McFarland & Co. in 1999.*

Joe Jackson is probably the best example in baseball history of how misleading the concept of batting average can be. The statement that his supporters seem to favor the most is the following: "Joe Jackson has the third highest career batting average in baseball history, after Ty Cobb and Rogers Hornsby." The implication of the statement is that this fact somehow establishes his credentials to be considered in the same class as these two great players. Unfortunately for Shoeless Joe, a more careful analysis of his numbers reveals that in no way does he come close to the stature of these superstars.

The system in brief—My rating system is a set of simple, fan-friendly formulas that establishes how good a season a player had—including hitting, fielding, and playing time. It represents an objective view of a player's numbers. It does not use percentages or percentage-based statistics like batting average, but instead applies a more mathematically sound approach.

The offensive season score is the sum of a player's total bases, runs scored, runs batted in, stolen bases, and half of his walks. Since the result is a sum, the system automatically takes playing time into account. A total of 600 is a great offensive year. Mickey Mantle had five such seasons. Babe Ruth and Lou Gehrig are the only players to have ten.

The defensive score is the combined result of putouts, assists, double plays, and errors, calculated appropriately for each position. A total of 400 is a

Transcendental Graphics

Joe Jackson

great defensive year. Mantle had five. Willie Mays had nine. Tris Speaker had ten.

Career scores are the average of a player's ten highest combined season scores. Ruth has the highest rating, at 1,110. Mays is second, at 1,101.

Using this system, I've determined that an 820 career score is the appropriate cut-off for Hall of Fame greatness. There are 105 position players in the Hall who have played in the twentieth century. Twenty-nine have career scores under 820. If Jacskon were elected tomorrow, he would rank ninety-third of 106.

(For a complete description of the rating system, contact Len Levin, SABR Research Library, 282 Doyle Avenue, Providence, RI 02906.)

Applying the system—Using this system, we can

compare Joe Jackson to other players to see just how good his numbers really were. Let's compare Jackson's numbers to those of Ruth, Ty Cobb, and Rogers Hornsby. My system ranks Ruth as the most effective player in baseball history, with Cobb ninth and Hornsby tenth.

Here are the numbers:

	Offense		Defense		Total
Babe Ruth	767	+	343	=	1,110
Ty Cobb	608	+	411	=	1,019
Rogers Hornsby	625	+	388	=	1,013
Joe Jackson	461	+	292	=	753

Joe Jackson played thirteen seasons in the major leagues. My system is based on a player's ten best seasons, so his poor showing is related to the fact that he played in 100 or more games in only nine of those seasons. However, Hank Greenberg had only nine seasons of 100 games, and he is a clear Hall of Famer with a total of 907.

Jackson's enduring myth is based on his batting average and the fact that he did have a few very good seasons. His career is similar to Hack Wilson's. Wilson played for only twelve years (1,348 games). Like Jackson, he had only nine seasons in which he played more than 100 games. Like Jackson, he had only a few good seasons. However, his best season (1930) was one of the best of all time: he hit 56 home runs and knocked in a still-record 190 runs. He had three 1,000 seasons. Jackson had none. Here is his career score:

Hack Wilson	478	+	302	=	780

Jackson's actual production does not justify his reputation. He had only two truly outstanding hitting seasons in which his offensive score was 600 or more: 1911 = 615 and 1912 = 604 (he also came close in 1920 with a score of 599). Cobb had five such seasons, Hornsby had six, Ted Williams had nine, and Hank Aaron had eight.

Jackson had only one 400 defensive season in the outfield. Tris Speaker had ten such seasons, Puckett had seven, DiMaggio had six, and even Babe Ruth had three.

And finally, Jackson never had even one great all-around 1,000 season. Mays had ten 1,000 seasons, the Babe had nine, and Gehrig and Jimmie Foxx had seven each.

I think Joe Jackson may be the best example in baseball history of "unfulfilled potential." During his playing days, many of his contemporaries were enthralled by his swing and spoke of him in glowing terms. Babe Ruth is reported to have said that he copied Jackson's swing. It appears that so many people were so sure that he *would be* one of the greats that they convinced themselves and most other people that he really was. But the numbers really do tell the tale. Shoeless Joe failed to live up to his potential.

How does Jackson compare with that other Hall of Fame outcast Pete Rose?

Pete Rose	507	+	392	=	899
Joe Jackson	461	+	292	=	753

Pete Rose has Hall of Fame numbers while Jackson does not.

How does Shoeless Joe's numbers compare to those of the two players selected by the Veterans Committee in 1998 for induction into the Hall of Fame?

George Davis	474	+	388	=	862
Larry Doby	475	+	373	=	848
Joe Jackson	461	+	292	=	753

Both Davis and Doby have legitimate Hall of Fame numbers.

If one were looking for a modern-day candidate for the Hall of Fame with whom to compare Jackson, the numbers indicate that Dwight Evans might be the choice. Look at their career numbers:

Dwight Evans	491	+	342	=	833
Joe Jackson	461	+	292	=	753

Evans and Jackson were both right fielders. Each player had two 600 offensive seasons among his ten best seasons and no 1,000 seasons. The numbers indicate that Evans was a more effective offensive player by thirty points and a more effective defensive player by fifty points. With a score of 833, Evans has Hall of Fame numbers. Even so, in the 1998 balloting for the Hall, Dwight Evans got only 49 votes (10.4 percent). His chances for election are low.

In conclusion, I am not saying that Joe Jackson should not be in the Hall of Fame. I am saying that he *does not have Hall of Fame numbers*. It may be that those who vote for the inductees will see other factors that will convince them to vote for him. Shoeless Joe's story is the stuff of which legends are made. In his case it appears that the legend may be greater than the ballplayer.

100 Wins, 100 Losses

The history of winning or losing big, and consecutively

Scott Nelson

One-hundred win seasons might be long-remembered highlights for any major league club. But 100-loss summers are soon forgotten—and with good reason. Still, there have been forty-one more big losers than winners in the past ninety-eight years. The century mark has been hit seventy-eight times by winning clubs and 119 times by losing teams.

It is probably not surprising to most followers of the game that the New York Yankees head the majors with fifteen 100-win seasons and just two 100-loss records, the last one in 1912. Next are the St. Louis Cardinals with six 100-win records. The Chicago Cubs boast five seasons of 100 wins, four of them in the century's first decade. Detroit, the old Philadelphia A's of Connie Mack, and the modern, relatively young American League Baltimore Orioles all claim five 100-win marks.

While the Philadelphia Phillies have the most 100-loss seasons, with fourteen, the old Boston Braves and Philadelphia A's aren't too far behind with eleven each.

Still, the Phils can claim one of only two instances of identical consecutive 100-win seasons, 101-61 records—in 1976-77. The Cardinals are the other claimant with identical 105-49 marks, in 1943-44.

American League teams hold a 41-37 edge on their NL rivals in 100-win seasons but also have sixty-five

100-defeat records to fifty-three for the NL.

Three clubs have rung up a record three straight 100-win seasons. Baltimore had 318 wins in 1969-71. The old Philadelphia A's, won 313 in 1929-31. And the Cardinals had 316 victories in 1942-44. Oakland missed by one victory getting three big ones in a row in 1988-90. The Yankees have had a pair of consecutive 100-win seasons four different times.

The most consecutive 100-loss seasons is five by the Phils in 1938-42. New York's Mets lost 100 games in each of their first four years, 1962-65, as did the expansion Washington Senators in 1961-64 and the 1909-12 Boston Braves.

In fact, the Mets fell down 100 times in five of their first six years, including their record 40-120 (.250) inaugural season. However, the 36-117-.235 Philadelphia A's of 1916 and the 1935 Boston Braves (38-115-.248) had even worse percentages.

There have been a number of seasons in which two teams (but never three) won or lost 100 games in the same league, most recently in 1998 when Atlanta and Houston each hit the century win mark. In 1993, the Mets and San Diego each suffered through more than 100 defeats.

Interestingly, the number of 100-win or loss records has jumped only a tad since the majors increased their schedules from 154 to 162 games. There were 1.90 of those records per season prior to 1961, 2.19 since then. The strike-shortened seasons aside, since 1960 there has been only one year—1992— in which there wasn't at least one 100-win or loss mark posted.

Scott Nelson is working on material that supports the contention that Babe Ruth's 60 home runs in 1927 were more significant thatn the records set by Mark McGwire and Sammy Sosa in 1998.

100 Wins, 100 Losses

AMERICAN LEAGUE

Team	100-win yrs.	Consecutive 100-win yrs.	100-loss yrs.	Consecutive 100- loss yrs.
NY	15	1927-28, 36-37, 41-42, 77-78	2	—
Baltimore	5	1969-71 (3), 79-80	2	—
Detroit	5	—	4	—
Philadelphia A's	5	1910-11, 29-31 (3)	11	1915-16, 19-21 (3)
Oakland	3	—	1	—
Boston	3	—	7	1925-27 (3)
Cleveland	2	—	5	—
KC Royals	1	—	0	—
Minnesota	1	—	1	—
Chicago	1	—	3	—
Texas	0	—	2	1972-73
Seattle	0	—	3	—
Toronto	0	—	3	1977-79 (3)
KC A's	0	—	4	1964-65
Washington I	0	—	5	—
Washington II	0	—	4	1961-64 (4)
St. Louis Browns	0	—	8	1910-12 (3)
Milwaukee	0	—	0	—
Anaheim	0	—	0	—
Totals:	**41**		**65**	

NATIONAL LEAGUE

Team	100-win yrs.	Consecutive 100-win yrs.	100-loss yrs.	Consecutive 100- loss yrs.
St. Louis	6	1942-44 (3)	2	1907-08
Chicago	5	1906-07, 09-10	2	—
New York Giants	4	1904-05, 12-13	0	—
Cincinnati	4	1975-76	1	—
Brooklyn	3	1941-42	2	—
New York Mets	3	—	6	1962-65 (4)
Los Angeles	2	—	0	—
San Francisco	2	—	1	—
Pittsburgh	2	—	5	1952-54 (3)
Philadelphia	2	1976-77	14	1927-28, 38-42 (5)
Atlanta	3	1997-98	2	—
Montreal	0	—	2	—
San Diego	0	—	5	1973-74
Boston	0	—	11	1909-12 (4)
Milwaukee Braves	0	—	0	—
Houston	1	—	0	—
Florida	0	—	1	—
Colorado	0	—	0	—
Totals:	**37**		**54**	

Eddie Rommel's Last Win

An extravagant farewell

Jerry Sulecki

Eddie Rommel

Eddie Rommel was a righthanded knuckleballer who won 171 games and lost 119 in a career that spanned thirteen seasons (1920-1932). He helped the Philadelphia Athletics win consecutive pennants in 1929, 1930, and 1931 and World Championships in 1929 and 1930.

At 6'2" and 197 pounds, he twice led the American League in wins, with 27 in 1922 and 21 in 1925. He also led the league three times in relief wins, with eight in 1922, 1928, and 1929.

That 171st and final win was a toughie. On July 10, 1932, Rommel gave up fifteen runs, twenty-nine hits, and nine walks while pitching the last seventeen innings of an eighteen-inning slugfest. Eddie surrendered nineteen singles, nine doubles, and a home run. He also threw two wild pitches and committed an error while stranding twenty-four baserunners.

At the plate, he was 3 for 7, scoring two runs and driving in one. He beat Wes Ferrell, who pitched 11-1/3 innings, giving up eight runs on twelve hits and four bases on balls. After four hours and five minutes, the A's had defeated the home town Cleveland Indians, 18-17, before an estimated gathering of 10,000.

Wait, there's more!—Johnny Burnett of Cleveland garnered nine hits (two doubles and seven singles) in eleven at bats, eight of them off Rommel and one off

Jerry Sulecki is an umpire, football official, grandfather, and Karen's husband in Concord Township, Ohio.

Lew Krause, Sr. Besides Burnett, four other players got at least five hits in this preposterous pitchers battle.

Jimmie Foxx of the A's was 6 for 9 with a double, three homers, four runs scored, and eight RBIs.

Al Simmons of the A's was 5 for 9—all singles—with four runs scored and two RBIs.

Ed Morgan of the Tribe was five for eleven with two doubles, scoring a run, and driving in four.

Earl Averill of the Indians was 5 for 9 with a home run, three runs scored, and four runs batted in.

Rommel committed Philadelphia's only error, while Cleveland made five.

The A's swatted twenty-five hits and Cleveland had thirty-three base knocks in a losing cause.

But wait, there's even more!—Rommel's seventeen-inning relief stint is the American League record. Johnny Burnett, who had two hits the day before, set another still-standing American League record: eleven hits in two consecutive games.

The first two games of this series were played in Philadelphia on Friday and Saturday, but this game was moved to Cleveland because Sunday baseball was outlawed in Pennsylvania. According to the newspaper accounts, Rommel remained in the game because Connie Mack brought only two pitchers to the game—Rommel and Krause, who started but pitched only the first inning.

Rommel's win was not only his last but his lone victory of 1932.

After hanging up his glove as a player, the "father of the knuckleball" once again joined the major leagues in 1938, this time as an umpire. Before retiring in 1959 after twenty-one fine seasons as an arbiter, Eddie Rommel would create more baseball history when he became the first major league umpire to wear glasses on the field, on April 26, 1956.

Sources:

Russell Schneider, *The Cleveland Indians Encyclopedia.* Temple University Press, Philadelphia (1996)

Mike Shatzkin, ed., *The Ballplayers*, William Morrow, NY (1990)

David Nemec and Pete Palmer, *1001 Fascinating Baseball Facts.* Longmeadow Press, Stamford, Ct. (1993)

Baseball Shrine off Beaten Path
by Bill Cunningham

If you're alive 50 years from today, and haven't anything more pressing to do, just for the hakes of it, take a ride over through the little town of Cooperstown, N.Y., and ask somebody whatever became of the baseball museum and all that Abner Doubleday business. I'll probably be too old to get about much by then, and I'd really like to know.

Understand, I'm not slamming the affair they're holding over in that New York hill country today. I'm all for ancient and historical things, shrines, vintage and heritage. The lordly British who, despite their gracious Queen and their friendly King, can be plenty uppity where and when American is concerned, have fathered the remark that this country, for one thing, has no ruins. I'm all for building these things and keeping history preserved, but why in Sam Hill place an item of this description in Cooperstown, N.Y.?

Yes, i know General Doubleday was born there, or pitched the first baseball there, or laid out the first diamond there or something, but so did Orville Wright fly the first airplane at a place called Kitty Hawk, N.C., and you don't have to go down there to a stretch of sandy beach to see Lindbergh's Spirit of St. Louis, do you?

Baseball is a game of the cities. If they even have a team in Cooperstown, N.Y., it must operate in some hotel league. This isn't to say that the classic birthplace of James Fenimore Cooper, the Society for the Prevention of Cruelty to Animals, a famous four-wheeled conveyance of another generation and sundry other items isn't beautiful, pleasant and thoroughly worthwhile place, for it is. But it is to say that it isn't, and it never will be, a baseball capitol, that the only people who will ever see the place and what it has to offer will be a lot of off-the-main-route motorists, with "Guests of Canada" stickers on their cars and that, therefore, all this pomp and circumstance and ballyhoo and bombastic word-age, air and typed, is little more than a Chamber of Commerce promotion that will be a complete waste in a national sense because the place is historically instead of strategically located.

If baseball wants to set up a hall of memories, and maybe it should, it should be located in New York, Boston, Chicago, Washington or some other major league city with touristic appeal. The Cooperstown boys, and it's a civic promotion strictly, hope to use the baseball shrine as dignified tourist bait. So far they've done a fine job. They got the thing under way with local money. They got the leagues and sundry other agencies to cooperate. They hired the highest priced press agent in the United States "to publicize" the event, and he did.

Today they have all living members of the Hall of Fame in the town. There'll be a baseball game played between picked teams of real major league stars. All the baseball big-wigs will be there without knowing exactly why. You can listen to some of the exercises on the radio, if your favorite, or even your unpopular station, has some unsold time at that hour.

And it's all very well, It will be a great jamboree.

But I still say drive around that way 50 years from today, count the cracks in the building, see how high the grass is around the door, and then write me a letter care of the Boston Post...

—Philip Bergen, from the Boston *Post*, June 12, 1939

Life Begins at 40 (or 35+)

The oldest players to get 200 hits in a season

Steve Krevisky

Paul Molitor's quest for 3,000 hits in his career led me to this research. His 200th hit in 1996 left him eleven short of 3,000, which he easily reached. He ended up with 225 hits in 1997, a career high (leading the AL in hits in the process), doing so at the age of forty. This was a truly remarkable season, and he has improved with age.

Molitor is now the second oldest player to reach 200 hits in one campaign (according to my research). The honor of being the the oldest to do so goes to Hall of Famer Sam Rice. (Rice finished thirteen hits short of 3,000 for his career, and might have played on to get it had he known he was so close to this mark.)

Rice was forty years old in 1930, when he tallied 207 hits. His 121 runs scored marked a career high, and his .349 BA was close to his career high of .350. He also had 55 walks with only 14 strikeouts, and a .407 on base average.

A ground rule for the list to the right is that all players had to be at least thirty-five years old at the start of the season. Many of these batters hit career highs in various categories in these seasons. For example, Tris Speaker's 1923 resulted in career highs in doubles (59) and RBIs (130). He also had a .469 OBA and .610 SA. Lefty O'Doul, Mickey Vernon, Al Oliver, and Tony Gwinn won batting titles, and Larry Lajoie may have, too, though AL President Ban

Johnson awarded the crown to Ty Cobb.

These players share the common denominator that they did not strike out much. None of these seasons was a fluke. All of these players were—or are—very good or great hitters.

Molitor chugged right through the 1998 season, stealing his 500th base to go with his 600+ doubles and 3,300+ hits.

Gwynn entered this list in 1997, when he became the oldest player to drive in 100 runs for the first time.

The oldest players to get 200 hits in a season

Player	Age	Year	AB	R	H	2B	3B	HR	RBI	BA
Rice	40	1930	593	121	207	35	13	1	73	.349
Molitor	39	1996	660	99	225	41	8	9	113	.341
Rose	38	1979	628	90	208	40	5	4	59	.331
Cobb	37	1924	625	115	211	38	10	4	74	.338
Gwynn	37	1997	592	97	220	49	2	17	119	.372
Wheat	37	1925	616	125	221	42	14	14	103	.359
Terry	36	1935	596	91	203	32	8	6	64	.341
Sisler	36	1929	629	67	205	40	8	2	79	.326
Lajoie	35	1910	591	94	227	51	7	4	76	.384
Oliver	36	1982	617	90	204	43	3	22	109	.331
Buckner	35	1985	673	89	201	46	3	16	110	.299
O'Doul	35	1932	595	120	219	32	8	21	90	.368
Speaker	35	1923	574	133	218	59	11	17	130	.380
Vernon	35	1953	608	101	205	43	11	15	115	.337

Steve Krevisky is a professor of mathematics at Middlexex Community-Technical College in Middletown, Connecticut. He has made presentations at many SABR regional and national meetings.

Predicting Postseason Results

Variables, favorites, and upsets

Stuart Shapiro

Before a World Series begins, everyone has a theory about why the team they root for will win.

"You can't beat the Braves with their pitching."

"But how about that lineup the Yankees have."

"Atlanta has been dominating opponents all year."

"Home field will make the difference."

We've all heard this kind of discussion and most of us have participated in it. Is there any way of predicting World Series winners that is substantially better than a coin flip? This article attempts to find one.

Similar to the common discussion before a postseason series is the one that takes place afterward. In this conversation, even the most remarkable upset is rationalized as inevitable.

"With Hershiser pitching like that, the Dodgers couldn't lose."

"There was no way the Cardinals were going to win any games in Minnesota."

Teams that pull off "upsets" quickly pass into baseball legend. We all have opinions about the greatest upsets in postseason history. The model that can be used to predict World Series winners can be used to show which teams were most in defiance of this prediction.

The tool used to accomplish these two goals is regression. Regression, in its various forms, takes one "dependent variable" and relates it to various "independent variables" to demonstrate a hypothesized causal relationship. The technique is used in the social sciences, for example, to relate education to income level, or auto sales to interest rates. The regression model results in coefficients for each of the independent variables that conveys the magnitude and direction of the effect of the independent variable upon the dependent variable. It also provides information that can be used to determine whether or not this relationship is statistically significant.

In this case, the dependent variable is whether a particular team won its postseason series. The dependent variable takes on the value of one if the team prevailed, and the value of zero if it lost. This type of regression model—where the dependent variable can only take on two values (zero or one)—is called a probit model. The data I use is for all postseason series from 1903 through 1992.

I examined a wide variety of independent variables, including differences between the two teams in batting average, home runs, slugging percentage, runs, wins, and ERA. To normalize the data, I divided team values by the league averages. For example:

ERAdif = AL champ ERA/AL League ERA - NL champ ERA/NL League ERA

The construction of variables for differences in the other team characteristics was identical. In addition, I included the home field advantage (called Alhome), and the difference between the percentage of wins garnered by the three top pitchers on each team (called t3pitdif). I included this in the model because

Stuart Shapiro *is a lifelong Yankee fan (hence the interest in postseason series) who is completing his Ph.D. in public policy at the Kennedy School of Government.*

I believe that in a short series a few strong starters can make a big difference.

The final model along with coefficients for the independent variables and t-statistics (explained below) can be seen in Table 1. It does not include differences in batting average and home runs because the effects of these variables were captured by the difference in slugging percentage. I found that differences in number of wins added no predictive power to the model.

Table 1. Final model

variable	coefficient	t-statistic
slgdif	-4.20	-1.61
eradif	-3.05	-2.38
t3pitdif	1.10	1.42
rundif	44.52	2.64
alhome	0.18	0.80
constant	-.04	

The first interesting thing to notice about the model is that with one exception all of the signs of the independent variables are as we would predict. A higher ERA means a team is less likely to win the series. More runs scored, the home field advantage, and a greater percentage of wins by your top three pitchers all make a team more likely to win the series. The one exception is slugging percentage. The higher a team's slugging percentage, the less likely it is to win the series. Perhaps teams that rely too much on power to generate wins find themselves at a disadvantage when matched up with other good teams.

Only two of the variables are significant at the 95 percentage level (a t-statistic of 1.96 or greater, or of -1.96 or lower). We can say with 95 percent certainty that the difference in ERAs and the difference in runs scored has a bearing on who will win a series. This confirms common sense. To beat your opponents you need to score and to stop them from scoring.

The model doesn't simply show us the relationship between team characteristics and the ability to win a postseason series. It also lets us calculate the probablity that each team entering a series will win it. These probabilities in turn let us test our model's effectiveness by calculating how often the team "most likely" to win a series actually did.

Out of the 128 postseason series used here, the model correctly predicts 83 winners, a success rate of 64.8 percent. This is far from perfect, but it's a success rate any prognosticator would be happy to achieve.

The model lets us locate the greatest postseason upsets, too, by noting the series in which the model was most incorrect in predicting the series winner.

I generated Table 2, which lists the teams that lost depite having the highest probablities of winning. Most of the entries agree with our common sense choices, but there are a few surprises.

Table 2. Greatest postseason upsets

Series Favorite	Probability of Winning
1906 Cubs	0.845
1975 A's (ALCS)	0.769
1987 Cardinals	0.746
1934 Tigers	0.745
1971 Orioles	0.711
1987 Tigers (ALCS)	0.701
1959 White Sox	0.698
1992 Braves	0.687
1954 Indians	0.683
1985 Cardinals	0.681

The great upsets pulled off by the 1906 White Sox and the 1954 Giants are on this list, as are the 1980s Cardinal losses to the Royals and Twins. (I do not have a variable for Don Denkinger umpiring first base). There were a few entries that I found surprising. Most people don't see the 1975 ALCS as a big upset. I think this is a case in which the model punishes the Red Sox for their large power advantage over the A's. The same may be true for the 1992 Braves, who most people thought were pretty evenly matched with that year's edition of the Blue Jays.

Finally what were the most lopsided postseason series ever? The following is a list of the nine teams that the model estimates to have at least a 75 percent chance of winning their series. As you can see, seven of the nine followed through between the lines. This list contains few surprises. The 1989 A's appear twice probably as much because of their weak opponents (Blue Jays and Giants) as their own dominance.

Table 3. Highest probabilities of winning.

1937 Yankees	0.845
1906 Cubs	0.844 (lost)
1970 Orioles	0.828
1905 Giants	0.801
1932 Yankees	0.781
1989 A's	0.780
1974 Dodgers	0.775 (NLCS)
1989 A's	0.774 (ALCS)
1975 A's	0.769 (ALCS, lost)

Where Did They Come From?

Hall of Famers in the minors

John E. Spalding

Most players who are enshrined in the Baseball Hall of Fame honed their skills in the minor leagues before they reached the majors.

Only twenty-eight of the players whose plaques are displayed in Cooperstown began their careers at the top and four of them were shipped back to the minors for more seasoning. The others graduated from thirty-four minor leagues. As you might expect, many came from the highest classification circuits, the International League (27), American Association (23), Pacific Coast League (18), Southern Association (18) and Texas League (11).

For the players who moved back and forth between the big leagues and the minors before settling at the top, I used the criteria reported in *Awards Voting* by Bill Deane, published by SABR in 1988, to determine their status as true major league rookies. There were no formal rookie guidelines before 1957, but I applied Deane's criteria—a maximum of 45 innings pitched in the major leagues or 75 times at bat—to all players except Billy Williams, who did not exceed the limitation of 90 times at bat in effect during his rookie year.

Players farmed out to the minors after exceeding the rookie minimums are identified by an asterisk (*) followed by the name(s) of the league(s) where they appeared. If a player worked in more than one minor league in the same season, the one in which he played the most games is shown.

John E. Spalding *is a retired newspaper reporter and editor who has written five books about the Pacific Coast League.*

There were 235 members in the Hall of Fame after the 1998 induction ceremony. Not included in this study are executives, umpires and other notables, as well as managers Joe McCarthy, Earl Weaver and Harry Wright and Negro League players Cool Papa Bell, Ray Dandridge, Bill Foster, Josh Gibson, Judy Johnson, Buck Leonard, John Lloyd and Willie Wells, who did not play in the major leagues.

Following is a list of 168 Hall of Fame players and managers showing the minor league team where they drew a paycheck immediately before graduating to the majors.

Atlantic Association (1)
Jesse Burkett (Worcester, 1889)

Atlantic League (2)
Jack Chesbro (Richmond, 1899)
Honus Wagner (Paterson, 1897)

American Association (23)
Roy Campanella (St. Paul, 1948)
Earle Combs (Louisville, 1923)
Leo Durocher (St. Paul, 1927)
Rick Ferrell (Columbus, 1928)
Whitey Ford (Kansas City, 1950)
Bob Gibson (Omaha, 1959)
Jesse Haines (Kansas City, 1919; Cincinnati, 5 IP, 1918)
Billy Hamilton (Kansas City, 1889)
Billy Herman (Louisville, 1931)

Miller Huggins (St. Paul, 1903)
Hugh Jennings (Louisville, 1891)
Fred Lindstrom (Toledo, 1923)
Rube Marquard (Indianapolis, 1908)
Willie Mays (Minneapolis, 1951)
Pee Wee Reese (Louisville, 1939)
Phil Rizzuto (Kansas City, 1940)
Ray Schalk (Milwaukee, 1912)
Enos Slaughter (Columbus, 1937)
Duke Snider (St. Paul, 1947)
Bill Terry (Toledo, 1923)
Hoyt Wilhelm (Minneapolis, 1951)
Ted Williams (Minneapolis, 1938)
Carl Yastrzemski (Minneapolis, 1960)

California League (1)
Clark Griffith (Oakland, 1893)

California State League—Outlaw (1)
Harry Hooper (Sacramento, 1908)

Carolina League (1)
Rod Carew (Wilson, 1966)

Central League (4)
Max Carey (South Bend, 1910)
Chuck Klein (Fort Wayne, 1928)
Bill McKechnie (Wheeling, 1909; Pittsburgh, 8 AB
1907; *American Association, 1912-13)
Edd Roush (Evansville, 1913)

Eastern League (6)
Richie Ashburn (Utica, 1947)
Lou Gehrig (Hartford, 1921)
Gabby Hartnett (Worcester, 1921)
Bob Lemon (Wilkes-Barre, 1941)
Warren Spahn (Hartford, 1942)
Early Wynn (Springfield, 1941; Washington, 20 IP,
1939)

Eastern Shore League (1)
Red Ruffing (Dover, 1924; Boston, 23 IP, 1924)

Florida State League (1)
Catfish Hunter (Daytona Beach, 1964)

Illinois-Iowa League (1)
John McGraw (Cedar Rapids, 1891)

Indiana League (1)
Cap Anson (Marshalltown, 1870)

International Association (2)
Pud Galvin (Buffalo, 1878)
Ned Hanlon (Albany, 1879)

International League—called Eastern League before 1911 (27)
Johnny Bench (Buffalo, 1967)
Yogi Berra (Newark, 1946)
Jim Bottomley (Syracuse, 1922)
Lou Boudreau (Buffalo, 1939; Cleveland, 1 AB, 1938)
Jim Bunning (Buffalo, 1955; *American Association, 1956)
Roberto Clemente (Montreal, 1954)
Jimmy Collins (Buffalo, 1894)
Don Drysdale (Montreal, 1955)
Jimmie Foxx (Providence, 1925; Philadelphia AL, 9 AB, 1925)
Charley Gehringer (Toronto, 1925; Detroit, 13 AB, 1924)
Lefty Grove (Baltimore, 1924)
Bucky Harris (Buffalo, 1919)
Monte Irvin (Jersey City, 1949)
Willie Keeler (Binghamton, 1892; *Eastern League, 1893)
Ralph Kiner (Toronto, 1943)
Tommy Lasorda (Montreal, 1954; *American Association, 1956-57; Pacific Coast League, 1957; International League, 1958-60)
Connie Mack (Hartford, 1886)
John Mize (Rochester, 1935)
Stan Musial (Rochester, 1941)
Jackie Robinson (Montreal, 1946)
Babe Ruth (Baltimore and Providence, 1914)
Tom Seaver (Jacksonville, 1966)
Red Schoendienst (Rochester, 1944)
Willie Stargell (Columbus, 1962)
Ed Walsh (Newark, 1903)
Vic Willis (Syracuse, 1897)
Ross Youngs (Rochester, 1917)

Inter-State League (3)
Elmer Flick (Dayton, 1897)
George Kell (Lancaster, 1943)
Robin Roberts (Wilmington, 1948)

League Alliance (1)
John Montgomery Ward (Athletics, 1877)

Middle Atlantic League (1)
Joe Cronin (Johnstown, 1925)

National Association (3)
Buck Ewing (Rochester, 1880)
Tim Keefe (Albany, 1880)
Mickey Welch (Holyoke, 1879)

New England League (4)
Hugh Duffy (Salem and Lowell, 1887)
Nap Lajoie (Fall River, 1896)
Rabbit Maranville (New Bedford, 1912)
Wilbert Robinson (Haverhill, 1885)

New York State League (2)
Grover Cleveland Alexander (Syracuse, 1910)
Johnny Evers (Troy, 1902)

Northern League (2)
Lou Brock (St. Cloud, 1961)
Jim Palmer (Aberdeen, 1964; *International, 1967-
68; Florida State, 1967-68; Eastern, 1968)

Northwest League—operated in Midwest (2)
John Clarkson (Saginaw, 1884)
Charles Radbourne (Dubuque, 1879)

Northwestern League (2)
Harry Heilmann (Portland, 1913; *Pacific Coast
League, 1915)
George Kelly (Victoria, 1915)

Pacific Coast League (18)
Earl Averill (San Francisco, 1928)
Dave Bancroft (Portland, 1914)
Steve Carlton (Tulsa, 1966; St. Louis NL, 25 IP,
1965)
Mickey Cochrane (Portland, 1924)
Stan Coveleski (Portland, 1915; Philadelphia AL,
21 IP, 1912)
Joe DiMaggio (San Francisco, 1935)
Bob Doerr (San Diego, 1936)
Lefty Gomez (San Francisco, 1929)
Babe Herman (Seattle, 1925)
Ferguson Jenkins (Arkansas, 1965)
Tony Lazzeri (Salt Lake City, 1925)
Ernie Lombardi (Oakland, 1929)
Juan Marichal (Tacoma, 1960)
Phil Niekro (Denver, 1964; Milwaukee NL, 15 IP,
1964; *International League, 1966)
Gaylord Perry (Tacoma, 1963; San Francisco, 43 IP,
1962)
Mike Schmidt (Eugene, 1972)
Paul Waner (San Francisco, 1925)
Willie McCovey (Phoenix, 1959; *PCL, 1960)

Pacific Northwest League (1)
Joe Tinker (Portland, 1901)

South Atlantic League (5)
Hank Aaron (Jacksonville, 1953)
Ty Cobb (Augusta, 1905)
Goose Goslin (Columbia, 1921)
Frank Robinson (Columbia, 1955)
Lloyd Waner (Columbia, 1926)

Southern Association (18)
Luis Aparicio (Memphis, 1955)
Luke Appling (Atlanta, 1930)
Fred Clarke (Savannah, 1894)
Kiki Cuyler (Nashville, 1923; Pittsburgh, 3 AB,
1921; Pittsburgh, 0 AB, 1922)
Bill Dickey (Little Rock, 1928)
Rollie Fingers (Birmingham, 1968)
Burleigh Grimes (Birmingham, 1916)
Waite Hoyt (Nashville, 1918)
Reggie Jackson (Birmingham, 1967)
Travis Jackson (Little Rock, 1922)
Al Lopez (Atlanta, 1929)
Eddie Mathews (Atlanta, 1951)
Joe Sewell (New Orleans, 1920)
Tris Speaker (Little Rock, 1908; Boston AL, 19 AB,
1907)
Casey Stengel (Montgomery, 1912)
Pie Traynor (Birmingham, 1921; Pittsburgh, 52 AB,
1920)
Dazzy Vance (New Orleans, 1921; Pittsburgh NL, 2
IP, 1915; New York AL, 30 IP, 1915, 1918)
Zack Wheat (Mobile, 1909)

Texas League (11)
Dizzy Dean (Houston, 1931; St. Louis NL, 9 IP,
1930)
Hank Greenberg (Beaumont, 1932; Detroit, 1 AB,
1930)
Chick Hafey (Houston, 1924)
Carl Hubbell (Beaumont, 1928)
Joe Medwick (Houston, 1932)
Joe Morgan (San Antonio, 1964)
Hal Newhouser (Beaumont, 1939)
Brooks Robinson (San Antonio, 1957; Baltimore,
66 AB, 1955-56; *Pacific Coast League, 1959)
Al Simmons (Shreveport, 1923)
Don Sutton (Albuquerque, 1965; *Pacific Coast
League, 1968)
Billy Williams (Houston, 1960; Chicago NL, 33
AB, 1959)

Tri-State League (3)
Frank Baker (Reading, 1908)
Ed Delahanty (Wheeling, 1888)
Cy Young (Canton, 1890)

Virginia League (3)
Christy Mathewson (Norfolk, 1900)
Sam Rice (Petersburg, 1915)
Hack Wilson (Portsmouth, 1923; *American Association, 1925)

Western Association (8)
Jake Beckley (St. Louis, 1888)
Rogers Hornsby (Denison, 1915)
Addie Joss (Toledo, 1901)
Joe Kelley (Omaha, 1892; Boston NL, 45 AB, 1891)
Mickey Mantle (Joplin, 1950; *American Association, 1951)
Joe McGinnity (Peoria, 1898)
Kid Nichols (Omaha, 1889)
Sam Thompson (Indianapolis, 1885)

Western League (5)
Mordecai Brown (Omaha, 1902)
Red Faber (Des Moines, 1913
Nellie Fox (Lincoln, 1948; Philadelphia AL, 3 AB, 1947)
Heinie Manush (Omaha, 1922)
Arky Vaughan (Wichita, 1931)

Western League—renamed American League in 1900 (2)
Sam Crawford (Columbus and Grand Rapids, 1899)
Rube Waddell (Columbus and Grand Rapids, 1899; *California League, 1902)

Started in majors without minor league experience (26)
Ernie Banks (Chicago NL, 1953)
Chief Bender (Philadelphia AL, 1903)
Dan Brouthers (Troy, 1879)

Frank Chance (Chicago, 1898)
Roger Connor (Troy, 1880)
Candy Cummings (New York Mutuals, National Association, 1872)
George Davis (Cleveland NL, 1890)
Larry Doby (Cleveland AL, 1947; Negro Leagues)
Bob Feller (Cleveland, 1936)
Frank Frisch (New York NL, 1919)
Walter Johnson (Washington, 1907)
Al Kaline (Detroit, 1953)
Mike Kelly (Cincinnati, 1878)
Sandy Koufax (Brooklyn, 1955)
Ted Lyons (Chicago AL, 1923)
Tommy McCarthy (Boston, Union Association, 1884)
Jim O'Rourke (Middletown, National Association, 1872)
Mel Ott (New York NL, 1926)
Satchel Paige (Cleveland, 1948; Negro Leagues)
Eddie Plank (Philadelphia AL, 1901)
Eppa Rixey (Philadelphia NL, 1912)
Amos Rusie (Indianapolis, 1889)
George Sisler (St. Louis AL, 1915)
Al Spalding (Boston, National Association, 1871)
Bobby Wallace (Cleveland NL, 1894)
George Wright (Boston, National Association, 1871)

Started in majors, but were sent to minors (4)
Roger Bresnahan (Washington NL, 16 AB, 1897; Toledo, Interstate, 1898; Minneapolis, Western, 1899)
Eddie Collins (Philadelphia AL, 15 AB, 1906; Newark, Eastern, 1907)
Harmon Killebrew (Washington AL, 192 AB, 1954-56, and Washington AL, 62 AB, 1957-58; Charlotte, Sally, 1956; Chattanooga, Southern, 1957-58; Indianapolis, American Association, 1958)
Herb Pennock (Philadelphia AL, 278 IP, 1912-15; and Boston AL, 14 IP, 1915; Providence, International, 1915; Buffalo, International, 1916)

From a Researcher's Notebook

Al Kermisch

Titanic Disaster Cast Dark Spell Over 1912 Opener

On April 14, 1910, William Howard Taft initiated the custom of the President throwing out the first ball to open the baseball season in Washington. An enthusiastic crowd of 12,028 let out a great roar as the President tossed the sphere. The Senators responded by defeating the Philadelphia Athletics, 3-0, behind the one-hit pitching of Walter Johnson. In 1911, while training in Atlanta, the ball club received word that National Park at 7th Street and Florida Avenue had been destroyed by fire, the grandstand and bleachers burned to the ground. But new stands were erected in time to start the season on April 12, 1911. President Taft again threw out the first ball as the Senators beat the Boston Red Sox, 8-5, before 12,021.

In 1912 Washington was scheduled to open on the road for only the third time in its twelve years in the American League and the first time since 1908. While the club was on the road the great Titanic disaster occurred on April 14, ending any chance that President Taft would attend the home opener scheduled for April 18. The sinking of the Titanic was particularly painful to President Taft since his trustful military attache, Major Archibald Butt, had gone down with the ship. The President had sent Butt on a diplomatic mission to the Vatican. Major Butt was one of the heroes of the disaster, spending many hours assisting women and children into life boats, and when the ship broke apart Major Butt jumped into the sea and drowned.

The Senators started slowly under their new manager, Clark Griffith, in 1912, but when the club secured first baseman Chick Gandil from Montreal of the International League the team caught fire. After winning the second game of a doubleheader in Boston on May 30, the Senators astounded the baseball world by reeling of sixteen consecutive victories on the road. When they returned to Washington thousands greeted them at Union Station. On June 18, a crowd of 15,516 was on hand for a game with Philadelphia. President Taft made up for missing the home opener and threw out the first ball as the Senators made it seventeen wins in a row, 5-4.

Another Four Strikeout Inning For Bobby Mathews

Diminutive Bobby Mathews, one of the star pitchers of early professional league baseball, is the first pitcher listed in the record book for striking out four batters in an inning. On September 30, 1885, he fanned four Pittsburgh batters in one frame as he won 8-1 in an American Association game. However, Mathews had struck out four in one inning three years earlier while pitching for the Boston National League club. In a game at Buffalo on September 18, 1882, he

Al Kermisch *got his greatest thrill as a youngster when he saw Babe Ruth hit a home run in Washington.*

fanned four batters in one inning as he beat the local club, 8-2. The Providence *Evening Press* noted that "Mathews struck out White, Force, Galvin and Foley in one inning, but the latter got his base on a passed ball by Deasley."

On another occasion Mathews fanned four batters in one inning, but one batter who reached first after the catcher missed the third strike was later called out for kicking the ball after an appeal to the umpire. The game took place in Baltimore on May 7, 1883, as the Athletics won, 8-1, in an American Association game. John Fox opened the first inning for the home club by reaching first when catcher Ed Rowan missed the third strike. Lew Say also reached first safely as Rowan again missed the third strike. But the Athletics protested that Say had accidentally kicked the ball on his way to first and umpire Ben Sommer called Say out. Later in the inning Mathews struck out Phil Baker and Dan Stearns.

Ruth and Koenig Tangled In Exhibition Game

On September 5, 1926, the New York Yankees were trounced in an exhibition game by the minor league Baltimore Orioles, 18-9. The game was highlighted by a brisk tussle between Babe Ruth and Mark Koenig, who was in his first full year as Yankee shortstop. Ruth played first base and as the game progressed he was annoyed by the sloppy play of Koenig, who loafed on several plays. Ruth wanted to speed up the game to enable the Yankees to catch a train to New York.

The Baltimore *American* described the event as follows:

"The run-in between the two players occurred as the Yankees came to bat in the eighth inning. According to several rooters in range of hearing, the Babe was ragging Koenig for easing up. As they descended into the dugout, Koenig is said to have leaped upon Ruth and a tussle ensued. Babe merely held his attacker's arms helpless until other players separated the pair. Koenig was banished from the game and it required several minutes for the bluecoats to clear the diamond for play."

When Ruth came to bat in the ninth inning he was unjustly greeted with hoots and jeers. Ruth was close to tears at the outburst. He wasn't used to that kind of treatment in the city where he was born. The Babe had a bad day at the bat. He was 0 for 5, fanning twice and hitting into a double play. In batting practice Ruth hit a terrific drive over the clock in right-center, clearing the fence by twenty feet.

Koenig was the last of the 1927 Yankees to pass away. He died in 1993 at the age of 88. He was proud of being a member of that great club and always sang the praises of Ruth. It was the Babe who taunted the Cubs during the 1932 World Series for awarding Koenig only a half share of the series money. The Cubs rode Ruth unmercifully and inspired the Babe to hit the controversial "called shot" home run in the third game of the series in Chicago.

Phenomenal Smith Not With Baltimore Unions In 1884

The major league playing record of John F. "Phenomenal" Smith begins with a 3-3 record for Baltimore of the Union Association in 1884. But John did not play for Baltimore that year. There were two players by the name of Smith who played for the Baltimore Unions in 1884. The first one was 3-3 when he was released on May 30. At the time of his release he was referred to as "the Canadian pitcher." The other Smith, who pitched one game on June 5, was a local lad from the Actives of a Baltimore amateur league. He lost that game to the Boston Unions.

Phenomenal Smith did pitch for Baltimore of the American Association in 1887 and 1888. He won 39 and lost 49 for the two seasons. His best year was in 1887 when he won 25 and lost 30. On September 15 of that year Smith pitched two complete games and lost both to St. Louis by scores of 3-0 and 4-2.

John Smith's record indicates that he was born in Philadelphia, but his obituary in the Manchester *Union Leader* on April 4, 1952, stated that he was born in Strasbourg, Alsace-Lorraine, and lived in Philadelphia until he moved to Manchester in 1901. After he left the majors Smith managed and played the outfield in the minors. In 1896 he was an outfielder with Pawtucket of the New England League. He batted .406, second only to Nap Lajoie, who led the league with a .429 average. (Lajoie was sold to the Philadelphia Phillies in August of that season. The night he found out that he was going to the majors, he went out on the town and was arrested for using too much ginger in celebrating his departure.)

Smith was manager of Norfolk in the Virginia League in 1900. He signed twenty-year-old Christy Mathewson and the youngster blossomed under Smith's tutelage. Pitching under the name of "Mathews" Matty won 20 games while losing only two. On June 12, he pitched a 1-0 no-hit game against Hampton. Later in the season Smith sold Mathewson to the New York Giants.

Cubs and Tigers Played Exhibition Game after 1908 Series

When the Chicago Cubs defeated the Detroit Tigers four games to one to win the 1908 World Series, only 62,232 witnessed the series, the lowest total in modern World Series history. Moreover, the final game, played in Detroit, drew only 6,210 fans, the lowest attendance for a series game ever. For winning the series each of the twenty-one Chicago players received $1,317.58, while each of the twenty-one Detroit players got $870. On Sunday, October 18—four days after the final game in Detroit—the Cubs and Tigers played an exhibition game in Chicago. The Tigers won, 7-2, before a crowd of 6,864. The players divided the money evenly.

Before the game, players of both teams participated in a series of field events. The excitement ran very high as Ty Cobb, the Tigers' speed merchant, entered all three sprint races. As expected, he won all three. He bunted and ran to first in 3-1/5 seconds, beating Johnny Evers, Mordecai Brown, and Del Howard of the Cubs, and Davy Jones and George Winter of Detroit. Cobb then circled the bases against time in 13-4/5 seconds, topping the times of Evers and Winter. In the 100-yard dash Cobb won in 10-2/5 seconds (in a baseball uniform and cleats, of course), besting Jones and the Cubs' Solly Hofman. The other event of the day was the long-distance throw. Hofman won with 338 feet, Sam Crawford of the Tigers was second. The other contestants were Joe Tinker, Cobb, and Evers.

Oriole Farm Clubs Tops in Lengthy Extra-Inning Games

The longest extra-inning game by Baltimore in the majors is nineteen innings. In a game at Memorial Stadium on June 4, 1967, the Orioles defeated the Washington Senators, 7-5. However, minor league affiliates of the Orioles (Elmira in 1965, Miami in 1966, and Rochester in 1981) are tops in lengthy extra innings games.

On May 8, 1965, Elmira outlasted Springfield, 2-1, in twenty-seven innings in an Eastern League game at Elmira. The game lasted six hours and twenty-four minutes and was scoreless for twenty-five innings. Springfield broke through with a run in the twenty-sixth frame, but Elmira tied the score in the bottom of the inning. Elmira won the game in the next inning when Johnny Scruggs led off with a double, Ron Stone bunted him to third, and Larry Haney grounded to second scoring Scruggs. Earl Weaver managed Elmira and Andy Gilbert piloted Springfield.

In a Florida State League game in St. Petersburg on June 14, 1966, Miami outlasted the home club, 6-5, in twenty-nine innings. The game lasted six hours and fifty-nine minutes and ended at 2:24 AM. With the bases full and one out in the top of the twenty-ninth, Fred Rico hit a long fly to center fielder Archie Wade to score pitcher Mike Hebert from third. Herbert then retired three in a row to end the marathon. Billy DeMars managed Miami against Sparky Anderson, St. Petersburg.

On April 18-19, 1981, Pawtucket and Rochester of the International League battled through thirty-two innings in Pawtucket before play was stopped at 4:07 Easter morning with the score tied, 2-2. The game was resumed on June 23 in Pawtucket. Only one more inning was required to end the game as the home club scored in the bottom of the thirty-third. Marty Barrett was hit by a Steve Grilli pitch. Chico Walker singled Barrett to third and Dave Koza singled into short left field to score Barrett and end the longest game in Organized Baseball history. The elapsed time of the game was eight hours and twenty-five minutes. The opposing third basemen were Cal Ripken, Jr. for the Red Wings and Wade Boggs for the Red Sox. The managers were Joe Morgan, Pawtucket, and Doc Edwards, Rochester.

Pat Flaherty—Ballplayer, Soldier, And Actor

Pat Flaherty appeared in over 100 movies in a career that lasted from 1934 to 1955. His roles were usually small and very rarely did his name appear in the credits, but he was always in demand. Flaherty was a natural for pictures with a sports theme. A tall, good-looking individual, he had pitched in the minors for a half dozen years. Despite the fact that he never appeared in a major league game he was regarded as a prospect and twice went to spring training with the Washington Senators and once with the Boston Red Sox. Flaherty was in many sports pictures, including *Gentleman Jim*, *Pride of the Yankees*, *The Jackie Robinson Story*, *The Stratton Story*, *It Happened in Flatbush*, *Navy Blue and Gold*, *The Babe Ruth Story*, and *The Winning Team*. In *The Stratton Story* he played the opposing manager who told his players to bunt on the one-legged pitcher.

Flaherty was born in Washington, D.C. on March 8, 1897 and died in New York on December 2, 1970. In World War I, Pat was an army aviator, stationed at Park Field, Tennessee, where he was injured in an accident. He went on to serve in both World War II and the Korean War, reaching the rank of major. In 1919 Flaherty was a star pitcher with the Baltimore Drydocks, an outstanding independent team managed by former major league pitcher Sam Frock. During the 1918 and 1919 seasons the team included, at one time or another, such top-notch players as Joe Judge, Frank Schulte, Johnny Bates, Dave Danforth, Fritz Maisel, Tommy Thomas, Clarence "Lefty" Russell and future Hall of Famers Waite Hoyt and Bucky Harris.

Pat was the older brother of Vincent X. Flaherty, a noted sports columnist and Hollywood screen writer, who collaborated on the screen play for *Jim Thorpe—All American*. After working as a columnist for the Washington *Times-Herald*, Vincent went west and took a similar job with the Los Angeles *Examiner* in 1945. He was the driving force behind the effort to bring major league baseball to Los Angeles. He even went as far as to predict that a major league team in Los Angeles could draw three million in one season. Unfortunately, he died in 1977, the year before the Dodgers became the first major league club to top that mark.

HAVE A SABR HOLIDAY SEASON

With the holidays approaching, don't you think you deserve a little baseball cheer? How 'bout spending a couple of hours around the fire with a good baseball book? Why not give yourself one of SABR's highly acclaimed minor league publications and reprints of the early BRJs? Or maybe send one to a friend? These stocking stuffers may just be the tonic that gets you through the months till Spring Training.

❑ *The Baseball Research Journal Reprint of Vol. 1-3*: Relive SABR history with the little-known first articles by SABR's first great researchers. Seminal articles that stand the test of time. 186 pages, $12.50 (postpaid) from SABR.

❑ *The Minor League Baseball Research Journal, Volume 1*: Twenty-plus page articles on The West Texas-New Mexico League; Ballparks of Los Angeles; The formation of the PCL and its first tumultuous season; and a great portrait of baseball gypsy Bill Sisler; and much, much more. (Limited quantities.) 126 pages, $11.45 (postpaid) from SABR.

❑ *The Minor League Baseball Research Journal, Volume 2, Going For the Fences: The Minor League Home Run Record Book*, by **Bob McConnell**: Everything you'd every want to know about minor league home runs by the premier expert on home runs. 186 pages, $12.50 (postpaid) from SABR.

❑ *The SABR Guide to Minor League Statistics*: A pure research tool that lists--league-by-league, and year-by-year--what statistics the major baseball guides carried. (Limited quantities.) 158 pages, $11.45 (postpaid) from SABR.

Have a happy holiday to one and all.

Mail orders to:
SABR, 812 Huron Rd E #719, Cleveland OH 44115